DATE			

COMPARATIVE WORK SYSTEMS

Ideologies and Reality in Eastern Europe

Alexander J. Matejko

PRAEGER SPECIAL STUDIES • PRAEGER SCIENTIFIC

New York • Philadelphia • Eastbourne, UK
Toronto • Hong Kong • Tokyo • Sydney

Library of Congress Cataloging in Publication Data

Matejko, Alexander J.
   Comparative work systems.

   Bibliography: p.
   Includes index.
   1. Industrial sociology—Europe, Eastern.
   2. Labor and laboring classes—Europe, Eastern.
   3. Social classes—Europe, Eastern. I. Title.
   HD6957.E82M37 1985   306'.36'0947   85-6354
   ISBN 0-03-004492-8 (alk. paper)

Published and Distributed by the
Praeger Publishers Division
(ISBN Prefix 0-275)
of Greenwood Press, Inc.,
Westport, Connecticut

Published in 1986 by Praeger Publishers
CBS Educational and Professional Publishing, a Division of CBS Inc.
521 Fifth Avenue, New York, NY 10175 USA

INTERNATIONAL OFFICES

Orders from outside the United States should be sent to the appropriate address listed below. Orders from areas not listed below should be placed through CBS International Publishing, 383 Madison Ave., New York, NY 10175 USA

Australia, New Zealand
Holt Saunders, Pty. Ltd., 9 Waltham St., Artarmon, N.S.W. 2064, Sydney, Australia

Canada
Holt, Rinehart & Winston of Canada, 55 Horner Ave., Toronto, Ontario, Canada M8Z 4X6

Europe, the Middle East, & Africa
Holt Saunders, Ltd., 1 St. Anne's Road, Eastbourne, East Sussex, England BN21 3UN

Japan
Holt Saunders, Ltd., Ichibancho Central Building, 22-1 Ichibancho, 3rd Floor, Chiyodaku, Tokyo, Japan

Hong Kong, Southeast Asia
Holt Saunders Asia, Ltd., 10 Fl, Intercontinental Plaza, 94 Granville Road, Tsim Sha Tsui East, Kowloon, Hong Kong

Manuscript submissions should be sent to the Editorial Director, Praeger Publishers, 521 Fifth Avenue, New York, NY 10175 USA

ACKNOWLEDGMENTS

In the first chapter material was used from chapter 2, "Organization of Work Relations," of Beyond Bureaucracy? by Alexander J. Matejko, Cologne: Verlag für Gesellschaftsarchitektur, 1984. Materials on Sociotechnics, Vol. 1. In chapter 2 some fragments were incorporated from the article "The Impact of Authoritarian Rule on Basic Social Strata in East Europe," Canadian Slavonic Papers, 1979, XXI, 2: 197-224 and several quotations are from Russia Under the Old Regime by Richard Pipes (London: Weidenfeld and Nicolson, 1974) and from The Russian Tradition by Tibor Szamuely (London: Secker and Warburg, 1974). In chapter 4 some fragments were incorporated in a modified form from Social Change and Stratification in Eastern Europe by A. Matejko (Praeger 1974), now out of print. In chapter 5 some fragments were incorporated from "Marxists and Christians: A Dialogue?" found in Marx and Marxism, ed. by A. Jain and A. Matejko, New York: Praeger, as well as several quotations from Main Currents of Marxism by Leszek Kolakowski (Oxford: Clarendon Press, 1978).

CONTENTS

INTRODUCTION

The socioeconomic order currently existing in eastern Europe originated from the radical rejection of the local ideological and social tradition. Communism has been a great experiment in reshaping the socioeconomic base of a society from its foundations. The almost total elimination of the private sector under communism has completely changed the social structure of eastern European societies. Only in Poland and, to some extent, in Hungary are private earners numerous.

This book is an attempt to trace the impact of the communist socio-political and economic organization on Polish society. The main thesis of this book is that the profound transformation by communists of the sociomoral fabric of Polish society has proved to be impossible despite the imposition by force of an omnipotent organizational machinery. State socialist bureaucracy has been oriented predominantly toward its own survival that is unable to penetrate the deeper motives of people, offer them a morally convincing stimulation or encourage the substantial voluntary contributions to the continuous improvement of the system.

The dilemma of spontaneity versus formalization is valid for all societies. However, under Soviet state socialism this dilemma becomes acutely important because of the elimination of the private sector and the restriction of civil liberties. In eastern Europe under Soviet communism the traditional socioeconomic and political structures of societies that are located there has been completely changed. The purpose of this book is to introduce interested readers to the problems that arise within societies because of a contradiction between spontaneous social changes dictated by industrialization, educational growth, higher professional skills, etc., and the imposition on societies of rigid state Socialist work structures. The Polish case seems to be particularly illuminating in this respect.

This book was written with the intention to analyze the Polish case in relation to major differences of work systems at the international and cross-cultural level, mainly the differences between the western free market systems and the Soviet state socialist systems. The work done before by Wilczynski (1983) seems to be particularly important in this respect and therefore the generalizations made by this author will be here summarized, as an introduction to the topic.

There is an obvious need to compare the structural characteristics of various types of societies. Labor force participation is higher in the communist countries because of the mass mobilization to implement ambitious goals. Labor turnover varies widely from one country to another irrespective of the social system; in general, it is higher with a higher stage of economic development; it is usually highest in construction, transport, trade, and industry and lowest in agriculture, forestry, and public administration. Under communism there is now a tendency to replace penalties and formal restrictions with incentives because the former appear to be counter-productive. Working hours are shortest in the west and longest in the developing countries, with the communist countries falling roughly in the middle. All around the world authoritarianism prevents genuine humanization of work, and dissatisfied workers indulge in absenteeism. Collective bargaining is most developed in the industrialized west and least developed in authoritarian systems.

There is a growing interest in industrial democracy, but its implementation remains restricted or distorted. The socialization of the means of production has not overcome the employee-employer conflict or workers' alienation either. In communist countries the degree of workers' participation in management is surprisingly small, except in Yugoslavia. The hierarchical concentration of power effectively prevents any substantial initiative and participation at the bottom; when workers are less educated and less assertive, participation can be effective only with the support of strong trade unions. Workers' participation has resulted in neither spectacular gains to the workers nor disastrous effects on production and social organization. In a centralized system unreserved workers' participation in management is not feasible.

The higher the stage of economic development, the greater the proportion of the working population engaged in industry and services. Generally labor productivity grows, but there are several obstacles in this respect based on the specificity of a given system (for example, hoarded labor under communism); in both free market and the command economies technological unemployment (hidden or open) has become a major problem. For example, in the Soviet bloc countries hoarded labor constitutes between 5 and 20 percent of total employment.

As a matter of fact, Marx's predictions of the increasing misery of the proletariat under capitalism and labor liberation under state socialism has not occurred. Under state socialism there is a conflict of interests between the rulers, promoting investments at the expense of consumers, and the actual producers, who are skillfully using the formal incentive system to improve their actual wages without necessarily producing more. Tough informal bargaining in this respect is a reality. Within total incomes the role of fringe benefits is growing all around the world; under communism authorities tend to enhance the effectiveness of individual material incentives to produce more. The incentive differentiation is greater among managerial and specialist personnel than among blue-collar workers and office personnel. The share of incentives in total wage earning under communism is large, and in fact surprising when considering the ideological commitment to egalitarianism. Considerable income disparities exist under capitalism as well as socialism, however, under socialism personal income disparities are smaller, and the spread in wage scales is generally narrower. Under the economic reform the disparities have tended to increase in most socialist countries, which contrasts with the capitalist tendency for the differences to decrease.

The standard of living of the working people depends not only on the level of development and the resource potential but also on the proportion of national income devoted to consumption, defense expenditures, working time, taxes, savings, availability of goods and services on the market, actual productivity of labor, the distribution of personal income, social consumption (formal and actual), availability of jobs, etc.

Inflation appears both under capitalism and socialism and is rooted in the growing contradiction between the demand and the supply. Socialist governments have much more power to withstand the pressure toward higher real wages. Capitalist market economies tend to give preference to fighting inflation rather than unemployment, while in the socialist centrally planned economies full employment takes precedence over inflation.

In capitalist countries industrial disputes are greater within the areas where the development and degree of labor's participation in political movements and management is substantial. A considerable social and economic inequality is also a contributing factor. Under state socialism there is a general tendency to restrict strikes or exclude them entirely. The more industrialized and democratic a country, the more elaborate a system of dispute settlement it has.

There are about 20 million migrant workers in the world, mostly in northwestern Europe, the U.S., and West Africa; some labor-importing countries depend on them heavily, and several labor-exporting countries heavily depend on the transfer of savings; however, labor migration has only a marginal effect on the economic modernization of labor-exporting countries.

The above mentioned general observations by Wilczynski (1983) should inspire much more comparative research. As already mentioned, the models of socialism and capitalism offered so far do not appear to be satisfactory. Official libertarian intentions and the reality of command and centralization under "socialism," when taken together, lead to a quite perplexing model. In some respects the "command" economies, as understood by Heilbroner (1980), share features, regardless of whether it is communism, Nazism, democracy at war, or a racist state. On the other hand, a mild form of state socialism, as, for example, in Hungary or Yugoslavia, has many common features with the free market economies.[1]

Contrary to what, for example, David Lane argues in The Socialist Industrial State (1976), this book does not claim that socialism in eastern Europe is a well-functioning model with some minor defects that will be gradually eliminated. The reliance on bureaucracy and coercion, the elimination or at least a very serious curtailment of civil rights, and the monopolization of socioeconomic, cultural, political and ideological life by one party that is self-appointed and entirely free from any public scrutiny have allowed the rulers of eastern Europe to mobilize all social resources for one goal: the building of a quasi-perfect work structure at the full disposal of the top elite. In reality such a structure has also led to the evident dysfunctions of the whole system: Consumer needs have been neglected for the sake of the state's and party's grandiose ambitions; Democratic mechanism for exchanging people in power is absent; the promises of the Marxist-Leninist doctrine, which is in permanent contradiction with reality, go unfulfilled; initiatives that originate outside the dissatisfying bureaucratic set-up are curtailed; spontaneity is suppressed and pushed into marginal or even into underground positions by formalism and the artificial nature of the whole structure. This built-in artificiality makes the state socialist work structure vulnerable to any external and internal threats and, therefore, makes the issue of survival the main preoccupation. Innovation trends are discouraged and the inability to incorporate them into the structure becomes evident.

The communist order in eastern Europe officially pretends to be progressive, but actually it constitutes a peculiar blend of new and old. The conservative and even reactionary nature of the system was a shock for the western New Left, which has experienced similar shocks, becoming disillusioned first with Maoist China, then Pol Pot's Cambodia, etc. (Levitt 1984). This book will try to show how much can be explained by looking into the particularities of the changing work structure.

The new eastern European generations enter the historical scene by moving from the traditionally lower class locations to the new, upwardly mobile positions in the socioeconomic and political hierarchy secured for them within the existing system. For several decades this wide-spread social mobility has been one of the main attractions of Soviet communism, as well as its source of power and mass support. At the higher stages of socioeconomic development, this whole social transformation becomes a more and more complicated matter, and its advantage for the system appears quite questionable.

The materialistic nature of Soviet communism inspires mass expectations that exercise a growing pressure on the ruling elites. Under Stalinism these expectations were kept under control by a mass terror whose development, however, endangered the ruling elite themselves more and more. Therefore, finally the decision makers had to stop using terror as the main controlling device, at least among the party ranks. By introducing some freedoms, improving the standard of living gradually, promoting modern technology, and adequately training people to make use of it, the rulers expose themselves to the rising demands articulated by various groups.

The issue of interest articulation is particularly complicated under Soviet state socialism because of the limits on self-expression and public criticism. Formally, no caucuses and coalitions are allowed unless originally sanctioned by the power elite. Therefore, it is common to use the informal or semiformal ways of interest articulation, which are highly dysfunctional in bureaucratic systems and add to the trouble instead of reducing it. This problem will be explained in the appropriate sections of the book.

The social structure of work relations under Soviet state socialism is the focus of this book, and the mutual relations between various strata, groups, and institutions are treated here as the blend of "old" and "new," however, without necessarily assuming (as is usually done by doctrinaire socialists) that under state socialism "old" is really disappearing unavoidably from the historical scene. Here the social structure will be understood as "a system of human relationships, distances and hierarchies (conceived) in both an organized and unorganized form" (Ossowski 1963, 11) and will be treated as influenced by two opposing tendencies: one oriented toward social equality, and the other oriented toward social inequality. Those who approve the existing order usually accept also the inequality. Those who question the existing order tend to see the inequality as unjust (Ossowski 1963, 197). Contemporary eastern Europe does not differ in this respect from the rest of the world even though the state socialist order established there at the end of World War II is quite egalitarian in some respects.

In many countries the state socialist ideology has become a very important factor of socioeconomic growth. In the name of state socialism the existing order is put aside to make room for the new ruling elites. The Marxist ideology accompanies the one party system, rationalized by the ruling elite as the best assurance of internal peace, order, equality, and common welfare. Manual workers, whose numbers rapidly grow with the progress of urbanization and industrialization, are deprived of effective collective bargaining, autonomous trade unions, and freedom of political choice, but the system lures them in with the promise that in the long run they will be better off.

Industrialization is closely related to the numerical growth of blue-collar workers, and this creates several problems for the ruling elite of both capitalism and state socialism. As long as manual workers represent a minority in agrarian-peasant societies, they must accept the conditions imposed by leaders. However, along with economic progress, some basic social transformations have occurred in industrializing and urbanizing societies. The numerical growth of manual workers makes a potentially strong pressure group within a given society. Yet, the bureaucratization of the nationalized economy multiplies the number of office workers, who are generally in an even worse socioeconomic situation than manual workers because they are more dispersed, less organized, and much more directly dependent on their bosses. Leaders of state socialist countries have good reasons to be anxious about how long they will be able to stay in control; these leaders govern in the name of working masses but in most cases the masses do not elect their own rulers. Everything may function relatively well as long as the leadership is able to assure some basic mass satisfaction. However, under the pressure of growing needs and aspirations, wide-spread dissatisfaction becomes more common as may be seen, particularly in Poland.

The relative social equilibrium in the eastern European countries depends not only on the authoritarian rule of the communist party but also, at least to some extent, on the changing relationships between all the major socioeconomic strata. For example, in the USSR, during the period 1939-83, within the total population, blue-collar workers have grown from 34 percent to 61 percent and collective farmers together with craftsmen in the coops have declined from 47 percent to 13 percent (SSSR 1984, 13). It is a very important analytic question how various strata make claims on the whole system and how their demands are aggregated into the system. For example, in Poland private farmers resist the official state and party authority as a veto group, but they were allowed to organize themselves into a coherent pressure force only temporarily in 1981. The intelligentsia all around the Soviet bloc is much too differentiated internally to be able to act in a coherent manner. People who have learned how to manipulate the system for their own benefit are, of course, not really interested in any reforms that would undermine their vested interests.

The ruling elites of eastern Europe constantly create new social tensions, sometimes quite unintentionally. Measures oriented toward egalitarianism lead to certain elitist consequences. Planning that is too strict and much too detailed gives rise to chaos. The doctrinaire propaganda depoliticizes people instead of making them more committed. All these paradoxes are not results of the ineptitude or of the doctrinaire approach of the elite but rather are caused by the application of a centralistic and highly authoritarian system to modern and relatively well-developed societies. There is a growing cleavage between the authoritarian style of managing people and the pluralistic nature of new emerging social structures. Most people work in nonagricultural pursuits within the nationalized economy, and they are dependent on the state as the monopolistic employer. In Poland, with her private agriculture, even farmers trade mostly with the state. The large numbers of working married women strengthens the economic dependence of the families on the state. At the same time, expectations regarding housing, buying power of incomes, promotion, leisure, and opportunities for the young are growing faster than the state's ability and willingness to satisfy them. Even in the popular culture achieved progress is not keeping pace with growing demands. The cultural facilities are overcrowded. There is a growing gap between the progress of the cultural sophistication, especially among the young people, and the quality of cultural supply.

The one-sided emphasis in eastern Europe on heavy industry and the negligence of these governments in the fields of consumption and services have both led to structural imbalances that may, in the long run, undermine a politicized work system that has so far remained relatively stable and secure. Soviet-bloc leaders have been quite successful in keeping the potentially disruptive forces under control. However, any further deterioration of mass consumption, and particularly of the food supply, may make the working people even more prone to opposition. The progovernmental trade union leadership depends not on the support of union workers, but on loyalty to the party. The informal public opinion is vulnerable to the extravagance of the ruling circles and their lavish consumption. The inadequate standard of living among most of the population and the affluent life-style of the leaders are at the root of growing dissatisfaction. The survival of the system depends primarily on the strength and loyalty of people who serve as party functionaries in the army, on the police force, in bureaucratic positions, etc.

The future of the present day status quo in eastern Europe depends mainly on the structural balance between social forces committed to change and forces that either want to preserve the status quo or tend to remain quiet. The rapid growth of the manual workers stratum and its relation to the system is of crucial importance in this respect. In the Marxist meaning of social class, blue-collar workers do not differ from white-collar workers because both of them are in the same position relative to the means of production as hired labor. The differences between both categories of workers in salary versus wage payments, fringe benefits, length of vacations and of the probationary period, notice of termination of employment, etc., have been gradually diminished in the Soviet-bloc countries and in several cases totally abolished. The position of white-collar workers used to be privileged in all these aspects, but now the privileges depend on seniority in a given enterprise, on the level of education, skills, and efficiency. This is the case in a formal sense at least, but in practice political leverage and the informal grapevine play a very important role.

By comparison with the situation before World War II, blue-collar workers have increased their numerical participation in the society; they have acquired considerable opportunities for social advancement, and they have ameliorated their position with respect to the traditionally higher classes. And yet, with all this, the bureaucratic regime has not given them an authentic chance to socially dignify physical labor and achieve a decent standard of living. The establishment's principles of action are based not in the nature of labor, its needs and requirements, but in the historical necessity of consolidating power at the top level. People who are members of the communist establishment and its main supporters trace their ancestry to the traditionally lower classes; but genealogy per se is not yet evidence of unity or disparity of concrete interests.

By subordinating the interests of the labor force to its utter dictatorship, the communist bureaucracy has created a system in which upward flight of blue-collar workers and farmers to the intelligentsia spheres has taken on a particular attraction. And these elitist spheres are highly differentiated. The bureaucratic system dominates, for after all, even the creative professions have become bureaucratized. To be sure, the white-collar ranks are continually growing but this originates much more from the progress of bureaucracy than from the technological and organizational progress.

All the above mentioned problems, aspects, and dimensions of the eastern European state socialism are discussed in detail in this book based not only on the statistical data, various surveys, and studies but also on the long experience of the author who lived in eastern Europe continuously until 1968, taught at the University of Warsaw (sociology of work and organizations), trained the managerial cadres in sociology and human relations, acted as a managerial consultant, did several research studies, and visited various eastern European countries several times on study trips and visiting lectures. The author published in 1974 Social Change and Stratification in Eastern Europe, An Interpretive Analysis of Poland and Her Neighbors (Praeger), now out of print. Some much-updated parts of that book are incorporated into chapter 4.

The first chapter deals with the work systems in general from a broad comparative perspective. Depending on the material basis, power of involved partners, freedom of action available to them, the values desired by partners, and the type of relationship commonly practiced (conflictual or cooperative), work systems differ widely in response to the local circumstances. These systems are products of the long-term historical developments and can be explained only from the perspective of various specific limits, necessities, established procedures and other reinforcements gradually accumulating in the process of bargaining.

Most attention is given in this first chapter to the western patterns to expose their difference with the communist work systems. Quite often the latter are interpreted in the literature without enough understanding of actually how much they are conditioned by the one party rule, dependence of all employees on the omnipotent state, lack of free trade unions, low wage policy, the great role of productivity bonuses in wages, etc.

The next chapters deal exclusively with the communist experience, particularly the Polish reality. It is up to the reader to make final conclusions about the advantages and disadvantages of both work systems, western and eastern, in the stimulation of working people and the coordination of their efforts. Basic problems in the west and in the east are very different, and this is due to a considerable extent to the different amount of personal freedom. The highly competitive and antagonistic nature of the western system has its obvious disadvantages. However, the "peaceful" and "cooperative" nature of the eastern system enforced by the power of the state and party apparatus has probably even many more disadvantages.

The second chapter introduces the readers to the historical origins of the present day social structures in eastern Europe. A comparison of Russia and Poland helps in understanding how much the past experiences of various societies of eastern Europe are diversified and how much the present day intersocietal tensions may be explained by the differences of historical background. To make readers fully aware of how risky it is to apply western criteria to the eastern European reality, some comparisons are provided between various countries.

The third chapter considers the dilemma between egalitarianism, officially presented in Eastern Europe as the basic social creed, and the practice of elitism rationalized by the rulers as "temporarily" unavoidable. It is shown here how the bargaining between various pressure groups within the state socialist system makes elitism something unescapable in the long run, and how a genuine democratization has been constantly postponed to the unforeseeable future. Group interests depend in their relative strength on a given group position in the bureaucratic hierarchy and, as happens all around the world, the stronger win and the weaker lose. It is necessary to mention that among the weaker are women, young people, ethnic minorities, nonparty members, etc. The constellation of groups changes under the varying historical circumstances, but the principle of elitism remains more or less the same.

Chapter 4 deals with the workers as a diversified conglomerate of various occupational categories; some of them traditionally were treated as "brain workers" in eastern Europe as distinct from "manual workers." Here first of all the identity of the intelligentsia is emphasized as a distinctive stratum maintaining the aspiration to be spiritual leaders of society. The competition in this respect between the class-conscious members of the intelligentsia and the bureaucratic state and party functionaries is almost unavoidable and explains many aspects of work structures in eastern Europe. Social relations within the ranks of the intelligentsia are explained in some case studies (actors, journalists, scientists) done by the author during his stay in Poland. Regarding the rest of the white-collar workers, their growing diversification and proletarization is the subject of attention. The bureaucracy has remained so far at the primitive technological and organizational level, hence the very great number of employees are needed to keep it intact. The irritation experienced in eastern Europe by most of the population when dealing with bureaucracy darkens the prestige of those who are servants of the state.

In the same chapter Poles working manually are treated: farmers, blue-collar workers, people in services. Most of these workers have their roots in the peasantry and they or their parents or grandparents moved to towns and into nonagricultural occupations not so long ago. Many face adaptational problems aggravated by the fact that during the whole period of socialist industrialization priority was given to heavy industry and military investments at the expense of housing, production of consumer goods, quality of services, etc.

There are several important differences among working people depending on age and generation, location, ethnic background, religiosity, etc. Different subgroups have been exposed at differing degrees to the official Marxist ideology, opportunities for social advancement, involvement in the party, and influence of the traditional values of intelligentsia. The class identity of the blue-collar workers is generally vague even if officially they are supposed to constitute collectively the ruling class and to reign over the party as an executor of their collective will. In reality the blue-collar workers form a "silent class," and the content of this chapter should provide an understanding as to why this happens. The more detailed treatment of manual workers and farmers may be found in A. Matejko, "The Hard Working People: Manual Workers and Farmers," 1983.

The fifth chapter analyzes the role of Polish sociologists within the social reality of eastern Europe. Their contribution is of a professional nature but under the peculiar circumstances of state socialism, they must avoid being identified with any direct or indirect opposition. This leads to several moral conflicts and anxieties from which there are no easy escapes. Taking into consideration the role conflicts of eastern European sociologists, it is necessary to interpret the message of their writings with adequate caution.

In the epilogue an attempt is made to inspire the readers to make for themselves the large scale conclusions that come in general from any revolutionary transformation of work systems in societies. What is the social and moral cost when people are treated as the objects of experimentation promoted by small privileged groups free from any control and vitally interested in staying in power? Who has the right to impose in an authoritarian way his/her own model of society claiming it to be perfect and, therefore, not open to any debate? The careful and critical study of the eastern European experience is vital for understanding the hidden nature of pitfalls that await us along the way to a better society, as well as to a better man.

NOTES

1. Wilczynski (1983) has taken too seriously the official declarations of the communist countries in the construction of his own scheme of comparative analysis. In several places in his book he makes critical observations and comments regarding the practice of socialism (elimination of free unions, low wage policy, lack of actual participation, etc.) but at the same time he does not correct his own model accordingly. If in the individual cases there is so much difference between ideal and reality, then why still treat the ideal as the basis of an interpretive analysis? One of the reasons for inconsistency is the fact the Wilczynski probably incorporated the Polish events (Solidarity, etc.) later on when the basic framework of analysis was ready.

Wilczynski quotes various sources from the communist countries without enough criticism regarding the reliability of facts and sincerity of insights. He makes the readers aware that the communist party elite on many occasions has proved to be insensitive and even vindictive to popular demands for better working and living conditions (p. 12), but this does not prevent him from treating socialism as a highly socialized system. Too much dependence on empirical facts quoted uncritically from various sources and not enough analysis and explanation seem to be the major weaknesses of this otherwise quite valuable book.

REFERENCES

Lane, David. The Socialist Industrial State. Towards a Political Sociology of State Socialism. London: Allen & Unwin. 1976.

Levitt, Cyril. Children of Privilege. Student Revolt in the Sixties. A Study of Student Movements in Canada, the United States, and West Germany. Toronto: University of Toronto Press. 1984.

Matejko, Alexander, J. "The Hard Working People: Manual Workers and Farmers," in Solidarity, ed. by Ajit Jain, Baton Rouge: Oracle Press, 1983, pp. 36-93.

Ossowki, Stanislav. Class Structure in the Social Consciousness. London: Routledge & Kegan Paul. 1963.

SSSR w cifrah 1983, Moscow: Finansy i statistika, 1984.

Wilczynski, Jozef. Comparative Industrial Relations. Ideologies, Institutions, Practices and Problems Under Different Social Systems with Special Reference to Socialist Planned Economies. London: The Macmillan Press, 1983.

1 VARIETY OF WORK SYSTEMS

THE COMPARISON OF PATTERNS

There is a variety of industrial relations models that fairly respond efficiently to the variety of circumstances. The "paternalistic" model, based on a far reaching dependence of employees on the employer, seems to be historically obsolete, but it still survives in some parts of the world, particularly Japan. The model of an "antagonistic cooperation" between unions and employers is still dominant in western countries but is widely criticized for its shortcomings: too much antagonism and too little cooperation. In state socialist societies the model of full cooperation between unions and the state (unions as a transmission of the ruling party to the working masses) prevails. But the enforcement of industrial peace by the ruling elite involves several disadvantages revealed in the early 1980s by the revolt of Polish blue collar workers promoting their Solidarity.

It is not an easy task to reconcile the organizational freedom of workers with the preservation of industrial peace; civil rights applied to the workplace with the high organizational efficiency; managerial prerogatives with the democratic spirit; control by workers of their own union organizations with an effective bargaining practice; technological progress with tenure and seniority rights; freedom of initiative with the state interference on behalf of the public good; good human relations with an effective work discipline; employment policy with the economy of the enterprise. The existing models of industrial relations in the west as well as in the east become more and more questioned from inside and outside.

Efficiency-oriented critics in the west blame the existing "antagonistic cooperation" model for tolerating waste, prolonging the bargain-

1

ing procedure, and complicating it, as well as antagonizing relations between various partners. The defendants of labor claim that the collusion of interests represented by the state and the private entrepreneurs leads to the suppression of the genuine labor interests. As long as organized labor is part of the play, the actual welfare of the rank-and-file is open to harm.

In the communist countries the model based on enforced cooperation is the source of different worries. The ruling circles complain that workers look for any occasion to be paid for nothing; there is a high labor turnover, and the output remains relatively low; there is much waste and neglect of duties. The opposition claims that the suppression of free trade unions and the elimination of a genuine bargaining demoralize people and contribute to low efficiency: People who are not represented and remain the objects of exploitation do not have much reason to commit themselves to work. The authorities apply several incentives and pressures for the labor power to work hard, but their impact remains quite limited. There is a permanent shortage of labor and the nationalized enterprises compete among themselves in the recruitment of workers.

The developing countries also have their own problems with the labor relations systems. As long as the hired labor remains a minority in traditional societies consisting mainly of peasants, trade unions represent collective interests quite opposed to the welfare of the poor majority—especially when the standard of living enjoyed by the workers is much higher than the average (Matejko 1976). The authoritarian nature of political systems imposes another restriction on organized labor. The corruption and inability of the union leadership also is an issue. In the labor markets favorable to the employer, organized workers have to compete with the unorganized candidates for employment. Under such general conditions, the existing labor relations system becomes more a liability than an asset.

All of these circumstances make the improvement of industrial relations very important from the standpoint of public interest, despite all possible reservations. Organized workers "selling themselves" to the employer may endanger not only their own well-being but also weaken the chances for other workers. On the other hand, prolonged conflict and aggravation of mutual relations with the employer would be harmful in the long run to all interested partners. Occupational groups that defend at any cost their privileged positions antagonize the rest of society, disrupt the existing order, and hide various inefficiencies as long as they serve vested interests.

The antagonization of mutual relations between the industrial partners may lead to the major social transformations; for example, to the nationalization of the whole economy or at least its most strategic parts. This does not necessarily mean a much better economy.

The substitution of private business by the omnipotent state apparatus may be a necessity in some underdeveloped countries that lack their own entrepreneurs, but this does not seem an effective solution in the long run. The universal blueprints formulated on the basis of some doctrines quite often do not allow any flexibility, and, therefore, they soon reach their limits of adequacy.

The incremental improvement of industrial relations may have much appeal to the practically oriented but will not work in the long run without some foresight and vision. The basic question is how to achieve a cooperation between all involved partners without upsetting the balance of power between them. The employer may be eager to improve the quality of working life but remains anxious regarding any issues dealing with the share of control. The unions may be open to technological improvements but will not accept the reduction of personnel. The state may be willing to leave much autonomy to the industrial partners but remains very sensitive to any turmoil. The shareholders may be open to the improvement of the living standard for the labor force but do not want to lose money for the benefit of higher wages.

The pluralistic arrangement of industrial relations, at least in the western framework, seems to remain as a permanent feature. Even in the collectively owned enterprises, industrial disputes are taken for granted and sometimes even lead to strikes. The limitation of these disputes by the law is treated by the general public with a suspicion. Except in some special circumstances, the abolishment of the right to strike is far from being popular. Collective bargaining at various levels and the wide application of peaceful procedures to prevent the aggravation of tensions are commonly treated as the reasonable remedies.

There is a constant challenge to the smooth cooperation in industry from the changing endeavors of various partners that are not necessarily in agreement with the rationale dictated by the market, profit making, and technology. With the constant growth of industrial production on the world scale (over three times in the period 1960-80), societies become more artificial and mutual relationships existing between industrial partners (employees, government, unions, clients, etc.) are more and more vulnerable. Very often only the external interference, exercised mostly by the state, manages to prevent a major disaster. The objective necessity of pluralism of decision making remains in a constant conflict with the long range concerns dictating centralization.

According to some gloomy predictions, pluralism is bound to disappear for the benefit of "peace and order" maintained by authoritarian regimes. On the other hand, the believers in democracy expect participation and decentralization to prevail all over the world because of their economic and humanitarian advantages. So far, the industrialized world seems to be more divergent than convergent, and there is not much chance for any unification in this respect.

Affluence of industrialized societies is a debatable issue. The pockets of poverty and the social inequalities remain evident under capitalism as well as under socialism, and in addition affluence is undermined by the unlimited growth of human aquisitiveness, generating inflation, dissatisfaction, tensions between various groups, etc. The civilization based on growth faces its limit, commercialization in the west as well as politicization in the east are self-defeating. "Convergence and divergence, continuity and change, similarities and differences are not poles apart but appear to be intrinsic features of the industrial world" (Hirszowicz 1981, 25).

THE UNEMPLOYMENT AND ITS
IMPACT ON INDUSTRIAL RELATIONS

Any restructuralization of the modern labor relations has to take into consideration the changing social background and the disproportions that grow under the impact of the slow down. The main blow for the poorer countries has been the sudden change in job prospects. Also, in the relatively rich countries the wide-spread unemployment is evident; in the developed market economies the rate of unemployment has grown on average in the period of 1970-82 from 3 percent to 8 percent. The demand of jobs has been growing steadily because of the rising material aspirations and the improvement of skills.

The young are particularly handicapped. Not only do they suffer an evident lack of perspectives, but they also enter as a generation the epoch of growing collective burdens. Unemployment compensation (60 to 70 percent of the average earnings) constitutes a growing burden on the developed countries. They are now much less able than before to absorb the immigrants and migrant workers; measures are taken to cut illegal immigration.

The quality of industrial relations in developing countries may have a major effect on those countries growth opportunities. The system vulnerable to inefficiency and corruption contributes to low output. Unions overly dependent on external powers, the state administration and the ruling party and military, are insensitive to the rank and file. Lack of an adequate link between the bottom and the top makes communication virtually impossible. The internal differentations of the labor power depending on organization, income, ethnicity, religion, and privilege contributes to the tensions. With the progress of urbanization, mobility, and education the public demands upon the industrial relations system multiply and make obsolete many traditional arrangements, for example protectionism. The moral and social constraints related to the traditional bonds cease to exist, organizational rules, welfare institutions, modernized religion, etc., need to substitute for them.

Problems characteristic of the industrial regions of the developed world are also grave, but they have a different character and a different background. Contrary to the immense inertia that characterizes precapitalist societies, the modern economic mechanism is flexible, sensitive, and development-oriented but at the same time unable to react positively to various limitations. One limitation arises from the growth of expectations faster than their satisfaction. For example, in the U.S. during the 1960s and the 1970s the consumption of durable goods grew much faster than the real disposable income. The eagerness of people to earn more and to spend more remains much ahead of the slowing down of industrial efficiency in the great western industrial democracies.

There is also a great concentration of power and wealth in the economy. One hundred of the biggest U.S. firms are the source of almost half of the sales of the whole industrial sector. About one-third of the nation's work force is employed by big business. The leading 800 firms employ roughly as many persons as the remaining 14 million proprietorships, partnerships, and smaller businesses. Twenty percent of the population owns about 76 percent of total wealth.[1] In the period 1929-72 the share of total personal wealth owned by the top one percent of the population has declined from 36 percent to 21 percent, but the concentration of economic power remains the fact of life.

In addition, the public sector plays a major role in the U.S. Taxes are in the proportion to final sales 1.0:3.2, and the employment in government to the employment in private business (excluding agriculture) is in the proportion of 1.0:4.6. In the period 1950-80 the number of people employed by the government has grown from 6.4 million to 16.2 million, and this does not include a large number of people working for the government indirectly. In a whole variety of ways the government influences the well-being of the nation. Governmental intervention has become matter of fact, including transfer payments, which have grown in the period 1929-80 from less than one percent to about 10 percent of GNP. People feel more and more entitled to take advantage of the government, and this new philosophy of "entitlement" has replaced the older one of "rugged individualism."

Governmental purchases have declined in the period 1960-81 from 23 percent to 19 percent of the GNP, but they represent a very powerful vehicle of influence. The role of transfer payments in the personal income of Americans has grown between 1960-81 from 7 percent to 14 percent; saving has declined in the period 1970-81 from 8 percent to 5 percent of the disposable personal income (much less than in western Europe or in Japan).

In the democratic American society there is an evident pressure toward equality, but the income distribution in U.S. housholds in the period 1967-81 did not change much. Those at the bottom (less than $10,000 annually) still constitute, as before, 25 percent of all households, and those at the top ($35,000 and more) have improved their share from 14 percent to 19 percent (among blacks from 4 percent to 9 percent). Inflation contributed to the feeling of injustice even though the real average income declined only by 4 percent.

Due to the growing responsibility of the government for the general performance of the economy, the pain of a crisis is less evident than before. However, at the same time the material aspirations of people are definitely growing and this imposes some significant pressures. In the period 1960-81 U.S. personal consumption expenditures per capita both on durable goods and services doubled while the real per capita disposable personal income grew only by 60 percent. The economy, which depends more and more on services, does not allow for any dramatic improvement of productivity except the major reconstruction of the economy on the basis of heavy investment.

The U.S. economy depends to a growing extent on its relations with the world, not only in oil but also in other items. (In Canada exports have grown in the period 1968-82 from 18 percent to 30 percent of the GNP, but her share in world trade has diminished from 5.2 percent to 3.6 percent.) American overseas production assets may be as much as $300 billion, and U.S. direct investment has moved toward Europe (45 percent of the whole U.S. external investment) in 1980 in comparison with only 18 percent in 1929); manufacturing and petroleum together constitute two-thirds of this investment. There is a vital problem of how to reconcile the U.S. interests with the growing ambition of developing countries to run their own business in the way most suitable for them. Difficulties are unavoidable. "It is not capitalism alone that is in crisis, but all modern industrial society," (Heilbroner and Thurow 1982, 239). There is an obvious need to establish good working conditions between the government and the private business, and the Japanese experience shows that it is possible.

With the growing level of general education and higher material aspirations, there is more pressure in the labor market to find some jobs that would allow the living standard to be maintained or improved, achieve a career, move to a better social position. In the economy that is not developing fast enough, it is difficult for people to secure what they want. A growing number of people in society want and have to work. In the U.S. population the percent of those not in the labor force has declined in the period 1950-82 from 40 percent to 36 percent; in the same period the percent of unemployed has grown from 3 percent to 6 percent. The decline of agriculture (from 7 percent to 2 percent) and the growth of female employment are the most obvious structural changes of the labor force. It is necessary to mention that the U.S. economy is in much better shape than in other western countries. For example, in the period 1950–1983, employment has grown in the U.S. by 71 percent in comparison to only 17 percent in West Germany (Die Zeit, 1985, 13, pt. 3).

THE HISTORICAL CHANGE OF INDUSTRIAL RELATIONS

In developed countries, during the formative decades of the late nineteenth and early twentieth centuries, the control of labor moved gradually higher up the management hierarchy, reflecting the more integrated and interdependent nature of the new production systems. Managers were pushed to the front line of supervising production; the increased centralization of pay systems within companies produced a need to develop personnel policies and skills. The progressing segmentation of the market under capitalism favored the establishment of internal labor markets, bureaucratic patterns of management, and the modernized versions of paternalism. There was a thrust toward welfare capitalism associated with the emergence of large corporations in the early years of the twentieth century—primarily in the U.S. (Gospel and Littler 1983, 189).

Paternalism on the one side and the enlightened employment policy administered directly by the employer on the other side took over gradually, especially in large factories. "Managers in America and elsewhere changed their views about delegation and came to regard the organization of work processes and the direction of "labour" as functions which they had to control in the interests of maximum profitability. . . . Rationalized organization would find better ways of working and regulate labour more closely, thus raising its productivity" (Hill 1981, 24). According to Clawson (1980), rationalization in administration was arbitrarily imposed upon working people against their will, interest, and sense of justice. This is only partially true because any progress meets resistance and usually remains a painful process. The imputation of sinister motives to innovators like F. W. Taylor and others does not lead far enough in understanding the historical processes.

In the U.S. the bureaucratic control succeeded to stabilize labor/capital relations even in the 1920s. The internal promotion system became more rigid than in Japan. The German pattern was characterized by the welding together of Taylorism and welfarism. It was in the large German corporations, like Krupp and Siemens, that bureaucratic patterns of management and internal labor market developed (Littler 1982, 191).

The new fabric of a "scientific" control presented a mixture of hierarchy, rules, a systematic division of labor, written records and communications, maximum fragmentation of jobs, divorce of planning and doing, divorce of direct and indirect labor, minimization of skill requirements and job-learning time, as well as the reduction of material handling to a minimum. As long as there was not too much resistance to it, and the cost of reform remained lower than the expected benefits, the employers showed a willingness to implement scientific management in their enterprises. It is significant that "most union officials accepted the given frameworks of capitalist and managerial power and, moreover, had little conception that neo-Taylorite schemes would alter the structure of control over the labour process" (Littler 1982, 189). The internal labor contractor and the traditional foreman constituted a much more important source of resistance than the unions.

The process of work bureaucratization in the U.S. as well as in the U.K. has contributed considerably to the destruction of traditional authority and group relationships. It was impossible to infuse the existing levels of group solidarity with commitment to the same values as the formal organization. Contrary to the tactics applied by the Japanese employers, the dynamic of deskilling in the west has led to decollectivization and a gap between the enterprise and its employees. The progressive reification of mutual relationships in the quadrangle, that is, employer-employees-trade unions-government provided a suitable ground for the antagonistic mutual relationship, and bureaucratization was the only answer. "The bureaucratization of the employment relationships has (partly) been a union attempt to exercise leverage on hiring, firing and promotions and to fight off the commodification of labour" (Littler 1982, 195).

Under such conditions there was no room for paternalism, ideological control, and "groupism" that gained an upper hand in Japan. This was not a matter of determinism but a specific managerial strategy chosen to fit existing circumstances. Trends initiated many years ago have had a validity until today and shape the labor markets.

In the U.S. the bureaucratization of industry occurred two decades earlier than in the U.K. This happened during the expansionary period of large production corporations. Taylorism and systematic management "offered solutions to the exigencies of managerial control and coordination, and they minimized the economic impact of labour turnover by structuring work organization around a mobile, shifting, immigrant labour force. The impetus behind many bureaucratic innovations was management's attempt to free itself from uncertainty in the labour market" (Littler 1982, 185). Due to the favorable economic conditions and the positive cooperation of unions, it was possible to achieve more organizational innovation than in the case of the U.K.

The development in Great Britain in this respect was much different than in other western developed countries. For example, in the

British engineering industry, the fragmented structure of established firms, the relative weakness of mass demand in the home market and the opportunities to evade foreign competition by moving into nonEuropean markets discouraged for a long time mass production and major capital investment into it. There was widespread trade union hostility toward any development of any internal labor market. The continued familial framework of many British industries meant that the development of new organizational forms was impeded (Gospel and Littler 1983, 84). There was a thrust toward welfarism and paternalistic strategies in some British industries during the early decades of the twentieth century, but it failed to become a major strategy.

The detailed analysis of "scientific management" applications, particularly in the U.K., shows its significance in the progressing bureaucratization of the structure of control, but not the employment relationship. The process of determining and fixing effort levels met resistance from the delegated forms of control (labor contracting etc.), lower and middle management, as well as workers themselves. Labor intensification proved to have a crucial effect on the structures of control and this endangered many people involved.

The elaborate bureaucratic rules applied to work became a matter of necessity. In the U.K. there was much less utilization of work organization experts than in the U.S., but the Bedaux system gained relative success. "In Britain, the organizational outcome of the transition process was neo-Taylorite forms of industrial organization, compromised by the continued informal power of shopfloor foreman. Also in the British case, work-groups were unanchored into the system, and proved impenetrable obstacles to centralized managerial control" (Littler 1982, 158).

The Soviet system of industrial relations as practiced in the U.S.S.R. and the satellite countries differs much from the west. Soviet society remains basically uneven, and the rigidity of gradation has a negative effect on its functioning. Contrary to the official creed, there is not much of an authentic mobility reflecting the ambitions, skills, and actual contributions of people to the general well-being. A permanent location of the majority in the unprivileged socioeconomic strata is a common fact in the Soviet Union, and inequality is growing due to differences in life opportunities. The groups already privileged are able to reinforce an uneven distribution of rewards and inequality of access to the most desirable positions. The passport system has been strengthened. The distribution of goods and opportunities has become more rigid instead of relaxed. An "organized consensus" keeps people well under control within "a political compromise between the state and the people in which basic social groups accept the existing distribution of power and their estrangement from the decision-making process in exchange for job security, some workers' rights, upward mobility, and a slow but steady rise in living standards" (Zaslavsky 1982, viii).

The internal passport system, which effectively prevents the collective farms from losing their labor power, the difference between open and closed enterprises, the ethnic ascription, the element of fear—all of these keep the citizens quiet, marginalized, suppressed, or exiled. The far-reaching atomization of society allows the ruling elite to preserve its privileged position, but economic efficiency is sacrificed for the sake of internal stability.

The system is producing a growing number of specialists for whom there are no attractive jobs under an economy that is losing its previous vigor. It is becoming more and more difficult to subsidize the low prices of basic foodstuffs, insure the availability of jobs, and tolerate the black market practices of the population to improve their living standard at the expense of public interest.

The historical compromise between the regime and the population does not have much chance to continue, especially with the tough measures initiated by Andropov and probably being followed by Gorbachev. There is not much more room for socioeconomic expansion of the kind that would keep people relatively well settled and satisfied. Young people are more and more tempted to escape from the countryside but they manage it only in an informal way. The "closed city" policy reduces the chance of territorial mobility. The cities are overcrowded with specialists while at the same time several branches of industry are suffering a shortage of them. The inhabitants of great cities enjoy privileges that are denied the remaining population. The state maintains a large number of people who in reality are not useful. So far the socioeconomic groups remain fragmented and do not have any chance to struggle collectively for an adequate share in society.

The recent attempts to strengthen labor discipline represent a delayed effort to rescue the situation. However, they are very much against the unspoken traditional social contract maintained for many years between the ruling elite and the population.

Because all social activity is impossible without party-state mediation, there is not much interest in the development of autonomous pressure groups. People individually strive to be upgraded and this exercises an effective pressure on the government. To keep the status seekers happy, it is necessary to open more room for them, establish the reliable criteria of promotion, and multiply the attractive resources (new jobs, housing, sponsored holidays, bonuses, etc.). There is a strong element of manipulation in the governmental policy regarding various groups and categories of the population.

Farmers are hated for charging too much for their agricultural and dairy products offered on the open market. Skilled industrial workers envy those who earn more in mining or construction. The animosities existing between various occupations and territorial groups show the weakness of the Soviet society that is unable to produce enough to satisfy the basic needs of the whole population.

THE JAPANESE EXPERIENCE AND ITS VALIDITY

The Japanese case is different from the previous ones. "In Japan, the employer strategy was one of incorporation: utilizing existing social relationships for production purposes, and maintaining an ideological control. . . . Commitment to skill dissolved into commitment to organization and organizational status" (Littler 1982: 160). Instead of superseding the powers of the contractors and traditional foremen, centralizing managerial control, deskilling part of the work force, and assuming a minimum relationship between the organization and the shopfloor workers, as happened in the Anglo-Saxon countries, the Japanese companies used the social solidarity principle, incorporated the previous labor contractors (oyakata) into the enterprises, and took advantage of the already existing work groups. There was no place in this arrangement for the resistance of the foremen who, as in the U.K., had inherited many of the powers and privileges of the labor contractors.

Is it possible to transplant the Japanese experience to different cultural and socioeconomic circumstances? Will western workers accept the Japanese style work ethic? A partial answer to this question is given by the first major survey of the Japanese firms in the U.K. (White and Trevor 1983).

There is a substantial difference between the Japanese-owned manufacturing companies and the financial subsidaries. In both cases only some elements of the Japanese management practice are implemented. "The keynote of Japanese personnel management in Britain has been a piecemeal pragmatism rather than any attempt to introduce a comprehensive Japanese system of employment" (White and Trevor 1983, 124). Local people hired by the Japanese are always very carefully selected. Financial companies tend to avoid any over-qualified personnel so that there would be no false expectations of promotion.

In these studies neither unusually beneficial employment practices nor exceptional levels of employee satisfaction could be identified. The advantage appeared in something different than creating particularly happy and contented workers or generating particularly strong feelings among workers that human relations in the company are given high priority (White and Trevor 1983, 127). The working practices of Japanese management based on an organized or orderly approach, an emphasis on detail, an overriding priority attached to quality, and a punctilious sense of discipline appeared as the basic asset appreciated by blue-collar workers. The effect depended on the combination not on this or that practices in isolation. The Japanese style of management based on personal good example coming from the top down the whole hierarchy was highly appreciated by British workers even when it imposed upon them high demands. "The need for fulfillment through commitment to work is not moribund, as so many commentators have for long assumed; it is merely waiting to be called into play" (White and Trevor 1983, 130).

It is significant that the British white-collar workers in the financial subsidiaries react negatively to the same style that is welcomed by the British blue-collar workers in the manufacturing companies. It seems that the white-collar workers are just less open to the high work ethic. "Employees sometimes expressed puzzlement about the Japanese emphasis on certain particulars, and did not see them as part of a whole style of work. . . . British white-collar workers have a different, and more instrumental outlook to work than British blue-collar workers. This instrumental outlook may in some cases take a form of preoccupation with material rewards, in others with career progression" (White and Trevor 1983, 130). The Japanese firms gain acceptance and support for their methods of management only among people ready to appreciate the full commitment to work. In the manufacturing firms "reactions to management were more favourable the greater the Japanese influence and presence" (White and Trevor 1983, 131).

The leadership by example seems to be the main asset of Japanese companies in the U.K. A sense of equality was also appreciated, especially by the blue-collar workers. "What impressed workers was not the patronizing graces of egalitarianism but the fact that management evidently shared the same objectives, tasks and disciplines as themselves. . . . The conditions under which workers will see management as highly rational and effective were amply satisfied. . . . Japanese-style working practices and Japanese-style management are part and parcel of one concerted system to achieve effective production. It is on those simple terms that both win the support of the British workers" (White and Trevor 1983, 132).

It is not easy to apply the Japanese experience to the developing western countries; one must remember that "behind the deceptive simplicity of specific Japanese-style working practices, there is an elusive unity of method" (White and Trevor 1983, 135). The Japanese system demands a heavy involvement of management in daily details, and the western supervisors are unprepared for it. A comprehensive and detailed knowledge of the design and control of production is taken for granted in the case of any Japanese manager. Close contact with day-to-day operations is expected even at the highest levels of management.

There is an obvious need to revitalize the notion of detailed practical exercise combined with the managerial knowledge and experience. There is a need to reconcile managerial delegation with management by detail and also to make management strong not by power but by expertise. The whole system has to be task-oriented. Leadership is mainly a problem of implementing it in practice. The performance of work groups can be affected much more by the design, planning, and control of work than by an exterior process of motivation. Much that is now taught to managers under the rubric of motivation, leadership, and the behavioral sciences, could perhaps be profitably replaced by new topics in the design and operation of production systems.

Discipline and a shared outlook within the Japanese system bring together supervisors and subordinates, generalists and narrow specialists, people representing various disciplines and different educational levels. This is exactly what seems to be missing in the modern western world. The career path based only on individual achievement is in basic disagreement with team work. It seems necessary to question several traditional assumptions to become really open to absorb and digest several useful aspects of the Japanese style of management.

THE ISSUE OF CONTROL

Any labor process contains elements of cooperation as well as conflict, and it is necessary to consider both these strands and their significance in various settings. The dominant form of control exercised in a given setting is the major factor. "By taking account of patterns of control we, then, can explain why certain activities are possible only in certain circumstances. . . . The analyst needs a measure of the ability of workers to resist management and to attain their own ends" (Edwards and Scullion 1982, 271). It is necessary to look into the multifaceted nature of workers' relations with management; the struggle for control may be conducted very differently under the same general type of management structure (Edwards and Scullion 1982, 273).

The control of the labor process reflects the power relations, and, depending on the goodwill and ability of the involved partners, this control may be more or less peaceful. "The ways in which differences of interest affect the fabric of social and economic life are various and display no simple or universal manifestation in the conduct of industrial relations" (Hill 1981, 14). According to C. R. Littler, "The linkage between the logic of capital accumulation and transformations of the labour process is an indirect and varying one" (Littler 1982, 34). For Littler the capitalist reality is more complex than the vision shared by H. Braverman (1974), Clawson (1980) and others who see a unilinear decline from a homogeneously skilled working class of the nineteenth century to the homogeneously unskilled working class of the twentieth century. "Braverman completely abandons any attempt to locate contradictory tendencies within the capitalist mode of production or contradictions within specific strategies of control. . . . Capitalism is in a perpetual tension between treating labour as a commodity and treating it as a non-commodity, that is as a continuing social relationship between employer and workers" (Littler 1982, 29, 32).

The frontier of factory control is much shaped by the interaction between employer strategies and the particular strategies followed by workers. Both kinds of strategies affect each other and produce some particular patterns of control. "Workplace activities have to be related to the frontier of control before their significance as forms of 'conflict' can be understood" (Edwards and Scullion 1982, 274).

Forms of social control over the structural constraints are crucial in understanding how the constraints work in practice. Within the existing constraints, the management rules primary among them, the workers have some freedom to act and they choose between various alternatives depending on the variety of circumstances. "The shopfloor has to develop a very particular form of control before certain forms of action, and the systems of argument that go with them, become possible" (Edwards and Scullion 1982, 279-80). Actions and structure interact and actors have a certain freedom of choice within the context of constraints located at the various levels of the structure. At the most general level the structure of market relationships permits some forms of workplace control to develop and inhibits others.

No simple causal line can be traced from stages in the development of capitalism to changes in management structure and strategy. Littler says, "In practice and in history, social groups and factions, such as managers and trade unions, mediate any relationship between the development of capitalism and changes in work organization and industrial relations" (Gospel and Littler 1983, 193). H. F. Gospel says something similar stating, "Rather than seeking an elegant typology, it is probably more historically accurate to look at the problems and opportunities which have confronted management over time and at the mix of strategies with which they have experimented. The combination of strategies has been highly complex, and employers have searched in a zig-zag backwards and forwards movement between them" (Gospel and Littler 1983, 12).

This is a much different approach than those taken by Braverman (1974) and Edwards (1979) who in their Marxist analyses "substitute for the broad processes of capitalism a single, overall trend namely an imperative of control of the labour process without specifying the nature and basis of this imperative" (Gospel and Littler 1983, 193). Detailed studies of particular historical sequences revealing the variety of factors and circumstances that influence the choice of strategies taken by the organized employers as well as the organized labor are greatly needed.

Littler makes a distinction between three levels of work structuralization: the area of work design, the formal authority structure of the factory, the relation of job positions to the labor market. "Whilst there is a tendency for changes in job design, control structures and employment relations to go together, this is only a tendency and not a necessity. . . . The introduction of new technology formed the base for the erection of bureaucratic structures of control, nevertheless the bureaucratization of the administration of production does not entail deskilling" (Littler 1982, 43). Skill may mean work routines, a socially constructed status, or control over process and products. The task range and discretionary content are the two dimensions of an objective notion of skill.

When dealing with the concept of bureaucracy, Littler claims that "it is necessary to theorize levels of legitimation and a concept of everyday compliance which may or may not exist within an overall framework of legitimation but is certainly not theoretically identical. 'Loyal' employees may go on strike whilst apathetic employees may not" (Littler 1982, 46).

Legitimation may be organized based or culturally based. The achievement of consent is a matter of modus vivendi between management and shopfloor that may have little to do with generating or reflecting large scale legitimations (Littler 1982, 39). "Actual shopfloor behaviour and relationships must be seen then not as consequences of the unilateral imposition by management on a passive workforce of specifications and prescriptions, but a two-way exchange in which an accommodation concerning the meaning and relevance of such prescriptions is achieved in exchange for some level of commitment to the existing distribution of authority, and to working objectives" (Littler 1982, 42).

From this perspective, the bureaucratization of the structure of control and the bureaucratization of the employment relations are two different processes. The dependency of workers is at a maximum when the employer has control over every aspect of the workers' lives and they are in no position to organize a collective opposition. On the other hand, the indirect employment and control, based on domestic system or an internal contract may make workers even more dependent than the direct employment and control. As long as subcontracting of management prevails in industry, the only nexus between the two sides of industry, employers and employees, is a naked self-interest.

One must look closer at the historically changing modes of labor control, the deskilling process, the conceptualization of the process of change under advanced capitalism, the organizational forms in industry and dominant managerial strategies, the cross-cultural comparisons of the development of labor control in various countries, the nature and effects of worker resistance to employer control strategies, the links and correspondence between labor market structures, and the labor process. We will review here some of the recent comparative studies in this respect.

THE CONFRONTATION

The spread of a rationalized mode of organization has contributed to the progressing depersonalization. By incorporating compulsion into the organization of the workplace it was possible to achieve more order and predictability; but at the same time the diversity of interests between various partners of the production process became even more accentuated.

Low mutual trust is now a matter of fact in capitalist enterprises and under state socialism. The work place is highly vulnerable to tensions and shows low adaptability to changing circumstances. Genuine cooperation becomes something unnatural because partners blindly follow their own self-interests and totally ignore the public good. When facing difficulties with their employees, employers prefer to substitute them with machines and transfer the responsibility for the discharged workers to the welfare state.[2]

The art of management has acquired a manipulatory character devoid of the ethical considerations. The notion of a community of interests including all partners is only a myth suitable for public relations and is very far from the daily reality.

It is necessary to make a clear distinction between the industrial conflict as confrontation between two or more opposite power centers striving for scarce resources, and the workplace deviance that is mostly "sub-cultural rather than contra-cultural; it reflects dominant values and norms as much as or more than opposes them" (Watson 1980, 245). Many working people adapt to their working conditions, release their frustrations and do not have to be in conflict. Dissatisfactions may be mobilized under suitable circumstances to serve as motives for the conflict-oriented activities, but this is not something unavoidable. The logic of work satisfaction (or dissatisfaction) has some connections with the logic of interest struggle, but both of them remain autonomous phenomena.

To keep their self-respect, the working people develop some defense mechanisms that rescue them from dispair and loss of esteem. There are also several rationalizations used to justify deeds that may be difficult to accept another way. However, all these phenomena should not be identified as necessarily conflictual.

The formation of groups and coalitions—from the defensive cliques and assertive cabals up to the formal institutions like trade unions, etc.—is mostly related in the industrial field to the gradual change from the diffuse master-servant relationship (status contract) to the much more specific functional relationship (purposive contract) of a depersonalized nature. The unequal power basis evolving within the hierarchical organizations has stimulated many categories of working people to establish their own institutional representation.

The instrumental collectivism of all these new socio-organizational forms was a response to the power of employers endangering the individual employees. The widespread industrial conflict has become actually possible only with the multiplication of the power centers; as long as the power of the employer remained unchallenged, there was no room for a conflict, except some sporadic outbursts of dissatisfaction or violence.

The ability of employees to collectively challenge the employer depends on several objective and subjective circumstances: the dependence of the employer on people representing specific skills; the control by the employees of the strategically important positions; the communication between the employees; the employees' ability and willingness to act together, etc. Various groups and categories of employees differ widely in their willingness and skill to promote the conflictual actions. Some of them are ready for the informal dealings (for example, a slow down), but any formalized appearance remains beyond their capacity. A strike usually needs much organization and resources to be successfully implemented. In this respect the judgment of a union quite often may differ substantially from the emotional readiness of local workers to act radically against the employer.

Depending on the major frame of reference—unitary, based on the harmony of interests; pluralist, based on the conciliation of various interests; and radical, based on the conflict arising from the major inequalities and imbalances of power—the role of industrial conflict may be approached from a variety of perspectives (Fox 1974). For example, the distinction between interest groups that are supposed to cooperate with each other from the autonomic positions (the pluralist perspective) assumes some equality of condition and opportunity, not substantive and material conflict of interests, freedom from external steering. This may be sometimes true, but very often it is not. Several authors, for example Watson (1980, 231), therefore question the validity of any analytical framework that assumes a stable balance of power between employers and employed.

In the conflict between unions and employers the breakdown of bargaining may be caused by several factors, but the level of pay is usually the major factor. For example, in the U.K. during the period of 1966-79 the share of pay issue has grown from accounting for 67 percent to accounting for 94 percent of days lost due to strikes (Hirszowicz 1981, 204). The demonstrations of protest play a major public relations function, and both sides are eager to gain allies. The frequency of work stoppages depends not only on the strike-proneness of various occupational groups and branches of the economy but also on the strategic considerations taken by the unions and employers. For example, when the employers do not care much to get their workers back, they may allow a strike to continue longer than when the production is badly needed.

In general it is possible to say that in the well-to-do democratic societies strikes have become a tolerated waste, treated as a necessary nuisance to keep human freedoms intact. Much more waste occurs from sickness and accidents, as well as the unemployment, than from the strikes.

On the other hand, now "strikes are more disruptive in economic and social terms than ever before. The growing 'systemness' of Western economies makes them much more vulnerable to prolonged strikes in key industries" (Hirszowicz 1981, 221). With the decline of growth in western countries, there is a drive to lower the level of strikes, especially in the essential services.

Another question is to what extent the unions are able and willing to control the striking activities promoted by the rank and file. Usually unions have a hard time convincing workers to strike and to show their dissatisfaction not necessarily only with the employer but possibly also with the union. "When a revolt takes place this may be regarded as a symptom of a more serious conflict that is not confined to the formal opposition of minority-majority rights but arises out of contradictions and signals the shortcomings of existing institutions" (Hirszowicz 1981, 226).

In the confrontation between organized employees and employers several factors count, such as how many people will join a collective action, who will sponsor it, how dedicated people will be to their common cause, etc. These factors differ widely among various economic branches, occupations, enterprises, and whole societies.

For example, in France the work stoppages are treated by law much more tolerantly than in the Anglo-Saxon countries or in West Germany. This does not necessarily mean that France suffers much because of strikes: For several years the time lost on strikes has not grown above 2.5 percent of total absenteeism and 0.002 of the whole yearly work time. France has many more strikes than West Germany, Austria, Holland, or the Netherlands but far fewer than the U.S., the U.K., Canada, and Italy. The strikes in France have a local character and last for a short time because they give an outlet to the dissatisfaction of employees and, as in several other countries, serve primarily as a weapon of collective bargaining. The average strike in France mobilizes no more than 200 employees and lasts from three to five days. Skilled male manual workers 25 to 40 years old most commonly strike. However, with the changes of the labor force other groups (women, unskilled workers, etc.) are becoming more common among the strikers (Reynaud 1982, 22).

Blue-collar workers even in France are quite often instrumentally oriented, and the success of the union or party organization depends on the ability to satisfy workers' specific expectations. "Militant class consciousness and protest are more likely to remain only latent—to be mobilized only in major crises" (De Angelis 1982, 238). The total socialist and communist vote in the legislative and presidential elections in France has remained around 40 percent or less. In present day France, despite the socialists being in power, many blue-collar workers are reticent. The quality of the "organizational weapon" plays a major role in the mobilization of French workers, and the relative success of communists in the past was because of this weapon.

There is a fluidity of partisan alignments and voting intentions, as well as the strength of patriotic, religious, conventional moral, and authority values among the blue-collar workers. The left is not the only political option for many blue-collar workers, and this is particularly valid for the communities in which a home-centered and privatized existence prevails.

Many blue-collar workers quit the union when they do not need it immediately. The support of the union "is often seen as an unpleasant duty, whose obligation is discharged by voting for a union list in plant committee elections and by sympathizing with other workers elsewhere when they strike for their rights—and occasionally by striking oneself when there is little risk involved, and when there is a good chance to win" (De Angelis 1982, 226).

Blue-collar workers in the developed market societies are far from being polarized as Marx predicted, and their appearance in the whole variety of roles (consumers, citizens, etc.) contributes to the pragmatic nature of labor conflicts. According to Crouch,

> Whatever the value of Marxist contributions, they are marred by two crucial characteristics: the assumption that all issues can be reduced to those of capital and labour, and the search for revolutionary consciousness. . . . To construct an entire theory of trade unionism around a nonexistent phenomenon—the revolutionary working class—is to produce something of limited usefulness in understanding the real day-to-day choices of trade unions and their members (1983, 37; 219-20).

The unions have to be down to earth in order to succeed. "A choice of strategy is not just a choice between goals, but a choice between goals set in the context of the means needed to secure them" (Crouch 1983, 37; 139). The actual chance to win at bargaining may be more probable in some areas than in the others, and so unions concentrate their pressure on the fields particularly well controled by them. The level of negotiation also is of great validity in this respect: In the case of a local negotiation different items play major roles than would be the case in a centralized negotiation.

Wage negotiations are the main concern of western unions in dealing with employers. Several aspects in addition to amount must be considered in this complicated issue. There is a great diversity of pay determination, as well as the traditional differences between the blue-collar workers and the white-collar workers. Payment by results makes establishments more vulnerable to strikes. All these factors make bargaining even more complicated. In addition to strikes, several other forms of conflict occur.

One of the potential sources of conflict is the relative autonomy of the levels of pay. Levels of pay and the financial or market circumstances of establishments are not set on a consistent relationship. The larger the establishment, the higher people are paid; the greater the proportion of women employed, the less people are paid. There is some tendency for earnings to be higher in places where union organization is strong. Payment and productivity do not necessarily go together and produce several tensions (Daniel and Millward 1983).

Unions have a political interest, but "the purpose of unions' political action is simply to ensure the non-interference of politics in their industrial activity" (Crouch 1983, 191). The wage-employment constraint directs unions to the political field to regulate the economy according to their interests. In this respect there is a major difference in perspective between union locals and the national leadership.

There is the near-inevitable drift of trade unions into politics, whether its members like it or not and whether its leaders take much interest in it or not. Through the friendly political parties the trade union movement can influence political developments that remain beyond its direct reach.

In the context of social democracy "a pattern of industrial relations seems to develop which does have some strange similarities with nineteenth century Catholic ideas of corporation; a fascinating irony given the old antagonism between socialism and Catholicism" (Crouch 1983, 207). Unions are likely to concede more to gain participation in the more important forums.

This growing "politicization" of unions makes them vulnerable to internal tensions if they are willing to sacrifice the immediate interests of their members, as well as the social causes, primarily the fate of the unemployed, to secure for themselves a warm place within the establishment. The shopfloor organizations have a vested interest to oppose corporatism, and under the present arrangement they become a major source of tension. "On several occasions union behaviour has implied that it is not worthwhile reaching deals with them since their arrangements will be upset by autonomous shop-floor action" (Crouch 1983, 219).

The state is taking a much more active role than before; the labor-management conflicts are getting more institutionalized, and a change in the nature of authority can also be felt. For example, in France, under the socialist rule cosponsored by communists, the role of the state in regulating labor problems has become particularly sensitive. On the one hand, the traditional socioeconomic inequalities remain intact and the state is cautious about aggravating the relationship it has with private entrepreneurs. On the other hand, the difficult economic situation of France makes it necessary to introduce several unpopular measures to correct the deteriorating balance of payments.

Between the trade unions and the employers the control issues are often much more conflictual than the economic issues. "Wage bargaining can be accommodated because it is not a zero-sum game with fixed resources where one side can only benefit at the cost of the other. But conflict over control cannot be moderated and regulated in the same way" (Hill 1981, 131). It is also important to remember that "patterns of behaviour reflect patterns of control, and that actions gain their significance as forms of conflict within particular structures of control" (Edwards and Scullion 1982, 282).

Biased, inoperable, or counter-productive policy suggestions arise very often from failure to recognize the underlying patterns of control. It is necessary to accept that conflict is part of a continuing struggle of vested interests and collective strivings. "The struggle for control takes a variety of forms and has a variety of consequences, and it is the outcome of the struggle, and not the implementation of this or that policy recommendation, which is crucial" (Edwards and Scullion 1982, 284). Conflict must be understood in context, and the general socioeconomic situation of the country plays a major role in this respect.

It is the nature of trade unions to have a limited perspective, and one finds that only in relatively few cases has a trade union become a platform suitable for a far-reaching job reform. Collective organization definitely has an effect on relative wage levels and the structure of wages, especially when unions are strong enough to exercise successful pressure on the employers.

Let's return to the French case already mentioned. Unions remain relatively weak and insecure even under the socialist government; many of their militant actions originate from insecurity and not from power; the politicization of unions shows that the traditional basis of their activities is not stable enough to act independently; several important categories of the working population remain beyond the scope of trade unionism; internal democracy within unions is either non-existent or underdeveloped.

Because industrial peace is not obligatory for the French bargaining powers, strikes are difficult to predict; many among the latter arise at the local level. Various unions coexist at the entreprise level, and this encourages them to be militant enough to make their members happy. The system of grievances is external and lacks the advantages of internal grievance systems. Strikes are a vital part of continuous bargaining and when militants promote divided trade unionism, often a semiformal political intervention is needed to find a temporary solution. The power game between unions and employers that develops under such conditions is not necessarily explained by the categories of different vested interests and rationalities. With changing circumstances, demands also change not merely to achieve something specific but also to improve one's position relative to the "adversary." The coalition of various interests may be quite shaky, particularly in the case of trade unions having a diversified membership. Achieving a satisfactory compromise may be difficult.

THE UNION POWER

One of the crucial questions related to the role of trade unions in modern society is how much they actually contribute to the organizational pluralization (Polanyi 1975). It is a well-known fact that the bureaucratic pattern leads to some malfunctions and distortions. By remaining beyond the control of management, unions are potentially able to correct the balance of power, if they are actually willing to do it. Unions have a different general orientation than the private or public businesses they are dealing with. The skills and resources available to unions differ greatly from those available to the business. The vested interests of union leadership do not necessarily encourage pluralization; sometimes union leaders cooperate closely with the business leaders due to personal interests. Unions usually represent a different social class than management.

"Organizations are devised by advantaged groups of society (and by their agents) to fulfill tasks which contribute to or at least do not undermine the prevailing societal pattern of advantage. The official patterns of organizational structure, the technology utilized and the people employed are all means chosen to fulfil these tasks" (Watson 1980, 223). The rule exercised in the business organizations by leadership is supposed to serve the specific interests, which are very different from the interests of labor, and quite often the former oppose the latter. "The ultimate constraint upon the way work organizations are structured in industrial capitalist societies is one which requires them to be involved in the maintaining and the reproducing of particular social structure" (Watson 1980, 223). For the class-conscious unions to accept the business creed means to serve different interests than the well-being of their own class.

Being a part of the power structure of society, unions and business remain distant as long as it is taken for granted that their respective powers are in mutual opposition. What is efficient from the perspective of a business may appear to be a waste from the position of a union. As long as there are profits, there is a chance for unions to push for an adequate share for labor. The general decline of business profits leads to the inquiries of whether it is within the capacity of business to offer some advantages to the organized workers. The general public usually looks unfavorably on unions that push for more under the conditions of an economic decline. Trying hard to look respectable (Vall 1970), unions have to adequately trim their demands.

There is more and more need in the union policy to consider the general well-being.

> The commitment of the unions to sectional interests poses serious problems when the welfare of society as a whole is concerned. . . . Unions are torn between loyalty to their own members, commitments to social welfare and commitment to the interests of the members of other unions—contradictions that manifest themselves in the ups and downs in union support for wage and price policies, in the factional struggles between Left and Right, and in the changing mood of the public when powerful unions exercise industrial muscle (Hirszowicz 1981, 185-86).

For the union leadership there is the great problem of how to keep members relatively happy and committed (which is difficult considering the prevailing instrumental approach toward members) and at the same time to not be troubled by people articulating their demands, trying to exercise some control, imposing restriction upon the leaders. The insecurity of union leadership positions differs in various countries (see Edelstein and Warner 1979) but there is a general tendency of the union administration to distance itself from the rank and file to secure for itself the freedom to maneuver in collective bargaining (Michels 1959). In the U.K. the bureaucratic tendencies are less pronounced because the union administration is much smaller than in North America and the elected union shop stewards are independent of the administration. Within the system of fragmented collective bargaining and multiunionism the local committees of shop stewards have much to say (Hirszowicz 1981, 197-200).

The growth of unions—from 43 percent of the labor force in 1960 to 54 percent in 1978 in the U.K., for example—has had a major impact on their functioning in several societies. In some fields unionization is almost total, for example in the Canadian public sector, and employee-employer relationships are under the influence of the potential unions represented. The growth of big unions (for example, in Canada in the period 1961-78 the unions of more than 30,000 members have grown from one-third to three-fifths of the total union population) has had major impact, especially when the employers are dispersed.

The growth in the 1970s of the work stoppages in number, length, and the scale—as seen in Canada and some other countries—illustrates the confrontation between two opposed images of society: one based on entrepreneurship free from any external interference and another closely controled by free associations, mainly trade unions. Should the public employer have full freedom to layoff workers who are not currently needed? How is technological and organizational progress possible without too much displacement of the labor force? All such questions are of vital importance for unions.

With the increasing proportion of the national product channeled to and distributed by the state (for example, in Canada in 1950 22 percent and in 1982 47 percent of the Gross National Expenditure was made by the government), the effectiveness of trade unionism depends more and more on its political weight; but in many countries the local trade unions are not adequately strong or prepared to gain some political leverage.

The power of unions depends to a large extent on being recognized by the employers as well as by the state. It took a long time and much effort for the unions to be recognized in several countries. In some cases this effort failed, as in the case of Polish Solidarity, which was dissolved by the authorities. But even in the countries that recognize free unionism, the recognition of unions differs among various branches of the economy.

In the U.K. ownership is the main source of variation in union recognition. In the nationalized industries union membership is almost universal and unions hold a strong position. Also in public administration the recognition is widespread. In the private sector recognition is lower but it varies (Daniel and Millward 1983, 279). In the private sector independent establishments are substantially less likely to recognize unions than establishments that constitute the parts of larger organizations. More and more people are required to be members of trade unions to obtain or retain their jobs; 27 percent of all employed people are in the closed shops and among the manual workers alone, 44 percent.

The data produced by the 1980 survey of workplaces with at least 25 employees covering public services, private services, nationalized industries, and the private manufacturing sector show the growing scope and depth of organization in British industrial relations (Daniel and Millward 1983). The acceptance of unionism by the public sector has had a major impact on the private sector, especially the large companies. For example, outside public employment, establishments with large numbers of employees tend strongly to be closed shops. Also, the larger the total organization, the more likely its particular establishments run closed shops (Daniel and Millward 1983, 282). The check-off arrangement (deduction by the enterprises of the trade union dues from the payroll) is also becoming more and more common. The role of union stewards is emphasized, especially regarding the power of their local committees through which they are able to exercise pressure on management as well as union.

According to the survey, the bulk of personnel work is done by people who are not specialists. Formal educational or professional qualifications play little part. At the same time there has been a substantial growth of joint consultative committees (available in 37 percent of workplaces), which is at odds with the traditional British system of industrial relations. Shop steward representation is on the increase. More than one-half of the employees are in work places that have a joint consultative committee and trade union recognition.

There is a disparity between the necessity of the trade union movement to act at the national and international levels, and its decentralized and mass participatory level (Crouch 1983, 217). However, there is no reason to underestimate the potential of modern trade unionism to adapt itself to the external changes within the environment.

Of course, the burden of conservatism remains heavy, particularly in the relationship to union and shopfloor democracy. But with the increasing educational level of the union membership, some internal reforms become unavoidable and sooner or later the new forms of union participation and management have to appear. This is already evident in those unions that appeal to semiprofessionals and depend on the new model of leadership free from the authoritarian bias for their attractiveness.

There is some difference of orientation between the leaders and the led. "The union's central interest is securing its capacity to make deals, while the members' interest is in the substantive outcome" (Crouch 1983, 176), leaders have to restrain members' immediate pursuit of material gains to gain more room for the broader union policy. Leaders at various levels within the union hierarchy differ on this perspective. There are various intensities of activization in the union and different spheres of interest.

The national leadership has priorities that are the reverse of those of the shopfloor organization. As long as the control is remote to the union members, they prefer to gain cash than collective power, but for the leadership the latter is of crucial importance in the long run as long as the organizational weapon remains under their control.

On the other hand union leadership is able to bargain with the employers from the position of a collective power only as long as the membership is willing to follow. The integration of shop floor activity within the national unions is in the vested interest of both leadership and the rank and file; it is not justified to treat unions as unavoidably broken internally.

Modern unions, particularly in the democratic west, are the permanent parts of the existing system, having a vested interest to cooperate with other parts but at the same time following their own goals and concerns. The problem of trade unionism in the U.S. is— according to Rees (1977)—its partial neglect of some basic functions in raising the social conscience, responding to the changing needs of working people, deepening industrial democracy, etc. He claims that even the economic losses imposed by unions are not too high a price to pay for their successful protection of workers against arbitrary treatment by employers. Wage control by unions is a way to keep the great mass of manual workers committed to the preservation of the existing system (Rees 1977, 187). "There are grave dangers in doing nothing about waste and the growth of unchecked power; there are also dangers that unwise treatment can be worse than the disease" (Rees 1977, 188).

THE UNION TACTICS

To become attractive to its actual or potential membership, the union has to offer tangible benefits, reduce the relative costs of membership, and increase the disadvantage of not being a member. As long as the union recruitment depends on specific occupational communities in which there are some pressures and counterpressures, unions do not have to suffer the disadvantages of recruiting from an anonymous mass population. The reality of the union that the individual worker encounters is often a face-to-face group (Crouch 1983, 65). In his or her personal decision he or she takes into consideration the factor of loyalty toward colleagues.

The ease to use the union organization and the dependence on an organization toward achieving goals play major roles in the decision to join the union and to stay with it. For example, if collective bargaining is widespread and concerned with important issues, there is more interest among the workers to join the unions. On the other hand the low degree of dependence on employment, as among some groups of women, will discourage the interest in joining unions.

As long as the collective may be helpful in the problem solving at the individual or group level, there is a great chance that people will join the union to gain rewards not available by acting alone. With the unions gaining power in the society, they become more attractive to join. For example, in the U.K. "workers may now see unions as capable of protecting them from the implications of unemployment, which was not the case in previous periods of high unemployment" (Crouch 1983, 13).

The threat to withdraw labor remains the main tool at the disposal of the union, but it is more convenient to keep it at the level of a threat than to start a strike. The longer the strike, the weaker the workers' position. The employer usually is in a much stronger position than the union to endure a long strike. Trade unions are irredeemable bargainers: In order to gain something important to them, they have to manipulate their power and willingness to withhold the cooperation with the employer.

However, to reach their goals the unions have a vested interest in achieving some status quo. Defending an existing standard from attack is the basic union goal that is difficult to achieve without having adequate information from the employer.

The conservative bias characteristic of many unions, and seen especially in technological progress, takes its root from the defensive union position. "New goals will be adopted in place of old ones only when their relative attractiveness is very high, because unions will set a high price on the risk of novelty" (Crouch 1983, 127). The appetite to take all power in society diminishes with the affluence and recognition of unions as elements of the system.

With the growth of enterprises, both formalization and specialization play a major role. Greater employment in larger enterprises leads to greater formality in industrial relations practices and more specialized staff (Daniel and Millward 1983, 297). In a prolonged crisis large establishments suffer employment cuts, and this may have a major impact on industrial relations.

The fast progressing formalization of industrial relations procedures is unavoidable in relationships between unions and managements. Such formalization, though, leads to some dissatisfaction among the worker representatives and contributes to the negative assessment of industrial relations in general.

Bargaining is not limited to the manifest substance but also has something to do with the latent contest of power. Both sides try to achieve specific gains and at the same time improve their relative positions. Unions assert rights to gain more security, and the employers deny them these rights to preserve traditional controls. From this perspective the search for rights and regulation is an aspect of the search for control.

Unions may be accused of obtuseness for asking to have more

control and better pay but not being ready to request from members a sense of duty. However, in reality any promise in this respect may cost the unions dearly when they share responsibility with management and lose workers' confidence. "Many British managements seem to have been willing over a number of years to concede fairly extensive workplace controls to the workforce, the latter having enjoyed them at the expense of higher wages" (Crouch 1983, 158).

The internal arrangement within unions may be oligarchic, as R. Michels saw it, but not necessarily. The rationality of representation and the rationality of administration are not mutually exclusive. Union leaders try to reach some balance between the two rationalities rather than maximize either at the expense of the other. The members will simply leave when the leaders care only about themselves. "Elimination of the possibility of exit may render voice more powerful, by forcing the discontented to use their energies to get improvements rather than simply going elsewhere" (Crouch 1983, 171). Michels' assertion that union members are always trapped and incapable of either acting autonomously or doing anything to arrest the progressive neglect of their representation is not true.

With the unions based on a diversified membership, traditional social pressures cease to act as efficiently as before, and the unions have to look for other ways to get member loyalty. The socialization of people into the trade unions is a difficult task, particularly in those countries where workers can easily switch from one union to another. The unions are generally too poor to offer members several attractive advantages.

Within the trade union movement itself private interests do not go easily together with the collective interests. More often it is convenient for an individual worker or employee to leave to others the cost and the risk of taking an action, but afterwards, when the action succeeds, the individual participates in all advantages.

The likelihood of members joining in a strike depends on the mobilization potential of a given union. When there are not enough dedicated members, the strike becomes impossible. The collective advantages of a joint action may differ widely depending on how much people gain from the action. Unions follow the general model established by the leading collective bargainers according to its suitability for their given circumstances.

Strikes are for unions a great occasion to gradually change the circumstances. The union leadership has to fill the growing expectations of the involved partners. Strikes are just a manifestation of some deeper and contradictory trends in modern society. Authority relationships are being transformed to offer more power than before to the employees' representatives. The great social-political crisis in France of the late 1960s and the early 1970s showed that the traditional central authority being practiced was much less rooted than expected.

The shift from the blue collar to white collar predominance has for years been one of the most important challenges for the traditional trade unionism. The obvious differences between production workers and office staffs have led to some difficulties in mutual understanding. The industrial union must meet the problem of organizing white collars across a class barrier, although this barrier seems to be quite amorphous. To reach the white-collar worker spectrum, the union must appeal to interests and emotions quite different from those among blue-collar workers. The concern for status advancement and the interest in seniority rights are much greater among white-collar workers than among blue-collar workers. Education is valued especially highly among the professional white collars, and the differences in comparison to shop workers are consciously maintained. The strong mobility striving is a marked characteristic of office staff.

Until 1961 the UAW in the U.S. did little to gain white collars or to overcome the disapproving attitude of management toward white-collar worker organization. The union traded the eventual membership among white-collar ranks for bargaining gains of blue collars. Because of the widespread white-collar employee discontent with the Chrysler administration, by the early 1940s it was necessary for the UAW to unionize a large group of office and technical workers. However, in general, "a largely passive pattern was followed in the white collar area until 1961. Throughout the twenty years of significant UAW membership gains among white-collar workers, the developing white-collar bloc intermittently pressed for more decisive action. The International responded by temporizing delays and minor concessions" (Snyder 1973, 57-58). In the 1950s and 1960s the white collar union membership approximated 5 percent of the total, but only a little less than 1 percent of expenditures were allocated for the needs of this membership. "Over the initial twenty-year period the UAW failed to develop a bargaining program of unique interest to white-collar workers. Organizing techniques and publications aimed at office and technical employees were only slightly modified versions of those used with production workers" (Snyder 1973, 71).

The UAW improved the situation greatly in the 1960s by establishing within the union a white-collar department, appointing skilled leaders, developing better publications, and improving the white-collar worker structure (advisory councils etc.). It costs twice as much to organize white collars as it does to organize blue collars, and there are still widespread unfavorable attitudes toward unionization. All these circumstances limit the scope of unionization. About one-quarter of the potential members are unionized. However, there is quite an obvious progress.

Snyder is correct to emphasize that "for many union leaders the orthodox industrial union ideology can constitute a mental block to effective understanding of the white-collar problem" (Snyder 1973, 132). Organizing across class lines is a must for the trade unions. The internal union democracy within the UAW has allowed to establish a white-collar worker caucus and to push for the full acknowledgment of the white collar interests. The autonomy was granted to the white collar group and thus making it possible to achieve more than in other industrial unions.

Acceptance of the white collar difference is of crucial importance. "The industrial union needs to regard white-collar workers as at a different stage of attainment and aspiration—especially in terms of working conditions—than its blue-collar membership. On the other hand, blue-collar negotiated economic gains have, at certain points, forged ahead of lagging white-collar benefits" (Snyder 1973, 145). There is some evidence that the unionized white collars maintain quite good relationships with the administration yet do not hesitate to strike in the case of an ultimate necessity. The growing importance of white collars in the industrial trade unions will probably contribute in the long run to the improvement of the leadership, the rank and file participation in decision making, and increase innovation within unions.

NOTES

1. Statistical data here included are from the U.S. governmental publications.

2. It is worth mentioning that in the OECD countries during the years 1960-81 social spending (pensions, health, education, and unemployment benefits has grown on the average from 13 percent to 26 percent of the GDP. See Social Expenditures 1960-1990, Paris: OECD, 1985.

REFERENCES

Braverman, Harry. Labor and Monopoly Capital. The Degradation of Work in the Twentieth Century. New York: Monthly Review Press. 1974.

Clawson, Dan. Bureaucracy and Labor Process. The Transformation of U.S. Industry 1860-1920. New York: Monthly Review Press. 1980.

Crouch, Colin. Trade Unions. The Logic of Collective Action. Glasgow: Fontana Paperbacks. 1983.

Daniel, W. W. and Neil Millward. Workplace Industrial Relations in Britain. The DE/PSI/SSRC Survey. London: Heinemann Educational Books. 1983.

De Angelis, Richard A. Blue-Collar Workers and Politics. A French Paradox. London: Croom Helm. 1982.

Edelstein, J. D. and M. Warner. Comparative Union Democracy. New Brunswick: Transaction Books. 1979.

Edwards, R. Contested Terrain: The Transformation of the Workplace in the Twentieth Century. London: Heinemann. 1979.

Edwards, P. K. and H. Scullion. The Social Organization of Industrial Conflict. Control and Resistance in the Workplace. Oxford: Blackwell. 1982.

Fox, Alan. Beyond Contract. London: Faber. 1974.

Gospel, Howard F. and C. R. Littler, eds. Managerial Strategies and Industrial Relations. A Historical and Comparative Study. London: Heinemann. 1983.

Heilbroner, Robert L. and L. C. Thurow. Economics Explained. Englewood Cliffs: Prentice-Hall. 1982.

Hill, Stephen. Competition and Control at Work. The New Industrial Sociology. Cambridge: MIT Press. 1981.

Hirszowicz, Maria. Industrial Sociology. An Introduction. Oxford: Martin Robertson. 1981.

Littler, Craig R. The Development of the Labour Process in Capitalist Societies. A Comparative Study of the Transformation of Work Organization in Britain, Japan and the U.S.A. London: Heinemann Educational Books. 1982.

Matejko, Alexander J. The Social Upgrading of Zambians. Meerut: Sadhna Prakashan. 1976.

Michels, R. Political Parties. New York: Dover Publishers. 1959.

Polanyi, K. The Great Transformation. New York: Octagon Books. 1975.

Rees, Albert. The Economics of Trade Unions. Chicago: University of Chicago Press. 1977.

Report on the World Social Situation. New York: United Nations. Department of International Economic and Social Affairs. 1982.

Reynaud, Jean-Daniel. Sociologie des conflits du travail. Paris: Presses Universitaires de France. 1982.

Snyder, Carl Dean. White Collar Workers and the UAW. Urbana: University of Illinois Press. 1973.

Statistical Abstract of the United States 1982-1983. Washington: U.S. Bureau of the Census. 1982.

Vall, M. van de. Labor Organizations. Cambridge University Press. 1970.

Watson, Tony J. Sociology, Work and Industry. London: Routledge and Kegan Paul. 1980.

White, Michael and M. Trevor. Under Japanese Management. The Experience of Japanese Workers. London: Heinemann. 1983.

Zaslavsky, Victor. The Neo-Stalinist State. Class, Ethnicity, and Consensus in Soviet Society. Armonk: M. E. Sharpe. 1982.

2 VULNERABILITY OF STATE SOCIALISM

STATE AGAINST SOCIETY

Organization is an artificial tool to achieve some specific goals in an optimal way and in this respect it differs from the socio-moral bond. The mechanisms and processes through which human beings become members of the social order and by which they remain members allow human beings to stick together (Nisbet 1970, 45). In these mechanisms mutual need and trust play a major role. The sharing of a specific language and culture, the collective memory of the past, and the awareness of a national destiny make it possible for people to find something deeply common, and at the same time something that is different from other societies. The state as an organization claiming sovereignty, authority, and the right to use force to insure the effective exercise of its legitimate control (Theodorson and Theodorson 1969, 412) acts as a symbol for the nation as long as there is a meaningful relationship between the state and society.

In modern times we have more cases of basic disharmony between the state and society. The military junta that takes power by a coup d'etat and afterward prevents the democratic processes to develop is the most common case of such disharmony. In the totalitarian states there is a strong tendency to subdue the society. "The totalitarian state extends its influence over the whole of life, private as well as public, and exacts full submission of the individual to its demands" (Elliott 1975, 464). The tendency to "improve" the society by using the state resources has a long historical tradition, but only in modern times has it become a necessity dictated by the deterioration of family bonds, an urgency to mobilize the labor force, a need to improve consumer power, and the incapability of the local communities to help their poorer members, etc.

There are two contradictory tendencies in the present day relationship between the state and the society. On the one hand the government gradually takes over several functions traditionally belonging to the private sphere; this is partly due to the progressing division of labor and the fragmentation of life and partly due to centralization and planning. On the other hand with the growth of aspirations and skills of the population there is a mass tendency to question the traditional state authority and liberate society from the organizational patronage exercised by the governmental agencies. The formation of the distinct spheres of polity and economy has been the basic characteristic of the capitalist society (Giddens 1979, 110).

Now we see a corporatist arrangement based on the collusion of interests between the state and the various influential groups that need the governmental apparatus to reach their particularistic goals. On the other hand the state bureaucracy in its survival and its exercise of strength gains much from the cooperation of lobbies.

Under democratic conditions the groups dissatisfied with the power game promoted by the state bureaucrats and the lobbyists articulate their demands in a variety of ways, such as, propagating tax cuts, demanding reallocation of public expenditures, changing the unpopular laws or state policies, and also by influencing management through the shareholders meetings, etc. Mass movements take advantage of civil rights to exert adequate pressure that may sometimes become dysfunctional.

According to Revel (1984), the democratic west's survival is endangered. The Soviet expansion is not adequately recognized, and the treatment of subversives as mere opponents makes democracies very vulnerable to internal threats. There is an instinctive tendency to appease. History's lessons are neglected. Intellectual confusion and paralysis mislead people living under democracies.

Under communism the society is identified with the socialist state. According to the official doctrine, society is supposed to develop by an artificial process from a rudimentary to a more highly organized condition. This is done according to the master plan, which is formulated by the ruling party and exercised by the state. The loyalty and obedience of the population is necessary; the ultimate truth and judgment are reserved for the upper elite who, in turn, are illuminated by the Marxist teaching. The monopoly of doctrinal interpretation is one of the basic assumptions taken licensed through the interal working of the party. People who are against history interpreted in the official way are kept voiceless.

TABLE 2.1. Basic Data on Eastern Europe

	Bulgaria	Czech.	E. Germany	Hungary	Poland	Romania	Albania	Yugo.	USSR	E. Europe[1]	USA
Population estimate											
Mid-1984 millions	9	15.5	16.7	10.7	36.9	22.7	2.9	23	274	111	236.3
Crude birth rate[3]	14	15	14	12	19	15	2.8	16	20	16	16
Crude death rate[3]	11	12	14	14	9	10	7	9	10	11	9
Natural increase											
Annual (%)	0.3	0.4	0.0	-0.1	1.0	0.5	2.1	0.8	1.0	0.5	0.7
Population doubling											
Time in years	257	198	2,310	—	68	131	33	91	68	136	100
Population projected to 2000 in millions	9.4	16.5	16.9	10.9	40.9	25.4	3.8	24.6	316	120	268
Population projected to 2020 in millions	9.3	17.3	16.8	10.5	44.7	28.0	4.7	25.0	364	127	296
Infant mortality rate[4]	18.2	16.1	12.3	19.7	20.4	28.6	4.7	29.9	32	20	10.9
Total fertility rate[5]	2.0	2.1	1.9	1.8	2.3	2.2	3.9	2.1	2.5	2.1	1.8
% population under age 15	22	24	20	22	25	27	36	24	25	24	22
% population over age 64	12	12	15	13	10	10	5	9	10	12	12
Life expectancy at birth (years)	72	70	72	70	71	71	70	70	69	71	74
Urban population (%)	63	67	76	54	59	50	33	39	64	61	74
Per capital GNP, 1982 (US$)	—	—	—[6]	2,270	—[6]	2,560	—	2,800	5,940[2,6]	—	13,160[6]

[1] The mentioned countries except Albania, Yugoslavia and the USSR.
[2] 1981.
[3] Per 1,000 population.
[4] Deaths to infants under one year of age per 1,000 live births.
[5] The average number of children that would be born in each woman if each were to live through her childbearing age 15-49. Replacement level fertility is from 2.1 to 2.5.
[6] According to GIA, in 1983, GNP per capita in thousands US$ was in the U.S. – 14.1, USSR – 6.8, E. Germany – 9.3, Poland – 5.8 (The Economist, 1985, 294, 7386:111).

Source: 1984 World Population Data Sheet, Population Today, 1984, 12, 5.

THE COMMUNIST INSTITUTIONALIZATION OF SOCIETY

The allocation of administrative privileges and subordination of the whole society to the party hierarchy is the central feature of communist rule in eastern Europe. From this perspective the advance of the socialist order just leads to more enslavement, and this will continue as long as democratic freedom remains denied to the society. Sovereign bureaucracy dominant in the Soviet bloc is primarily focused on the maintenance of power at any cost (Voslensky 1984). The monohierarchical order of the party state remains in constant contradiction with several vital interests of the population that are prevented from being articulated. "The principal lesson that may be drawn from the history of communism in eastern Europe is that bureaucratic dictatorship tends to reconstruct society along bureaucratic lines, a simple truth that has been widely ignored by the apologists of communist policies" (Hirszowicz 1980, 36). The official hierarchy of people, who are equal only in their far-reaching dependence on the official centers of power, penetrates the whole society and suppresses any manifest spontaneity. Citizens remain free only in their efforts to gain official rewards for loyalty and blind obedience to the higher-ups. Societies are forced into a deceptive dream of totalitarian order on the basis of omnipotent control, omnipresent supervision, and all-pervasive power. The population is mobilized to obediently fulfill the tasks formulated by the ruling elite.

It would be interesting to know to what extent the society is really willing to be subdued. For example in the USSR, according to V. Zaslavsky, an "organized consensus" keeps people well under control within "a political compromise between the state and the people in which basic social groups accept the existing distribution of power and their estrangement from the decision-making process in exchange for job security, some workers' rights, upward mobility, and a slow but steady rise in living standards" (Zaslavsky 1982, VIII).

The distribution of attractive goods and opportunities becomes more rigid instead of relaxed. The propagation of the "Soviet way of life" is supposed to integrate Soviet citizens, but the inequality remains a drastic fact of life. For example, there is a considerable ethnoregional, socioeconomic fragmentation.

Nationalism is mostly a matter of convenience and people change their identities when there is a gain in it. "Both inequality generated by budgetary allocations and inequality generated by market relations bear heavily on the exacerbation of ethnic tensions, although the significance of these factors is quite different for members of different social classes" (Zaslavsky 1982, 109). The growing new middle class in the national republics has some vested interest in nationalism. They defend their own privileges against all others, especially against Russians.

Stalin erected the foundation of a bureaucratic rule, and even with the advancing diversification of organizational forms within the Soviet-bloc countries this tradition has managed to survive. So far the Soviet leadership has been able to preserve the model established in the early 1930s by adapting it to the somewhat changing circumstances. Soviet communism has become even more conservative than before, but its attractiveness inside and outside the Soviet bloc has considerably diminished. People become more sophisticated; their needs and aspirations are growing constantly. The ossified bureaucratic system is simply unable to successfully meet the challenges of feeding the population, providing attractive opportunities to the fast growing number of highly skilled experts, running present day technology, developing foreign trade, etc. Even the myth of social equality appears to be far from reality.

Within the state socialist societies several obvious inequalities perpetuate themselves because of the omnipotent bureaucracy (Kende and Strmiska, 1984). Communist parties are overwhelmingly founded on white-collar worker participation and commitment, but there is a long tradition of upgrading the lower classes and utilizing them for the benefit of the system.

> Contradictions are built into the system, owing to the way individual and collective incomes are allocated. Every section of the population may thus expect a larger share of the national product at the expense of other sections, administrative privilege being the best example of how the higher strata of the bureaucracy can use the means available to them for their own benefit. . . . Stratification appears as a divisive factor that at the same time operates as an integrative force of sorts by destroying the links between different occupational sectors and reinforcing their dependence on the power centre (Hirszowicz 1980, 118, 121).

The policy of segmenting society has its dysfunctions even if the state gains free hand in shaping the institutional framework according to the wish of the party rulers. The monopoly of mediation between various groups and categories of the population is a heavy burden for the state and party functionaries. It has become necessary to hand over some privileges from time to time to the lower ranks, which has led to jealousies, bitterness, and tensions. Reforms fail when they are resisted by those who may lose by the introduction of them. Instead of giving valuable goods and services, the government depends to a large extent on offering alcohol—a good business for the rulers but one with tragic social results.

The skilled blue-collar workers and several categories of professionals are handicapped by the bureaucratic routinization and the sacrifice of quality for quantity. Under such circumstances it is very difficult to move to a more sophisticated and productive economy. The resurrection of a civil society remains impossible, but it is difficult to imagine any genuine socioeconomic progress without some move in that direction.

Increasingly, the ruling elite is unable to maintain some balance between the supply of goods and their demand. In the USSR the ratio of total commodity stock to the population's deposits in savings banks has deteriorated in the period 1960-77 from 224 percent to 52 percent. In the period 1960-83 the retail trade turnover grew 3.6 times (food, 3.1 and other merchandise, 4.2), but at the same time, savings deposits grew 17 times (16 in the urban areas and 22 in the rural areas) (SSSR 1984, 189-90, 197). There is not enough goods and services on the market for the population to purchase. The primary producers benefit from the shortage of basic goods, leading to a considerable embitterment between Russians and other ethnic groups.

The need for some interesting work and the feeling of underutilization are definitely growing among the young people, but the Soviet economy so far has been unable and even unwilling to satisfy these growing aspirations. According to Yanowitch, "A highly authoritarian system of enterprise management ('one-man management') and the whole structure of centralized economic administration leave little scope for any real 'worker participation'" (Shapiro and Godson, eds. 1982, 153).

TOTALITARIANISM OR A MANIPULATIVE SOCIETY?

The nature of institutionalization under Soviet communism seems to differ quite profoundly from the totalitarian model as understood in the west. "It appears to be a system in which a growing number of highly skilled and artful people (techno-bureaucrats) both direct and participate in the administrative and policy-making processes of a Party and government that never stop expanding" (Siegler 1982, 265). This is a co-optative technobureaucracy in which the political leaders totally dominate the policymaking process. "The Party leaders seem to co-opt (that is, carefully to select) whatever outside opinions best satisfy their own particular interests and ultimate objectives. . . . The Party leaders have preserved their monopolistic hold on the substance of power" (Siegler 1982, 266-67).

Siegler seems to be right in claiming that co-optation as practiced in the USSR tends to share the burdens of power related to responsibility and have the ruling authorities' decisions effectively drafted and properly implemented. The legitimacy image of the ruling elite is supposed to improve by the formal participation of outsiders in the decision-making process. The party leadership maintains a strict control of appointments, policies, and the whole process of implementation. The professional party apparatus carefully screens everything that is allowed to happen (Voslensky 1984). The basic substance of policymaking power is totally controled by the party leadership through its watchdogs located in all vulnerable places.

This casts doubt on the interest group approach based on a highly debatable assumption that nonparty institutions are regularly preempting the vital substance of the party leadership's policymaking power. The evidence offered by the interest group theorists ignores the fact that the statements appearing in the Soviet press and supposedly representing the group interest are very often initiated and arranged by the party leadership for the sake of legitimacy. Several individuals are encouraged to present publicly their views the content and general orientation of which are in fact decided by the party leadership.

This process is directly opposite to what happens in the politically pluralist systems where the freely expressed views force change. In the Soviet system usually the change is first decided by the top of the hierarchy and only afterwards is the public forum artifically arranged.

The political leadership in the Soviet-bloc countries looks for a counsel that may be easily co-opted. The easiest solution in this respect is to inspire only those counsels that exactly fit into the intentions and plans of leaders. The Soviet interest groupings are, in fact, to a large extent inventions of the western observers who do not understand well enough the actual functioning of the Soviet system in which individuals are co-opted to share responsibility for helping the leadership formulate better policy.

It is something very different from the western interest group behavior based on the pluralism of power. "The individuals observed speaking out in the press may be doing nothing more than exercising their right (indeed their responsibility as experts on some subject) to help the party leadership put together the most effective policy. Either singularly or collectively they may have no intentions of coercing the leadership to do anything against its will" (Siegler 1982, 280).

The bureaucratic party state hampers economic growth even when it is genuinely interested in giving full support to this growth. The elimination of a grassroot social control makes for easier policymaking but exposes the whole system to some serious deviations. The lack of institutional flexibility triggers social conflicts. Overcentralization causes unavoidable delays in decision making. A defensive attitude of functionaries to clients, customers, and outsiders hampers efficiency. Organizational inducements are not harmonized with the nature of the tasks to be performed or with the needs and aspirations of performers. Rules and regulations grow excessively. Party organs are constantly busy interfering in the various organizational units—

much more of a nuisance than a real help. Bending the rules is a common practice. Informal and formal structures interpenetrate each other in a negative manner. The quest for spectacular achievements is the source of waste and cheating. Various vested interest groups exercise their pressure through planning, changing priorities, and introducing chaos. The social costs of many economic programs are not taken into consideration. The public interest has become a lip service.

All these contradictions are common in the societies based on the Soviet state socialism, preventing the implementation of a rational model of welfare and common well-being. The efficiency of this system is low except on some grandiose projects promoted at any cost by the ruling elite for their own self-aggrandizement. Socialism as dreamed of by its intellectual fathers appears in the form of a caricature.

THE BUILT-IN IMBALANCE

The contradiction between intelligentsia and bureaucracy is one of the factors of imbalance. On the other hand the ruling bureaucrats need experts whose number is constantly growing. On the other hand the members of the intelligentsia maintain the tradition of social consciousness that is foreign to bureaucratic communism and potentially endangers its rule. For example, in Poland "the educated and articulate carriers of opposition not only regard themselves as the heirs to the old Polish intelligentsia but for some observers they are the intelligentsia in the proper sense of the word. . . . As fighters for the cause and guardians of public interests they are encouraged and supported by members of the public who sympathize with their demands and expect them to be the advocates of social justice" (Hirszowicz 1980, 98).

Until recently the Soviet-bloc countries have participated much below their capacity in the world market. During the period 1970-82, the export per capita of the European state socialist countries has grown five times (in U.S. $) but still in 1982 it represented only 29 percent of the per capita export of industrial democracies (Maly 1984, 314). Actual export in stable prices has grown by three in Bulgaria and in Hungary, but less than doubled in the remaining state socialist countries in comparison with 266 percent in Japan, 216 percent in Austria etc. (Maly 1984, 368). The quality barrier has prevented them from competing effectively and improving their share in the international exchange of goods and services. The attempt during the 1970s to intensify the exchange outside the Soviet bloc has led to sizable trade deficits. The net hard-currency debt of Bulgaria, Czechoslovakia,

East Germany, Hungary, Poland, and Romania at the end of 1984 was
$50 billion (The Economist, 1985, 294, 7386: 88). Several east-central
European countries have already reached their debt-load limits, and
the prospects for further development do not seem very bright even
if "western banking confidence in all countries except Poland and
Romania gradually returned" (The Economist, 1985, 294, 7386: 88).
For the foreign-currency-poor countries of the east, the large grain
imports, especially those necessitated by crop failures, are a heavy
burden, requiring the expenditure of foreign currency reserves for
consumer purposes rather than for growth-promoting imports of
capital goods.

It is very difficult to imagine further growth of foreign trade
outside the Soviet bloc without some substantial internal reforms of
the economies. More barter transactions, intensified economic cooperation and joint ventures are possible only under much higher economic effectiveness, better management, and less bureaucracy. Several east-central European countries show a strong desire for even
closer cooperation with the western industrial nations. However, under
the current highly bureaucratized circumstances, this cooperation has
to suffer very substantially. The Polish case is very significant in this
respect and far from being unique. The tough local party control makes
almost impossible any further economic progress.

Within the Soviet bloc there is a considerable divergence of vested
interests, and a single economic organ does not have much chance to
succeed. In its own way each country resists supranational planning.
The introduction to the Soviet bloc of some nonEuropean countries has
created an additional difficulty in integrating the very poor with the
relatively rich. It was the wish of the USSR to impose some of their
aid burden on the other east-central European members, nearly all
of which enjoy higher consumption than herself.

According to H. Seton-Watson, in east-central Europe "culture
has become socialist in form and nationalist in content" (Drachkovitch,
ed. 1982, 181). The new rulers are "socialist nationalists" and the
powerful, latent nationalism is an explosive force. "Dislike of Russians, devotion to national cultures, and the desire for freer forms
of government are endemic in eastern Europe" (Drachkovitch, ed.
1982, 182). The question is how well the destructive power of nationalism serves the interest of the Soviet elite by preventing east-central
European nations from joining their forces against the oppressive
power of Moscow. On the other hand nationalism may play a very
positive role in stepping toward a much broader socialization.

In eastern Europe the presence of the Soviet military is the
guarantee of "Pax sovietica" (Jones 1981). The multilateral military
exercises and other forms of training have become a suitable means
to prevent the local military from taking control of their own territory.

This is an effective way to prevent east European regimes from achieving autonomy, as was illustrated by an effective utilization of the Polish army to defend the Soviet interests against the Polish free trade unionism. According to J. Erikson, "The East European military establishments perform a dual role as the military helpmates of the Soviet Union and as avenues (or barriers) to the covert control that in part determines Soviet policy and defines Soviet security interests" (Drachkovitch, ed. 1982, 154).

It is worthwhile to add here that the military establishment in east-central Europe is privileged enough to appreciate the Soviet dominance. Especially the military careers of the higher officers gain a great deal from Soviet sponsorship offered through the training channels, mutual exchange, semiformal contacts, etc. Therefore, it is not surprising that "of all the elites in eastern Europe, the military has more or less consistently cleaved to Moscow during political turbulence, occasionally in circumstances that turned them against domestic factions" (Drachkovitch, ed. 1982, 154). The Soviet military establishment has successfully incorporated the local military elite, using them for its interest but at the same time keeping them sufficiently distance. This was demonstrated in the Polish case: the local army was the last chance for the Soviet ruling elite to keep an effective control over the satellites.

The promotion of military power happens to the great expense of the welfare of the population. The whole welfare system in eastern Europe, and particularly in the USSR, is meritocratic and not an effective antipoverty program. "It offers little help, or even understanding, to the undeserving. There is little overt sympathy expressed for the inadequate or the incompetent, for those whom one might call social deviants. Few attempts are made to explain their behavior in terms of the social and economic pressures to which they are subject" (Drachkovitch, ed. 1982, 288).

Any opportunities for equalization of general welfare purposes have been traditionally treated as dysfunctional in the USSR. The welfare benefits are limited to those who deserve them due to the past contributions and to those who succeed in loyalty to the system. All old-age pensions, disability pensions and sick pay benefits require prior employment as a condition of entitlement. Cash transfers are intended to provide an alternative source of income for those suffering from temporary or permanent incapacity. Very little is devoted to those with exceptional needs. There is no payment of income support to those without work even when some 1.5-2.5 percent of the Soviet labor force is without work at any one time (due to the high level of labor turnover). There are substantial numbers of persons of pensionable age who are not in receipt of an old-age pension.

The workers and their families are obviously exposed to great hardships due to the highly inadequate and irregular delivery of goods to the market, shortage of medical facilities, rough working conditions, inadequate preschool child care facilities (especially in the rural areas), inadequacy of housing supply, etc.

What are the real chances for a young Soviet worker to go up the social hierarchy? From the 1950s until now the number of secondary school graduates has grown considerably due to the extension of secondary education. The yearly number of graduates in the USSR grew five times from the early 1950s to the early 1980s. However, the admission of candidates to postsecondary daytime education has diminished from around 60 percent to only around 15 percent of all secondary school graduates. The young people become disenchanted because the white collar offspring have a considerable advantage over the youth of the blue collar or peasant origin in the intense competition. According to Yanowitch, "Like educational systems in Western industrialized societies, the Soviet system simultaneously reproduces prevailing class inequalities and provides mobility opportunities for large numbers of working-class and peasant youth" (Schapiro and Godson, eds. 1982, 137).

Youngsters of an overwhelmingly proletarian background go to the vocational-technical schools. In 1983-84, in the USSR, 3.6 million young people have finished the general secondary school and 1.3 million have finished secondary technical school; 1.1 million were admitted to postsecondary educational establishments. Of these, 60 percent made the regular program and the rest made the evening program or the extention program. In 1960-84, the ratio of secondary school graduates to the regular program admittance at the postsecondary levels has changed from 6:1 to 7:1 (SSSR 1984, 218-223). "Children from upper-strata families are much more likely to continue on the path that leads to a higher education and are rarely found in schools that train youngsters for workers' trade" (Schapiro and Godson, eds. 1982, 140).

The fact that a large number of young working class people complete their secondary education but find no opportunity at the higher educational level enhances tension and envy. The youth of a proletarian background are discouraged even to apply to the institutions of higher education due to the small chance of passing the tough entrance examinations.

The final result is that the working class youth remain heavily underrepresented in the postsecondary daytime education. The evening and correspondence courses are more available to proletarians than the daytime courses, but this route to social upgrading is much harder. "Workers' and peasants' children are substantially underrepresented in institutions that provide the most direct route to professional and managerial positions," states M. Yanowitch (Schapiro and Godson, eds. 1982, 147).

The considerable differences between various eastern European countries in their standard of living, level of organization, and even reliability of statistics (for example, very poor in the case of Romania and relatively good in the case of Poland) have to be taken into consideration in the analysis of social services (Mieczkowski 1982). East Germany and Czechoslovakia are rich enough to offer more and better services than poorer countries. There are major differences between various countries in their quality of administration, the role of informal links, and the general care of people by the government. The dictate of employment policy over social services has fluctuated depending on the economic pressures, the current party line, and various local circumstances.

As long as the citizens in their survival depend on the state organized and subsidized services and not on their private consumption power, the actual supply of social services has to be considered from a totally different perspective than in consumer-oriented societies. According to official data, in the USSR the allowances and benefits received by the population from social consumption funds have grown four times per capita in the period 1960-83; in the official calculations of the whole income of wage and salary earners, indirect benefits represent 28 percent (29 percent among wage earners only) (SSSR 1984, 177). Mothers pay little for nurseries and kindergarten arrangements but their salaries are also relatively low. Social services in eastern Europe function primarily for the sake of labor mobilization and only secondarily for the benefit of the population that under the nondemocratic system does not have much say. The daily press of eastern Europe is full of complaints that working women have great difficulty in placing their children in kindergartens and also in finding part-time jobs. It is also common to illegally fire pregnant women. As long as the social services are not developed enough, women remain in a vicious circle of disadvantage.

So far women in eastern Europe experience great difficulties to adapt their outside career to the implicitly understood higher priority at family home. The exchange of roles and mutual help in the families appeals in eastern Europe only to a limited extent, and the burden of running the household remains mainly on women, even if most are gainfully employed full time outside their homes.

CHANCES OF REFORM

Is there any possibility to reform the status quo? Is there any perspective of a peaceful transition from Soviet mono-party state socialism to a pluralistic arrangement? The approach taken by the democratic opposition is of a piecemeal character but free from illusions. Hirszowicz (1980) is quite pessimistic. The party may change but without necessarily undermining the bureaucratic dictatorship. An increase in administrative pressure is usually enough to suppress disturbances within the system. The extension of privileges to ambitious individuals and groups leads to their co-optation. Modern technology offers some more sophisticated organizational and propagandistic weapons.

According to Kolakowski, "Communist totalitarianism cannot generate an internal renewal: it can be changed gradually, yet only under social pressure, as a result of resistance and struggle that wrest by inches, so to speak, some areas of civil society away from the omnipotence of the state and recreate centers of independent initiative outside its oppressive machinery" (Drachkovitch, ed. 1982, 52-53). As R. Wesson has emphasized (Drachkovitch, ed. 1982, 57), the communist parties following the line of Eurocommunism have found it advantageous to present themselves as democratically virtuous. The concern shown by the western leftists for human rights in the Soviet bloc has some positive value for the dissent in east-central Europe. Any suitable form that questions the authoritarian basis of communist governments opens more room for potential pluralism. "Eurocommunist ideas may have percolated invisibly and made it easier for the discontented to demand a more human face on communism without feeling disloyal to the state" (Drachkovitch, ed. 1982, 77).

East-central Europe has remained a vulnerable part of the Soviet bloc. Various resistance efforts so far, although without much success, have created a definite continuum. For example, even if the USSR managed to successfully halt the Hungarian resistance in 1956, in the long run this victory has been of a highly doubtful value. As Peter Kende says, "Unquestionably, the main result of 1956 in Western European political life was the recession of communism and the spread of anticommunist public opinion. . . . Budapest has laid a string of time bombs that keep on blowing up" (Kiraly and Jonas, eds. 1978, 134, 142).[1]

The Soviet communists' skill of illusion making operates only under the protective shield of nationalism, and this shield is missing in most of the east-central European countries under the Soviet dominance. According to Ulam, "Since World War II, East Central Europe has been a mirror reflecting both the weaknesses of the West's policies and the durability of its ideas; both the strength of Soviet communism as a scavenger of history feeding on others' achievements and failures and its inability to create a viable international order and political culture" (Drachkovitch, ed. 1982, 16). L. Kolakowski claims that "Communism as a real faith, as a collection of high values worth dying for, is dead among those who have experienced the realities of socialism" (Drachkovitch, ed. 1982, 47). The will of the ruling elite to maintain and extend its power is the only factor that counts. "Ideology is nothing but noise, an effort to fill the communication space with meaningless sound to prevent it from being filled with anything else" (Drachkovitch, ed. 1982, 48). [2]

The question is for how long, especially under the changing circumstances, the east European regimes will be successful in promoting the policy of segmenting the society by erecting a veritable network of administrative barriers between social, ethnic, and territorial groups. Under the deteriorating economic conditions the base of the "organized consensus" is shrinking (Zaslavsky 1982, 156). In the last few years productivity growth and the volume of production growth have declined; at the same time the employed labor force is constantly growing. In the European state socialist countries the nonagricultural workers in the labor force have grown during 1970-1981 from 72 percent to 80 percent. The economic activation is around 50 percent of the population, higher than in western Europe (Maly 1984, 314, 327).

The declining rate of economic growth in the Soviet bloc and a traditional dependence on manual labor that is much higher than in other developed countries make it difficult to keep workers and employees really satisfied. The technological progress meets the limits imposed by the economic disincentives as long as the dependence on human labor remains more profitable for the enterprises than the dependence on full mechanization.

In east-central Europe under communism there is an unavoidable and permanent contradiction between the democratic versus the authoritarian interpretation of the system. It is, as Brzezinski says, a struggle between sectarianism and universalism (Brzezinski 1970, 172). With the general progress toward industrialization and universal education, which is truly an achievement of communist ruling elite, the authoritarian style of management becomes more and more out of date. There is a growing awareness not only among intellectuals, but also among the rank and file that some kind of participatory democracy is the only solution.

One of the main difficulties in progressing toward this solution in eastern Europe, except Yugoslavia, is of a doctrinaire nature. Officially, there is participatory democracy in all fields of social life, beginning in the field of work. Therefore, why look for something new? If under socialism there is no alienation any more, then of course there is no need to join western social scientists in studying various ways of overcoming alienation. In many east European studies done from the Marxist orthodox viewpoint, it is just taken for granted that nationalization of production means leads automatically to overcoming of alienation (Osipow, ed. 1966).

The Soviet type hierarchical system of economy is nothing new in the historical sense. The premarket economies based on reciprocity, redistribution, or household were mostly hierarchical. Deciding to overthrow the commodity production, communists did not have much more choice than to reintroduce the hierarchical structure. "Workers' control without a market system is not a viable or possible organizational system. Once an economy is characterized by complexity, democratic discussion among large numbers of workers is not sufficient to integrate the economy" (Roberts 1971, 60). The hierarchical principle is also seen in noncommunist totalitarian systems and obviously seems to be closely related to the need for full control. The corporative principle advanced in the nineteenth century Catholic proposals is sometimes confused with the above-mentioned hierarchical principle. "Whereas the papal encyclical Rerum novarum (1891) had put forward the idea of a corporative structure along medieval lines, this is to say, decentralized and localized in authority, the Fascist conception was 'hierarchical' and all authority was derived from the head of a corporate state." (Friedrich and Brzezinski 1966, 257).

Obviously, it is difficult to accept the totalitarian solution even if it may look attractive as a revolutionary way of procuring rapid social change. There is too much sacrifice of basic human freedoms and values. There is also not enough room for worshipping anything other than the state and the ruling party. In the long run any totalitarianism is a self-defeating proposal because of its internal constraints and inconsistencies. The contradiction between a more or less idealistic ideology and the pragmatism of the power execution is especially evident in the Soviet type of communism. Political leaders in the Soviet bloc exercise their power in the name of their ideology but, in reality, follow the rules of political expediency.

A pragmatic approach becomes a necessity in a situation of a relative political stability. New generations grow up and their views differ widely from previous ones. The fanatical Stalinists "have gradually given way to hierarchically-trained, pseudo-intellectual party apparatchiki, primarily interested in their own power; these leaders in turn are coming under pressure from the younger generation of technically trained intelligentsia." (Brzezinski 1967, 500). There is a progressing disintegration of the whole system still not evident enough on the international scene, but deeply rooted in the economic failures and ineffective socialization.

Totalitarianism provides simplicity and clarity of a pseudo-religious nature. They often attract people who are either tired of the democratic process or just anxious to push for their own social and economic power by any means. It is obvious that virtually any totalitarianism contributes to social change of a substantial nature. "Totalitarianism is a system of revolution. It is a revolution which seeks to destroy the existing political order so that it can subsequently be revolutionized economically, socially, and culturally" (Friedrich and Brzezinski 1966, 181).

THE CRISIS OF AUTHORITARIANISM

Social systems are not very durable even within the rigid framework of state socialism (Lane 1976, Fainsod 1978, Hough 1977). They are exposed to pressures exercised by various groups and individuals who participate in them. The uncertainties of socialization, perennial scarcity of resources relative to individual aspirations, contrasting types of social orientation, and a variety of principles underlying the social organization (Moore 1964) all create problems to which there are no overall, continuous solutions. Institutionalization within systems leads to the establishment of collectivities, which have their own vested interests, as well as to shifts in the balance of power, and to the creation of "antisystems" (Eisenstadt 1970, 11), all of which challenge the status quo or just the opposite—they try to defend it as long as possible. The resources and activities are disembodied from their ascriptive frameworks; the differentiation takes place within systems in various ways through the main social system functions.

The belief that "the rulers' authority is its own justification and that their practices should be accepted by their subjects, without consultation or persuasion, because of the authority vested in them" (Fontana 1977, 44) has deep historical roots in several parts of eastern Europe. Potential reformers thus encounter obstacles that originate not only from the punitive nature of Soviet state socialism but also from the local traditions. The willingness of the masses to accept existing authority and at the same time to reject democratic alternatives differs among various nations, cultures, positions in the hierarchy, levels of education, and even in different age and sex categories. In the Soviet-bloc countries acceptance of official authority is based on the power of an omnipotent state and an incontestable one-party rule. It is highly impractical for people to question this authority when all organized forces of the society are mobilized against those who dare to articulate a significant dissent. This is valid for the USSR and East Germany but much less for Poland or Yugoslavia.

It should also be noted that as eastern European societies become more homogeneous in terms of their material, educational, and cultural attainment, it becomes more difficult for the rulers to play some social groups against others to preserve their own freedom from any social control. These communists who led revolutions, civil wars, and resistance movements against foreign invaders are no longer on the scene, and their inheritors appear to the masses to be just bureaucrats who were clever enough to climb to the top of the official pyramid ahead of their rivals. They lack the charisma and, therefore, have to depend to a growing extent on being artificially created by the mass media as heroes. Everything thus becomes a matter of mass manipulation which reduces authority to a set of devices, stratagems, and structures as well as allows the power holders to gain their end: control over citizens. The ideological charisma of the Soviet-bloc leadership becomes increasingly questionable if it has never really been tested in true elections. The mutual trust between the top and the bottom of the hierarchy is no longer a factor of considerable importance. Ideology is given lip service, widely idolized by the rulers as well as by the ruled without any genuine personal involvement or mutual moral obligation.

The legitimacy of authoritarianism as widely practiced in Soviet-dominated eastern Europe is constantly diminished by a number of related factors: the slowing down of the rate of economic growth, leaving unsatisfied the needs of the population for food, housing, etc.; the growing aspirations of the better-educated masses; the developing contacts with the outside world in at least some parts of the Soviet bloc; the inability of the rulers to promote successful reforms that would affect such vulnerable spots of the system as its stagnant agriculture, low productivity in industry, underdeveloped services, ossified bureaucracy, constant discouragement of spontaneity and individual or group initiative not directly inspired by the party.

The Soviet bloc is not free from a revolution of rising expectations. On the contrary, the young generations push for a higher standard of living that may be achieved only by structural reforms. The young generation of experts and even party activists are tired of authoritarian leaders who do not hesitate to waste national resources for the sake of their own aggrandizement. The rural population is underprivileged compared to the urban population. The absolute and relative number of the intelligentsia with higher education is constantly growing, but this stratum is not able to play an independent role within society. For example, in the USSR during 1959–84, the amount of people with postsecondary education among those ten years and older has grown from 2 to 8 percent and, among the work force, has grown from 3 to 12 percent (SSSR 1984, 14).

The authoritarian Soviet leaders sooner or later have to accept not only that socialism must become more economically efficient and humane, but also that some kind of a self-rule has to be tolerated. Obvious failures in the fulfillment of economic and social plans manifest themselves particularly in the inadequate food production in Poland and in most parts of the Soviet bloc. Military and police actions will not help in this respect; a much more constructive administrative and economic policy is badly needed. The real danger for the USSR comes from the evident inefficiency of a bureaucracy identified with the Soviet style of state socialism.

The Soviet argument used to justify the temporary introduction of martial law in Poland at the end of 1981 did not make much impression mainly because it missed the basic reason why present day Poles, including communists, committed themselves to reforms. The Polish economy is in a major crisis because it was mismanaged for years by doctrinaire party functionaries, rigid bureaucrats, and just plain crooks. However, it is not enough to change the people in power. This had been done several times before and finally did not work. The system has to be changed for the economy to recover and Poles to have enough to eat. Soviet leaders apparently do not grasp this obvious fact and try to stop reforms in Poland. But, in reality, these reforms are unavoidable in the long run.

The problem is that Soviet leaders do not have much chance left. The occupation of Poland by Soviet troops would only aggravate the economic and administrative problem, and the USSR does not have the resources to waste on such a hopeless project. The awareness that reform is an absolute must is so widespread in Poland that authoritarian hardliners supported by the USSR do not have any local appeal.

Even if the Polish situation goes to the heart of traditional Russian security fears by threatening the loss of Poland and perhaps other states, the answer is not in the obedient acceptance by Poles of the conditions dictated by the Soviet leadership. The failure of bureaucratic state socialism has become so obvious in the Polish case that even the fearful Soviet leaders must accept the necessity of an economic rescue operation. Such an operation does not necessarily have to be antiSoviet, although the USSR remains far from being popular in Poland. Goodwill and mutual cooperation based on the joint understanding of how important it is to achieve an economic and social equilibrium in Poland form the only reasonable remedy for the long term.

Contrary to what is claimed in official eastern European circles, the development of social systems under Soviet state socialism does not constitute a cumulative and unilinear process. According to official Marxist doctrine, these systems should make constant progress from the lower to the higher stages of development. However, D. W. Deutsch is right in claiming that in all social systems the old social, economic, and psychological commitments unavoidably become eroded and broken; then from time-to-time the mobilization of people for new commitments becomes possible and necessary (Deutsch 1961, 493-514; 1968, 398).

The rigid Soviet model of state socialism in eastern Europe shows several disadvantages (Selucky 1972, Hirszowicz 1980). With the exception of the temporary abandonment of widespread persecution of people by the secret police after Stalin's death, attempts to reform the system have not been very successful so far. The system has shown only a limited ability to learn from its own failures and to absorb innovations. Rather, there is a tendency to reduce any innovation to its previous state of affairs. This happened, for example, with the Czechoslovakian reforms of the late 1960s and the Polish reforms of the 1970s and the early 1980s.

Conflicts within eastern European state socialism are in general related to contradictions within the model or contradictions between the model and the social reality in eastern Europe. State socialism of the Soviet style shows an obvious inclination toward meritocracy, but a full introduction of meritocracy would seriously limit the political power elite. Spontaneous informal activity is tolerated by the system as long as it does not go "too far". The black market has existed and flourished in the Caucasus for decades. Many illegal activities thrive because their performers are protected by influential people. The practitioners, however, may be fired or even sent to jail during or after a political reshuffle. The mutual dependence of the rulers and the ruled quite often results in a strong coalition of informal mutual interests; it is rather counterproductive in economic and social senses, but it confirms the status quo.

The political system of east Europe so far has been unable to learn from its own errors and to change in a peaceful manner. The whole social system of work places has to be overhauled to produce more, faster, and more cheaply. The mobilization of specialists for performing this task is evident in several parts of eastern Europe. How much courage and ability will they show in dealing with "touchy" issues? To what degree will they be trusted by the rulers and by the masses? How will rank-and-file initiative be reconciled with the expertise of the specialists? All these issues are of great practical importance for the future of east Europe.

THE HISTORICAL ROOTS OF AUTHORITARIANISM

The ability and inclination of people in various east European countries to accept authority depends not only on the current situation but also on past experience. The dependence of the peasantry on a tiny group of omnipotent masters and the numerical insignificance of other social strata for centuries have contributed to the social passivity of the masses. Here one should make a clear distinction between countries based mainly on the peasantry (Russia, Romania, and Bulgaria), those that traditionally have had quite a large gentry class (Poland and Hungary), and those that have a substantial number of burghers (Bohemia and Germany).

There are two basic reasons why Soviet-bloc rulers have been highly hesitant so far to abandon the authoritarian tradition and engage in democratic reforms. One is the deeply rooted historical dependence of the masses on their rulers, particularly evident within the borders of the USSR. The other is the highly centralized nature of the Soviet sociopolitical and economic system that is so vulnerable to substantial transformation that it may collapse entirely instead of accepting a new shape. The Soviet ruling elite so far has not had either courage or imagination to appeal for mass support of reforms. The shortsighted dependence on mass aversion to any substantial innovation does not seem to offer a guaranty of permanent rule.

The authoritarian tradition in Russia is related mainly to Russia's position as a frontier society, to her constant struggle against invaders as well as the process of colonization or conquest of the neighboring areas. The Mongol concept of society based on the total submission of all people to the absolute ruler was skillfully adopted by the Russian princes to unite the country and make it powerful. "Russia was really conquered twice: first by the Mongol army, and then by the Mongol state idea" (Szamuely 1974, 18). This idea fits very well with the conditions of war and exploration of new territories, both of which necessitated the mobilization of all resources of the society. The permanent army in Russia even in the sixteenth and seventeenth centuries was much larger than any other European country's. "The grim struggle against the Tartar hordes dominates Russia's history" (Szamuely 1974, 27).

Traditionally in Russia all people have been expected to be compliant and powerless dependents of the state. Starting from the times of Ivan the Terrible, land was given as reward for serving the state. "The landholding nobleman was tied to the State by bonds of compulsion; he owed it a lifelong obligation of service, but received no privileges in return. . . . To the end the Russian aristocracy remained a class of serving nobility, occupied with their State duties, weak politically, legally and economically, incapable of playing an important independent role in the life of their country" (Szamuely 1974, 39, 41). On the other hand, the peasants in the sixteenth and seventeenth centuries became serfs, bound to land and paying regular taxes to the state. "In the eyes of the government the serfs occupied the same legal position as the land on which they worked; they were assets belonging to the State, but temporarily ceded into private ownership as a reward for military service. . . . The serf became in actual fact little better than a chattel slave, yet he always remained a subject of the Tsar. The pomeschhik, however unlimited his authority, held only secondary rights to the person of his serf, rights that were derived from the primary owner, the State" (Szamuely 1974, 44, 46). The village community played the role of state agent to mobilize the local resources to pay taxes. Also the townspeople, relatively very few in Russia, were wholly dependent on the state.

It is much easier to understand events in the Soviet Union today by considering that traditionally the ruler claimed to own the land and its inhabitants and that the state had a patrimonial character. None of the basic social groups of Russia, except the intelligentsia, was able and willing to compete with the state for power and privilege.

Immediately before their emancipation serfs in Russia constituted two-fifths of the total population. They were obliged to work for their masters or pay rent (two different categories of proprietary peasants). The lack of any legalized personal rights prevented peasants, and especially serfs among them, to develop an active role, even though they numerically dominated the society. Even after the emancipation the peasant remained separate from the society. He was very much indebted; he depended on the arbitrary power of bureaucrats; his ability to cultivate land in an economic way was limited by the low level of technology, illiteracy, and shortage of land.

The Russian nobility was too dependent on the monarchy to be able to develop an independent stand, as well as too much internally differentiated to be able to gain a significant power. In addition "land was not accumulated but relentlessly cut up into ever smaller lots, with the result that the overwhelming majority of dvoriane [nobility - A.M.] lacked economic independence and could not afford to live in the style of landed gentry" (Pipes 1974, 177). It is enough to mention that four-fifths of all nobility were impoverished and depended on the state for jobs. "The political philosophy of the mass of dvorianstvo was not that different from the peasantry's; both preferred unlimited autocracy to a constitutional arrangement, seeing behind the latter manipulations of private interests acting for their own benefit" (Pipes 1974, 185). After emancipation of peasants the nobility found it very difficult to manage their estates. Before the 1917 revolution self-employed peasants owned two-thirds of the cultivated private land and nine-tenths of the livestock.

The Russian state from the beginning controlled to a very large extent industry and trade. "Like everything else, trade and industry in Muscovy had to be carried out within the context of the patrimonal state, whose rulers regarded monopoly on productive wealth a natural complement to autocracy" (Pipes 1974, 194). The state used to farm out some branches of business to individuals, who, however, remained dependent on the crown. These individuals had common interest with the rulers, and both businessmen and the rulers were oriented against free trade. Cities were properties of the state, and the population of them paid taxes in a similar way as the rural population. However, a very considerable part of the urban population (three-fifths in the middle of the seventeenth century) were civil servants and military men because towns served primarily administrative and military purposes. The success in trade or industry was always related in Russia to the collaboration with the state, and this was a very important reason why the bourgeoisie never became a political entity.

The clergy had a similar position. The centrifugal trend of Orthodox Christianity tended to blur the distinction between church and state. "The Orthodox church never had the power and the cohesion needed to defend its interests from secular encroachments. Divided into many national branches, each separated from the rest by frontiers and barriers of language, each under its own hierarchy, it had little choice but to adapt itself to whatever temporal power it happened to live under" (Pipes 1974, 224). The church was not able to command the loyalty of the population because of its heavy dependence on the state, its antiintellectual character, and its inability to solve the problem of the Old Believers and Sectarians. "The ultimate result of the policies of the Russian Orthodox Church was not only to discredit it in the eyes of those who cared for social and political justice, but to create a spiritual vacuum. This vacuum was filled with secular ideologies which sought to realize on this earth the paradise that Christianity had promised to provide in the next" (Pipes 1974, 245).

All the above-mentioned social groups had some vested interests in supporting the patrimonial state.

> Dvoriane [the nobility - A.M.] looked to the autocracy
> to keep their serfs in place, to conquer new lands for
> distribution to them as pomestia, and to preserve their
> various exclusive rights; the merchants depended on the
> crown to grant them licenses and monopolies, and through
> high tariffs to protect their inefficient industries; the
> clergy had only the crown to safeguard their landed prop-
> erties and, after these were gone, to pay them subsidies
> and keep their flock by defecting. . . . The underprivi-
> leged, the mass of muzhiki, also preferred absolutism
> to any other form of government except anarchy. . . .
> For the impoverished dvoriane, the mass of petty traders
> and the overwhelming majority of peasants, constitution
> and parliament were a swindle which the rich and influ-
> ential tried to foist on the country to enable them to seize
> hold of the apparatus of political power for their personal
> benefit. Thus, everything made for conservative rigidity
> (Pipes 1974, 249-50).

The isolation from the rest of Europe, lack of local democratic forms of social life, and rule of the highly centralized state all have shaped the reality of Russia for centuries. The self-glorification has been an escape. "It has been hard for outsiders to realize that Russian national feeling is a spiritual emotion largely detached from the mundane things of life, that for centuries past, Russia has meant for her people much more than just a country to be loved and defended: 'Russia' was a state of mind, a secular ideal, a sacred idea, an object of almost religious belief—unfathomable by the mind, unmeasurable by the yardstick of nationality" (Szamuely 1974, 60).

The gap between those who control centers of power and those who shape the public opinion had grown in Russia with the progressing number of educated people. They cultivated their salons, university centers, circles, journals. They also controlled the organs of local self-government. The radicals among the intelligentsia gained influence with the progress of repression and the deterioration of the ruling circles. "The imperial government invariably over-reacted to radical challenges" (Pipes 1974, 275), and this alienated from it the average liberal members of the intelligentsia. Tactics applied by radicals for the first time successfully in Russia "paralyses the liberal centre and prods it into joint ranks with the left against the increasingly extreme right, thereby assuring, over the long haul, liberalism's self-destruction" (Pipes 1974, 275). Imperial Russia was only a prototype of a police state with many loopholes (foreign travel, private property, legal restrictions of oppression), but it was enough to radicalize the Russian society.

As may be seen, the tradition of one self-administered hierarchy is nothing new in Russia. Just the opposite, it has deep historical roots and the present day unihierarchical model of power in which there is no place for pluralism is the logical consequence of the historical development. According to Pipes, the intelligentsia was the only stratum relatively free in comparison with the rest of the population. The modern police state started to develop in Russia to defend the status quo against the intelligentsia; this means against those who had the particular sense of commitment to public welfare. Pipes defines a member of the intelligentsia as "someone not wholly preoccupied with his personal well being but at least as much and preferably much more concerned with that of society at large, and willing to the best of his ability, to work on society's behalf" (Pipes 1974, 253).

The revolutionary intelligentsia in the nineteenth century rejected the synonymity of Russia with the Orthodox Christianity but perpetuated the myth of Russia's unique historical role versus the rest of the world. This myth, together with the lack of any historical experience in pluralism, led to programs and solutions that were devoid of a truly democratic spirit. The concept dominant among Decembrists was not only egalitarian and crudely socialistic but also naturalistic and authoritarian. The division between the westerners and the slavophiles in midnineteenth century Russia hid a much deeper division between people of a liberal orientation and people who saw violence as the most suitable weapon to change Russian society. Peter the Great was a commonly accepted idol. The most influencial literary critics like Belinsky and Chernyshevsky praised the unlimited use of force. The typical Russian populism was very much influenced by the belief, especially among the young people, that only by force is it possible to achieve something socially meaningful. Decades of distrust of the socialists and acceptance of the emperor gave rise to this disillusionment among the common people.

Szamuely relates the power of the Russian revolutionary movement primarily to the social and moral nature of the Russian intelligentsia. "The Russian Revolution was the product of the intelligentsia, and the revolution was the intelligentsia's raison d'être. In no other European country did a social stratum exist that remained, through three or four generations, exclusively and specifically devoted to the idea of revolution" (Szamuely 1974, 143). Szamuely characterizes the Russian intelligentsia as a category of educated people who opted out from making a career in service to the state and shared a hostility toward the Tsarist autocracy. "The intelligentsia was not so much a class as a state of mind" (Szamuely 1974, 145). In the traditional Russian model there was no place for such people, and this led to the constantly growing internal tension. "Unlike the West, Russia had no interest groups capable of giving strength, support and substance to the intellectuals' protest, of acting as a channel between them and the body politic" (Szamuely 1974, 146).

The hatred of serfdom and the hostility toward the existing imperial order were basic unifying factors of the Russian intelligentsia. The gradual inflow of people from lower social strata into the intelligentsia had some impact in this respect but only a limited one. With the growth of the educational system also grew the number of people who remained an extraneous element within the body politic; they depended on the state much less than others, and at the same time they had enough time and social opportunities to develop a revolutionary activity. "The acceptance of revolutionary upheaval as the only solution to their country's problems sprang from the intelligentsia's rejection of the existing order, on the one hand, and their messianism, on the other" (Szamuely 1974, 154). The intelligentsia was devoted to the destruction of the status quo under the assumptions that anything else would be better and that force must be used to get rid of the current rulers. This conviction justified the progressive and leading role of the intelligentsia in the social change. It gave the group the justification for imposing upon common people its own ideological convictions. "Anything less than the absolute was inconceivable; pragmatism was an invention of the devil. . . . For the ideologues of the radical intelligentsia moderation was the supreme crime" (Szamuely 1974, 158, 159).

The intolerance reigned both among the state authorities and the intelligentsia, and in this climate there was no room for any conciliatory activity. Among the intelligentsia humanistic values were not appreciated enough. The revolutionary cause justified a very utilitarian approach to cultural and moral values. "The only thing that counted was utility, and the sole touchstone of utility was alleviation of the people's sufferings. . . . In this atmosphere of utilitarian morality the idea of the end justifying the means was accepted unquestionably, even enthusiastically" (Szamuely 1974, 166).

The subordination of the interests of the individual to those of society has been always very strong in Russia and has made her different in this respect from western counterparts and the more westernized eastern European countries. This prepared the ground for the messianic vision of a perfect society—first in its nationalistic-religious and imperial form, and then in its Marxist-collectivistic form.

It is interesting to note how the revolutionary myth has grown. The influence of Nechaev and the Revolutionary Catechism upon later generations of revolutionaries was profound. The failures of populist appeals to the people contributed heavily to the intelligentsia's full-scale return to the concept of an avant garde party in full conspiration. The Tkachev-Lavrov controversy was significant. Lavrov forecasted correctly the pitfalls of the minority revolution, but Tkachev much more realistically predicted the circumstances of the actual seizure of power by revolutionaries. Consequently, Narodnaya Volya and afterwards Lenin's Bolshevik Party followed the program of the revolutionary dictatorship. The main problem was how to gain the full control over the Russian state, whose role was always decisive in Russian history. "Throughout Russian history the state, or part of the Marxian 'superstructure' had been the force that created and shaped the economic 'basis'—and not the other way around. Capitalism and socialism were to be no exceptions" (Szamuely 1974, 415).

The communist bureaucracy inherited from the imperial rulers the trouble with the intelligentsia. Quite a number of people in Russia are not concerned about job security, high income, access to various additional privileges, or the activities of the nomenklatura.[3] The concern shown by these people for social justice provides a source of spontaneous social movement that is still small but that undermines quite substantially the legitimacy of the ruling elite. The citizens of Russia now as before have little direct influence on public affairs, and an extraordinary courage is needed by the members of the intelligentsia to claim some rights in this respect. "The Soviet state machine, the process of production and the producers, are directed by the party-state nomenklatura officials, who recruit by co-option from among the beneficiaries of higher education, and who in various ways benefit from privilege" (Nove 1975, 632). The fact that present day rulers "determine to a great extent the status, earnings and social position of various groups in society" (Nove 1975, 634), makes them close to the traditional position of the Russian emperor. They only lack the blessing of God, but they claim another the blessing of history and ideology.

The development of an alienated stratum of people that gained education and hated the power elite was not limited to Russia; in modern times it has become common all around the world. This phenomenon is of a particular political importance in societies characterized by chronic unemployment, deep disillusion of the people with the political leadership, general imbalance of social structures, and rapid social change. In Russia this rather limited category of people has contributed to the development of the effective revolutionary counterculture. This new counterculture took over from the traditional system several values and norms that were strong enough to survive all revolutionary changes. The spirit of imperial Russia with her intolerance, principalism, and authoritarianism is still flourishing under Marxist-Leninist rule. It is not so easy to escape from one's own past. History is omnipotent.

THE IMPACT OF AUTHORITARIAN COLLECTIVIZATION

In eastern Europe, under the dominance of the communists, ambitious industrialization and urbanization plans have been more or less successfully implemented at the expense of the peasant masses. In the USSR, during 1940-84, the rural population has dropped from 67 percent to 35 percent (SSSR 1984, 5). In the Soviet bloc during 1970-82, the industrial production has doubled but the rural production has grown only by 26 percent (Maly 1984, 313). The fulfillment of industrial plans has depended to a large extent on the successful recruitment of new manual workers from the peasantry or even from the white-collar labor force. During the late 1920s the Soviet regime decided to stop bargaining with private farmers and to enforce collectivization. In the very short period of 1928 to 1932 the number of collective farms jumped from 33,000 to 237,000, and the area sown by them increased from 1 percent in the late 1920s to almost 80 percent by the late 1930s. Most of the rest was cultivated by state farms (Laird 1958, 1982). From 1927-28 to 1931-32 the share of the socialized sector in the production of grain increased from 10 percent to 69 percent. Collective farms are under the very strict control of the party and state organs, although it is impossible to envision a situation in which a set of clear and enforceable central orders would cover every contingency. According to Stephen Osofsky,

> For many years, the theory of the kolkhoz as a cooperative not only excused the seeming anomaly in a socialist

society of a not even minimum wage for a large segment of the work force, but also allowed for these nonstate employees, the kolkhozniks, to remain uncovered by the state old-age pension and social security system in the main, although both guaranteed pay—the right to be paid in accordance with the quality and quantity of one's work—a cardinal principle of Soviet socialism, and the right to security in old age and in case of incapacity are vouchsafed as constitutional rights to all citizens in the Soviet constitution (Osofsky 1974, 5).

The rigid policy of the Soviet state against kolkhozes had been related to the fact that in the USSR there was never an autonomous and self-conscious kolkhoz movement. In the mid-1920s the local government of the countryside was in the hands of the communes, strengthened by the fact that they were no longer responsible for raising taxes, as had been the case in imperial Russia. During the enforced collectivization, the traditional commune was swept away as a genuine collective institution of peasantry. This commune, thanks to its popularity and support among the peasantry, managed to oppose the rural Soviets identified with communist rule and urban interests. Peasants, forced into the collective farms, could bring with them only a little of the communal experience; in addition, this experience was informal in the extreme and did not fit into the highly formalized framework of the kolkhoz (Male 1971).

The present day kolkhozes still suffer from being treated as a "lower" form of production that should sooner or later disappear to make room for a socially "higher" form of a state enterprise. The general policy of the Soviet authorities has been to amalgamate kolkhozes into larger units and afterwards to convert them into the state farms (Stuart 1972). From 1940 to 1983 the number of kolkhozes has greatly diminished (from 237,000 to 26,000), while the number of state farms has grown several times over (from 4,000 to 22,000). The latter have improved their share in animal production from 16 percent to 46 percent and in the remaining agricultural production from 10 percent to almost 40 percent during 1940-76. The total number of people employed in the collective farms has diminished from 29 million to 15 million, while employment in the state farms has grown from 2 million to 12 million during 1942-83.

The average size of a collective farm in the USSR is now much larger than that of the kibbutzes, consisting of almost 500 households on average (only eighty in 1940). The proportion of kolkhozes that consist of more than 500 households has grown from 30 percent in 1956 to 36 percent in 1976. As may be seen from these indicators of size, the kolkhoz is a big agricultural enterprise and is much less diversified than the industrial-agricultural kibbutz.

The autonomy of kolkhozes is illusory. There is constant control and interference from outside and the internal order in kolkhozes remains under the strict supervision of the party and state organs. The basic charter that contains principles of administration is prescribed from above and allows little room for improvization. Within the kolkhoz party organs transmit information and provide release of some frustrations of kolkhoz members. In the individual work brigades there are councils of an advisory character. The auditing commission carries out a complete financial-economic review at least four times each year. The main power, however, is the hands of the administration, external bodies (the regional party and state organs), and the local party organization. Chairmen of the kolkhozes are elected formally but in practice quite often are brought to the kolkhoz by the party representative and automatically included as members. Leaders of kolkhozes can be removed without the prior decision of the general "meeting" of kolkhozniks if it so suits the party organs. The party organs and the kolkhozniks may bargain regarding party nominees to the responsible positions but the strength of the bargaining parties is highly unequal in such a case.

Under N. S. Khrushchev procurement prices were substantially raised and the state cancelled several debts owned by the kolkhozes. The production targets imposed by the state started to be based on more realistic criteria, and for the first time officials considered ways of reducing petty external tutelage. The difficult working and living conditions of the kolkhoznik received some attention by top party officials. However, the view still prevailed among Soviet leaders that the bigger a collective farm the better it would perform economically and that private plots should be eliminated as soon as possible. After Khrushchev, restrictions on both the size of private plots and the number of private livestock were relaxed. Moreover, the social benefits available to the kolkhoznik came closer to those of the working class.

The intensity of labor utilization differs among kolkhozes. According to data from the mid-1960s, an able-bodied kolkhoznik worked from 135 days (in Georgia) to 261 days (in the northwest) each year. During the winter most of the people remain idle because there are no ways to utilize them effectively. The mechanization of the kolkhozes made very substantial progress but was partially offset by a permanent shortage of spare parts. From 1965 to 1975 the number of tractors grew by one-third and the aggregate horsepower capacity of tractor engines doubled. These growing investments in socialized farming, and particularly in the state farms, do not necessarily pay off because of the shortage of skilled labor, inadequate incentives, excessive administrative interference, and emphasis on the quantity of production rather than on its quality. For example, the starch content of Belorussian potatoes received in processing plants decreased down from 19 percent to 13 percent between 1940 and 1970, decreasing alcohol yield per ton of potatoes. The kolkhozes overfulfill their delivery plans, but they do not have an economic interest in producing good potatoes.

The growing educational level of the people in the Soviet countryside may in the long run have a considerable impact on the organizational forms of collective work in agriculture. In 1926 one-third of the men and two-thirds of the women in the countryside were illiterate. From 1959 to 1983 the percentage of kolkhozniks with at least some secondary education grew from 23 to 68 percent (from 40 to 80 percent among blue-collar workers).

These better educated people will probably have higher expectations concerning not only their standard of living but also the quality of their working life on the kolkhozes. The real income of an average kolkhoznik has grown: in 1970–83 by 64 percent in comparison with 43 percent income growth of an average wage and salary earner (SSSR 1984, 175). It is impossible to predict that the authoritarian rule of the kolkhozes will meet an increasing number of obstacles with the improvement of the material well–being of the collective farmers. The Soviet state badly needs these farms' contribution, which explains why long-term credits for capital investments in the kolkhozes almost tripled during the period 1965–75.

It is very difficult to encourage people to stay in rural areas when living conditions in the village remain much less attractive than those in the urban areas. From 1959–84 kolkhoz farmers (with members of the artisan co-ops) together with their families have decreased from 31 percent to 3 percent of the total population. Industrial production increased during the period 1975–83 by 37 percent; yet agricultural production grew only by 19 percent (SSSR 1984, 26). If the production figures for 1940 are taken as one, by 1983 the level of industrial production was 23, but agriculture had grown only to three and a half times in livestock and two and a half in the rest of agriculture. It is paradoxical that only 1 percent of the cultivated land under the control of the kolkhozes is at the private disposal of kolkhozniks but at the same time, according to 1983 data, 21 percent of cattle, 31 percent of dairy cows, 21 percent of pigs, and 21 percent of sheep and goats are owned privately. Kolkhozniks produce privately 29 percent of meat, 25 percent of milk, and 30 percent of eggs (SSSR 1984, 18).

THE IMPACT OF INDUSTRIALIZATION

In east-central Europe since the communist takeover the human resources have been mobilized to a very high degree for modernization identified with industrial progress and heavy investments. Agriculture no longer represents a substantial part of the Gross National Income. However, a disproportionately high percentage of the total labor force is still dedicated to agriculture, and the general agricultural productivity is low. The progress of urbanization, education, and sociocultural aspirations of the masses exert greater pressure on the ruling elite, which are expected by the rank and file to offer some better standard of living, and reinforce existing inequalities among the more than 100 million people who live in Poland, Czechoslovakia, East Germany, Hungary, and Romania.

The progressing industrialization of east-central Europe leads to the substantial reallocation of human resources and to the growing sophistication of the people. The current formal structure is much too bureaucratized and conservative in comparison with changing human needs and rapidly growing aspirations. From the Marxist standpoint it would be possible to say that the clash between the infrastructure and the superstructure is just unavoidable in the long run. However, another question is how well Marxist reasoning applies to the Soviet socioeconomic model of modern society. Blue collars are now the majority, and their standard of living is becoming similar to the standard of white collars. The traditional difference between town people and the peasants has substantially diminished. However, the reality is still very far from the ideal of social equality. Even though far fewer people in east-central Europe earn double the average income or more than in western countries, some new criteria of social stratification have become dominant. Political or administrative power offers some people the guaranty of substantial privileges that, in addition, are tax free. Various occupations differ in their relative income and the opportunity to gain fringe benefits. The distance between lowest and highest paid employees may be seen in various economic branches.

The main issue seems to be not how many people are economically better off than others but how well justified are the rewards to real contributions. How much agreement exists between the wishes of the establishment and the wishes of the population? It seems quite obvious that the east-central European establishments give special rewards to their loyal and useful supporters. On the other hand, there is also an official tendency to upgrade the incomes of blue collars, especially in the lower brackets, and to diminish the differences between the blue and white collars.

In the dialectical process of goal achievement the ruling elites in east-central Europe constantly create new social contradictions, even if it is against their will. The measured orientation toward equalitarianism leads to some elitist consequences. Strict planning contributes to chaos. The doctrinaire propaganda depoliticizes people instead of making them more committed. All these paradoxes result not so much from the ineptitude or the doctrinaire approach of the elite but probably primarily from the centralistic system applied to the modern and relatively well-developed societies. There is a growing cleavage between the authoritarian style of managing people and the pluralistic nature of emerging social structures.

FORMAL EQUALIZATION

Elimination of the private sector, except in the Polish agriculture, has led to the formal equalization of people. Only 2 to 6 percent of the people in east-central European countries ruled by communists earn more than double the average income. The structure of the family budget and even the household equipment became similar in all three major social categories: blue collars, white collars, and farmers. Because of the official policy to progressively upgrade the incomes of the blue collars, especially in the lower brackets of income, there are no longer the substantial differences between lower paid blue and white collars. In 1983, the Soviet industrial workers earned the same on the average for all people employed in industry, and the same was valid for state agriculture (SSSR 1983, 1984, 169).

How satisfied the people are with progressing equalization and what its functional meaning is are good questions. According to the available Polish survey data, blue collars are more in favor of equalization than white collars, and especially the members of the intelligentsia (Matejko 1974). It is very common among people who have social power (apparatchiks, members of profitable professions, decision makers) to use it to safeguard some semiformal or informal privileges. There is an apparent gap between the hierarchy of social prestige, based on the educational level (and the real contribution to the common well-being), and the hierarchy of socioeconomic power, based on privileges given or at least tolerated by the party. This gap is probably the main reason why the egalitarian aspirations among east-central European masses—the traditionally underprivileged class—are stronger than among the intelligentsia, especially in Poland (Matejko 1974, 14-26). The higher the social position, the harder it is to recognize the conflictual nature of the whole social structure. Even sociologists and other eastern European social scientists show some bias in this respect, probably dictated by their relatively privileged social standing.

On the other hand, any anticommunist orientation of some western sociologists prevents them from recognizing several obvious achievements of state socialism in eastern Europe. In the field of education a lot has been achieved and the whole educational system is now much more open to masses of people than before. The literacy teaching, learning, and research levels are now as advanced as in

some western countries. However, the totalitarian character of the
system obviously has its impact on everything. For example, in Poland the official contradiction between old (the Catholic church, etc.)
and new (the Communist Party, industrialization, urbanization, secularization, etc.) does not explain much since "conservatives" and
"progressives" are on both sides of the fence.

People who enjoy almost absolute power have the tendency to
attempt to retain it as long as possible, and over time they become
more and more "conservative." Absolute power corrupts absolutely.
To retain their power, the rulers look for support among the established social powers in the ranks of bureaucrats, secret police, military, highly paid specialists. In this situation the rest of society is
able to participate only in the modest role of more or less obedient
"servants." The situation may improve only when public opinion starts
to be of significance, and rules are enforced to recognize the urgent
social needs as articulated by the majority of society as has happened
in Poland and Hungary.

The whole issue of secularization cherished by some western
political scientists looks different in a democratic political system
than in an atheistic political establishment imposed with absolute rule
by the foreign might. In Poland for members of the intelligentsia secularization was for many years a must to obtain favors from the ruling
elite. The resignation from religious beliefs resulted in specific material goods and privileges gained. Several people earned good money
by promoting antireligious propaganda. Party members who occupied
white-collar positions were afraid to attend churches in public. They
went to another town to hold the church wedding ceremony in secret.
Open religious prosecutions in Poland have ceased, but it seems quite
obvious that the atheistic establishment tolerates Catholicism only for
tactical reasons and not because of some kind of ideological tolerance.
There is a constant fight for souls of Poles, and secularization is
widely utilized by the establishment to subdue people spiritually. The
humanistic and liberal criteria found in the U.S.A. do not fit well
enough into the east-central European situations.

However, the major issue is to what extremes people will go
to fulfill their expectations. Blue collars complain primarily of the
organizational ineffectiveness of their bureaucratized work places,
which prevents them from doing, and earning, more. Members of the
intelligentsia feel restricted in their ability to act and think freely.
The large mass of the status and well-being seekers who took advantage of opportunities opened by state socialist regimes, find themselves
limited to a common modest standard of living. The rigidity of a
bureaucratic set-up makes it practically impossible to develop any
substantial initiative that would fit within the given legal framework.
Therefore, extra-legal activities become a common phenomenon. One

of the best examples of it is the large number of people from neighboring countries who privately trade goods on any suitable occasion (excursions, visits, official travels).

People of east-central Europe probably agree on at least one specific issue: The system does not provide a high enough standard of living. Most of the indicators show constant improvement,[4] but that does not mean that people are satisfied. There is too wide a gap between the promises and the reality. There are also too much obvious waste and rigidity. Differences in the standard of living between various social strata and even various countries in the final analysis probably contribute to the inability of the whole system to enter the higher stages of common well-being. East Germany and Czechoslovakia are obviously better off than the remaining countries. It is particularly evident in the part of the household budget, as well as consumption of meat, industrial goods, furnishings, private transportation, saving money, the media, etc.

The fact that the people in east-central Europe do not "live by bread alone" may be true even to a larger extent than in many other parts of the world. Mass media, culture, leisure, and education are controlled by <u>apparatchiks</u> but actually are run by members of the intelligentsia who impose upon the masses their own tastes, aspirations, and practical choices. The young generation of blue collars and peasants becomes socialized primarily due to the intelligentsia, which runs the whole show even if it does not govern. The ideal of being culturally well polished and following the patterns of the "well mannered" people, who know how to taste life, has become paradoxically the latent function of the communist takeover. Neither the blue-collar workers class nor even the tiny minority of party and state bureaucrats but rather the intelligentsia has gained the most in terms of prestige, influence, attractiveness, and even numerical power. By generously subsidizing mass culture, education, media, sport, and leisure, the east-central European regimes contributed, against their own manifest intentions, to the establishment of social power, which represents a major challenge to the whole concept of the equalitarian totalitarianism.

THE WORKING CLASS

Growth of the working class in eastern Europe and the inability of Soviet-style state socialism to satisfy the growing material aspirations of its workers or even to solve the basic problem of food supply, have led to growing tension between blue-collar workers and the ruling class. This tension, contrary to previous expectations, becomes even more aggravated by economic progress. The reason is quite clear when it is recalled that the Soviet model does not meet the needs of a more sophisticated, developed society, particularly in the sphere of mass consumption and a democratic style of management.

To understand the socioeconomic situation of blue-collar workers in eastern Europe, it is necessary to analyze their living standard in a comparative perspective. This perspective, however, becomes fully meaningful only if it is realistic for people in terms of their specific life experiences. For Russian blue-collar workers, comparisons with their western colleagues do not have much appeal because there is practically no labor mobility across the Soviet borders. Soviet Jews are an exception, but there are not enough emigrants among them to break the rule. The story is different for East German blue-collar workers who can at least watch West German television programs and even have family visitors from west of the border once in a while.

The standard of living in East Germany is approximately 30 percent below the West German level. East German consumers still depend more on potatoes and bread than West Germans, but the major difference is in the number of cars, washing machines, refrigerators, and household gadgets. The state socialist planned economy allows prices of basic goods and services to remain low, particularly in the area of rented housing, but it limits consumption of a more sophisticated nature. According to 1972 data, food and drink expenditures in working families of four people, constituted 46 percent of the budget in East Germany but only 33 percent in West Germany; expenditures for pensioners were 46 percent and 35 percent respectively (Materialien 1974, 261-62).

The average income of an employee in East Germany was 37 percent lower than a West German counterpart in 1971. From 1960 to 1971 average income grew by 144 percent in West Germany but only by 41 percent in East Germany. East German households are maintained to a much greater extent by two wage earners. In 1971, 76 percent (much more than in West Germany) of East German women between the ages of fifteen and sixty were gainfully employed. In 1970 four-fifths of all East German wives of employed men were gainfully employed; one-third of them had part-time employment (Materialien 1974, 468).

The working class is deprived of its own institutions and subdued by control from outside, which makes it almost impossible to develop clear class consciousness. The ruling communist parties have a monopoly on this consciousness and are the only representatives allowed in the field. As long as the working class consists mainly of people who moved recently from the countryside to nonagricultural occupations, it is relatively easy to maintain party dominance. However, the increasing adaptation of newcomers to the industrial-urban conditions, the growing level of education and sophistication, as well as the maturing of a new generation, have made workers much more conscious of their power and have given them self-assurance, particularly in Poland. Unlike white-collar workers, they can move with relative ease from one employer to another without fear of negative consequences. They have less to lose and, in a fully employed economy, there is always a need for their labor. In the USSR, industrial blue-collar workers earned in 1983 an average of 201 rubles per month in comparison with the average income of 131 rubles in the health services, 139 rubles in education, 115 rubles in cultural (most of these services are done by women) (SSSR, 1984, 171).

Blue-collar workers in eastern Europe are in a situation of serious status incongruency, which has to be a factor of great concern for actual or potential rulers. Numerically, these workers prevail in the society but their class potential is not recognized. Party officials run the state, and the intelligentsia creates the most attractive values, norms, and patterns. In addition, the ruling establishment acts in the name of the workers and is particularly anxious to suppress any collective consciousness that might spontaneously develop among the blue-collar workers concerning their class interests. Contact between blue-collar workers and the intelligentsia is controlled by the ruling party, which has a special interest in preventing the creation of a class alliance that would endanger the political status quo. The sociocultural identity of blue-collar workers directly related to their material interests is now allowed to crystallize in a Soviet-style socialist society opposed to consumerism.

The workers' offspring aspire to enter either the bureaucracy or the creative intelligentsia, leaving their own stratum at the first opportunity. The manual worker is officially glorified, but at the same time his social position is not attractive to anybody, including himself/herself. As long as peasants were in an even worse situation, they strove to become blue-collar workers. Now the potential of the villages in terms of human resources is more or less exhausted (taking for granted the current low technological and organizational level of agriculture); the influx of people into the workers' stratum from the white-collar ranks has a negative character because these young people treat it as a form of social degradation, contributing to the workers' general dissatisfaction.

There are some growing similarities in the lifestyles of white-collar workers and blue-collar workers in eastern Europe thanks partially to the widespread viewing of television. The problem is that mass culture and mass entertainment, as provided by east European governments, do not fulfill the needs of blue-collar workers. What is offered on television, in theaters, and movie houses is a peculiar mixture of political propaganda, high-brow intellectual culture, and cheap nonsense.[5] The better-educated white-collar worker finds more entertainment here than the average manual worker. Governments sponsor a whole network of holiday hostels but, here again, such places are not always geared to the working class family and often are more popular among the white collar than blue-collar workers.

The main disadvantage for the blue-collar working class under the present day political system of eastern Europe is the loss of its bargaining power. Almost all workers are members of officially sponsored trade unions—except in Poland—but the activity of these unions is limited to the administration of various social welfare plans, agitation to work harder without additional financial benefits, dissemination of official propaganda, and reception and transfer of complaints into managerial channels. There is some token collective bargaining, but within the centrally planned Soviet-style system, there is no real place for unions in the decision-making process. Political control is so far-reaching and so tough that it is impossible—except in Poland—to maintain underground trade unions, such as those prevalent in Spain during the last years of Franco's rule. In Poland, even during the 1970-71 strikes in the dockyards, party members played the major role in providing leadership. Their appearance was a kind of security valve, indicating that the strikes were not politically oriented or directed against the Soviet-style status quo. Only afterwards, when blue-collar workers became irritated by the lack of adequate response from the authorities, did nonparty leaders assume leadership of the strikers (Sulik 1976, 65-77). This was particularly evident in the Solidarity movement during 1980-81.

It is necessary to emphasize that the only organizational and leadership experience available to blue-collar workers outside Poland is within the ranks of the ruling party. Even in the trade unions, acceptance by the leadership is dependent on being a reliable party member. The reshuffling within the party, especially at the top, usually provides a good opportunity for various pressure groups among the population to promote their own causes. On the other hand, parts of the population become consciously or unconsciously involved in the internal power struggle. For example, in Poland in 1968, the hidden internal party opposition used antisemitic propaganda in its maneuvers to gain power. In the Polish events of 1970-71, when blue-collar workers revolted against the rise in food prices, there were probably some elements of provocation sponsored by the opposition group. This group had a vested interest in providing evidence that the current party leadership was unable to control the situation and that Moscow should accept a change of leaders.

WHITE-COLLAR WORKERS

Engineers represent the largest group among present day east European intelligentsia, and this contributes to the technocratic orientation of east European societies (Hough 1977, 59-70). It is worth mentioning that one-third of all engineers in the USSR are women (and among medical doctors, three-quarters are women). The high popularity of technical professions among the young places pressure on the higher education system, which is able to accept only a portion of these candidates. The children of workers and peasants are handicapped on the entrance exams even if the authorities offer them some additional advantages. For example, in the USSR "throughout the 1960s probably not more than one in ten or one in eight of the university group (eighteen to twenty-five years) succeeded in gaining a higher education. And yet before the end of this decade, Soviet sociologists had shown that between forty-five and ninety-seven percent of pupils in the final year at school wanted to go on to higher education" (Churchward 1973, 37). Under these circumstances parents use every means possible, including bribes, to place their children in institutions of higher education.

There is a spontaneous tendency among the upper echelons of the white-collar workers' to secure a privileged professional position for their own offspring. The blue collar and peasant strata similarly desire to upgrade their children beyond their own level. The number of people in the middle of the social structure is constantly growing.

The constantly growing category of people "in the middle" has very little in common with the western-style middle class. Dependence on the state and the party prevents these people from gaining a reasonable measure of social autonomy; the amassing of wealth is either impossible or at least impractical; basic incomes are relatively low and moonlighting is unstable; pressure from the state to maximize economic growth at any cost suppresses the development of consumerism; economic security is often won by these people at the expense of personal freedom and family life; there is tough competition for all good jobs and various privileges; it is never certain whether children will be admitted to higher education.

Careerists and opportunists among the intelligentsia find better opportunities and recognition than people willing and able to formulate independent judgment. Party control and influence is a source of constant irritation and even disequilibrium because it often interferes with common sense and good intentions to fulfill professional obligations satisfactorily. The fulfillment of personal needs and aspirations is constantly frustrated by the ossified bureaucracy. Joining the party may help some people overcome status incongruity, but it does not provide a real solution to the essential problems of adapting to changing conditions and finding genuine self-fulfillment. It is significant that the percentage of party members varies depending on the tactical necessity to support one's occupational position by political leverage. In the mid-1960s, the percentage of party members among various segments of Soviet society were as follows: tertiary students—5 percent; medical doctors—22 percent; teachers—25 percent; engineers—42 percent, scientific workers in the Academy of Science—43 percent, and agricultural specialists—44 percent (Churchward 1973, 92). The party is highly selective in accepting new members and candidates are evaluated according to their relative attractiveness to the party as reliable individuals and as representatives of the socioeconomic and ethnic categories whose support is currently welcomed. For example, people from clerical circles are in general not welcomed (there are already too many of them in party ranks) but well-known experts and famous artists will almost always be admitted.

Real wages and salaries have grown from 1960 to 1975 by 50 to 70 percent (according to official statistics) in various eastern European countries. In 1976, among people employed in the Polish nationalized economy, around 80 percent earned from 0.5 to 1.5 of the average net (after tax) income. Only in such fields as construction and manufacturing was there a considerable percentage earning more than double the average net income, while around 10 percent of those in forestry, public housing administration and services, internal trade and agriculture earned less than 50 percent of the average net income.

The growth of educational and income levels and the gradual elimination of extremes in the material well-being[6] lead to a progressive homogeneity within the younger generation. Among those 20 to 29 years of age in the RSFSR, Estonia, Georgia, Moldavia, and Uzbek, well over half in the urban areas and not much less in the countryside possess at least secondary education while among those over 60 years old, the share of educated people is very low, particularly in the rural areas. On the basis of massive educational upgrading, cultural needs and aspirations have grown fairly quickly and have become multiethnic in character even though local customs concerning marriage and the family remain (Arutyunyan 1978, 15).[7]

CONCLUSIONS

State socialism of the Soviet style is based on the bureaucratic concept of universality and impersonality of rules associated with rationalist thinking. Decisions in this model are supposed to be made on the basis of deductive reasoning from an objectified, scientifically based knowledge as well as from a legal premise. The practice, well established in eastern Europe, of rigid authoritarianism has constantly been in disagreement with the above-mentioned model, and this has led to several internal conflicts.

Bureaucratization in eastern Europe is the direct outcome of the authoritarian command system. It defeats itself, however, because it goes too far. Under excessive formalization, people not only find their daily life to be difficult and cumbersome, but it becomes very complicated for them to achieve even the official goals. In western literature on eastern Europe there are several very good descriptions of how business managers cheat their superiors in fulfilling production quotas, bribe suppliers, lower the quality of products, etc. (Richman 1965; Conquest 1967). Even in the field of scientific research, much informal manipulation is necessary to secure the needed resources to satisfy the formal requirements of bureaucratic superiors and to reconcile the demands of science with those of the command system (Matejko 1973).

Industrialism in eastern Europe, like elsewhere, requires geographical mobility, expansion of economic opportunities, upward social mobility, substitution of formal agencies and facilities by more personalized arrangements, lessening of the individual's dependence on formal and informal relations, and emphasis on achievement over ascription and cliques (Goode 1963, 369-70). In eastern Europe only some of these requirements have been fulfilled. Until recently there was even no hope for peasants in the USSR to move freely. Upward social mobility is now less evident than during the first stage after the communist takeover. Achievement evaluations have constantly been challenged by party-imposed bureaucratic criteria, or informal criteria imposed by interest groups based on ethnicity, common origin, bureaucratic affiliations, family ties, friendship, etc.

The most important factor, however, is the gap between formal agencies and the needs of the population. It is not simply bureaucratic malfunctioning, but a question of for whom the agencies actually function. On the one hand formalization is promoted by the ruling elites as a guarantee of the obedient execution of their orders by lower echelons of the bureaucratic hierarchy. On the other hand lower bureaucrats treat formalization as a security device against anybody who may endanger their vulnerable positions. Liberalization and decentralization are against the vital interests of all those people who enjoy some privileges. "While greater individual freedom and protection of civil rights are among the strongest popular demands, concessions in this sphere are the most dangerous for the survival of the reformers, on the one hand, or of the system itself on the other" (Rakowska-Harmstone 1972, 327).

In daily life the ossified formal structure interferes with personal striving. The full normalization of relations between the individual and the omnipotent state is impossible in eastern Europe not only because of private ambitions and excessive institutional demands, but even more because of internal contradiction between many such demands that negate one another. Initiative leads to trouble for the people who originate and promote it. Therefore, exceptionally strong motives are necessary to develop entrepreneurship among present day east Europeans functioning within the framework of a bureaucratic empire. Private motives of an egoistic nature can act only under the pretense of some common good or, even better, as the fulfillment of party goals.

The ruling elite is caught in the unhappy dilemma of either accepting servile flattery, or rejecting it and creating considerable trouble for itself. For east European elites, self-perpetuation seems to be a much more attractive goal than reforms. The far-reaching submissiveness of lower bureaucratic echelons has been taken for granted for so long that substantial change of this state of affairs would be a shocking experience for the elite. "In order to remain in power the regime must change and evolve, but in order to preserve itself, everything must remain unchanged" (Amalrik 1969). The elite must "bribe their people away from their dreams to be able to choose freely among competing political alternatives" (Rakowska-Harmstone 1972, 327) but so far it has been sufficient to suppress the appearance of these alternatives.

The collectivist tradition of east European societies is an important asset for their rulers, and it quite effectively buttresses the official ideology. The pragmatists who gain power and influence within the ruling circles do not hesitate to use nationalism as an ideological weapon; the revisionists are effectively out-distanced by them in this respect. The case of Czechoslovakia is an exception because reformers there managed, for a while, to align the cause of reform with the national cause. However, so far the elites in eastern Europe are not willing or able to seek substantial reconciliation of mass needs with those of production. "There is no doubt from the point of view of its basic goals—i.e., those of maintaining and expanding the political and military power of the state—that the Soviet command system is functioning and yielding satisfactory results. It provides not results, however, in the solution of the human problems of socialism" (Selucky 1972, 175).

A superficial overview of Soviet-bloc countries, or China, may lead to the wrong impression that their working people have considerable opportunities for participation and activism. W. J. H. Sprott (1958), for example, was very much impressed by the activism of the rank and file within small groups organized by the party in China. [8] After all, the communist countries host a whole network of social organizations and institutions, with the plant party organization and union council at its head (Matejko 1969, 448-80). There are numerous committees and productivity meetings. Activists comprise only a very small percent of the total workforce, but their role is essential because the attainment of production and other goals by the enterprise depends largely on them. The activists tend to come from the ranks of workers who are more highly qualified and have better positions.

They are interested in demonstrating their keenness to advance their careers; the party and other organizations in the workplace wish to strengthen their positions by having competent and effective supporters.

Dealing with the social reality rather than the official model, one should distinguish between various types of activists: those who wish to further their careers in this way; those who have been pushed into participation by a greater or lesser degree of external pressure; and those who do not take their "activism" at all seriously. As J. Kulpinska says about Polish activists, "The motives of activism frequently relate to the opportunities for contact with management during meetings and campaigns at a level of relative 'equality.' Linked to this motive is usually that of gaining promotion or other privileges. Activism is treated as the means of advancement in the personnel hierarchy" (Szczepanski, ed. 1969, 275). People frequently engage in activism only for a limited period to achieve a specific goal, such as gaining enough credit to become eligible for staff housing. Some, however, take their activism very seriously and find themselves in trouble by obstinately fighting for lost causes or by annoying influential superiors.

This model of workers' activism has remained largely unchanged since the Stalinist period. The fact that it is unsuited to modern needs has been ignored for years by the party elite. In Poland, W. Gomulka once said that "we have never had a situation in which the working class and the individual workers of enterprise were completely deprived of opportunities to participate in the running of the national economy and of their workplaces, and in which they did not make use of these opportunities" (Nowe Drogi 1957, 6: 96, 10). It is obvious that Gomulka identified the working class with party action groups, and that in addition he did not wish to acknowledge the totalitarian bias of communism.

Any totalitarian system is based on the manipulation of masses dictated by vested interests of the ruling elite. Sooner or later a crisis occurs. In the case of Czechoslovakia this crisis was especially evident. Instead of achieving changes for the better, which were expected by the people who enthusiastically joined the Communist Party in the 1940s, there was a conspicuous economic decline in the 1960s. A noncompetitive command economy promoted an extensive but disastrous form of growth. Instead of orienting the whole economy to some specific needs of the masses, investment in heavy industry became a self-perpetuating goal.

In a model that reduces ordinary citizens to objects of manipulation, consumers are just applicants. The same is true in reality with producers. The function of the market as an information link is nullified under a planned economy system by the intervention between market and producer of a detailed plan that provides obligatory "information" overriding that obtained from the market. Here we have the conflict arising from the disintegration of <u>homo economicus</u>: as a consumer, he helps create a market demand for goods and services; as a producer, he fails to react to this demand (Selucky 1970, 39).

Soviet ideologists claim that the nationalization of the means of production has necessarily led to a substantial change in the whole economy and in its social content. This is substantially true but it did not lead necessarily to the benevolent results expected by Marx. P. C. Roberts is right in saying that "a capital market can be replaced under conditions of public ownership by another polycentric form, one that is simply more clumsy and less efficient from an economic standpoint because it cannot take as full advantage of explicit productivity signals" (Roberts 1971, 79). Instead of a market mechanism the Soviet bloc knows a mechanism of pressure groups and cliques competing with one another for favors. "This interplay of rival pressure groups, each supported by its own combination of political and economic (and personal) arguments, is similar in its organization to the competition of enterprises of individuals for private market" (Roberts 1971, 79).

The myth that it is possible to establish a perfect plan, which would match production to consumption and vice-versa, seems to be far from reality. Reasons for this are obvious in the power structure of society. A market mechanism of a representative democracy, or even authoritarianism practiced within the strict limits of humanitarian law, at least provides some checks and balances. Without them society is exposed to secret power struggles of pressure groups, each pursuing its vested interests. The central plan becomes the object of manipulation of groups that appear more powerful than others. Consumers do not have the freedom to organize themselves and to match the influences exercised by <u>apparatchiks</u>, planners, experts, the military, secret police, etc. This is exactly what has happened in the Soviet bloc. The individual becomes demoralized because the purpose of efforts is stultified, consumer needs are not satisfied, and the desire for self-fulfillment is constantly frustrated. This is the prime economic cause of that individualism that drives individuals, for all the collectivist ideology of Stalinism, into isolation, indifference, and "internal emigration," alienates them in a new and specific way from their environment, and produces a kind of social schizophrenia among those involved in production. Such people, living theoretically in a collective environment, flee after office hours into their own private refuges to escape at least for a few hours daily the manipulations of the bureaucrats (Selucky 1970, 40-41).

With the growing complexity and sophistication of modern east European societies, the authoritarian model for governing them shows its inadequacy and even its obsolescence. All members of society, including rulers, become victims. Of course, it is not in the interest of the rulers and their supporters to admit where the fault really lies.

These obvious inefficiencies, however, are handy for various groups struggling for power and are used against one another. This was the case with Khrushchev and Gomulka in 1956, Husak in 1968, Gierek in 1970, the antiGierek caucus in 1980, and Jaruzelski in 1984.

The Soviet model of society provides a good example of self-defeating prophecy. The authoritarian bureaucracy was originally supposed to serve as a means to promote industrialization, social equality, and common welfare. Later it was almost unavoidable that this same bureaucracy took power from the ideological elite and started to run the whole business for its own benefit. The widespread waste and inefficiency, deficiencies in materials, squandering of economic surplus, general unadaptation of production to needs, under-utilization of the intensive factors of economic growth, underdeveloped exports—all these factors responsible for slowing down the rate of economic growth are related to the authoritarian rule exercised by the bureaucracy. All social groups have to struggle against the bureaucracy to improve their relative position within the system. "By its very nature, the bureaucracy destroys social initiative since its rule is based on a monopoly of social organization and the atomization of independent social forces" (Kuron and Modzelewski 1972).

The application of direct coercion is becoming less frequent in modern societies (Peters 1978, 50). The increasing interdependence of various strata, groups, and individuals requires increased control and more effective socialization; this becomes a growing problem within the highly centralized Soviet system, which, in addition, claims ideological superiority over the rest of the world. "Double-talk" is practiced in the Soviet bloc and the formalistic appearance of the rules contrasts with much more flexible reality undermining the effectiveness of official socialization. Relations between the central bodies and other social entities takes on a semifeudal character, and this constantly contradicts the communist ideal of equality and fraternity of social strata liberated from the mutual exploitive relationships.

The individual strata artificially manipulated from the top of the bureaucratic hierarchy are not able to become responsible members of society, able and willing to fulfill their integrative functions. State and party agencies impose their will on society, and in this respect they continue under modern circumstances the traditions of imperial Russia. There is a growing contradiction between the need for at least some spontaneity and the administrative practice of direct or indirect coercion (Matejko 1977, 22-66). This contradiction also appears in the west, but the pluralistic nature of power and the relative autonomy of various strata effectively limit its negative consequences. The fact that social forces in the Soviet bloc either are fully dominated by their rulers or are pushed into a sub rosa position necessitates constant interference by central bodies and prevents these societies, as well as individual strata, from achieving a genuine identity. Socio-technics (Podgorecki 1975) of the Soviet bloc is focused too much on survival and not enough on efficiency, and this prevents the whole system from developing higher maturity (Matejko 1984).

NOTES

1. In order to compare the Hungarian revolution with several other phenomena of massive resistance to communism in eastern Europe, it would be necessary to look much closer into the changing social structure of the population as well as into the mechanism of group interests' articulation within the existing political system. The dissatisfaction of the Hungarian intelligentsia in the middle 1950s probably has more in common with what happened in Czechoslovakia in 1968 than what happened in Poland in 1970-71 or what happened in East Germany in 1953. A sharp sociological analysis of eastern Euro-pean riots and revolutions is badly needed to avoid the danger of mythologization.

2. Kolakowski, like Ulam, appreciates the power of nationalism but at the same time treats it as a major vulnerable spot. "National sentiments are the major forces of disintegration in the Soviet-domi-nated area" (Kolakowski 1978, 51). He does not see any possibility of an ideological renewal within the framework of official doctrine. "Polish workers proved to be completely immune to the verbiage of state ideology" (Kolakowski 1978, 52).

3. The ruling party keeps the list of responsible and well re-warded positions available exclusively for the carefully selected candidates moved from time to time from one nomenklatura position to another.

4. For example, according to the official Soviet data during the period 1970-83, the real incomes of kolkhozniks have grown by 64 percent and the real incomes of blue-collar and white-collar workers have grown by 43 percent. In 1970, only 18 percent of the population had the income of over 100 rubles per month, per person, and this has grown to 60 percent of the population in 1983 (SSSR 1984, 175).

5. The latter is the product of moonlighting by many artists and intellectuals, done purely for money and without concern for the quality of their performances.

6. In the USSR during the period 1970-83, the number of em-ployed people with at least secondary professional education has doubled and the same was valid for people with postsecondary educa-tion (SSSR, 1984, 172).

7. In the USSR in general, during the period 1970-84, the per-cent of the population, 10 years or older, with at least some secondary education has grown from 48 to 69 percent (SSSR, 1984, 14).

8. On the reality of political education in small groups, see D. Erdal, "I worked in Mao's China," Worldview (November 1977).

REFERENCES

Amalrik, Andrei. "Will the USSR Service Until 1984?" Survey 73, 1969.

Arutyunyan, Y. "Time and Nations." Soviet Life, June 1978: 14-15.

Bahro, Rudolf. The Alternative in Eastern Europe. London: New Left Books. 1978.

Brown, Archie and Michael Kaser, eds. The Soviet Union Since the Fall of Krushchev. London: Macmillan. 1975.

Brown, A. and G. Grey, eds. Political Culture and Political Change in Communist States. London: Macmillan. 1977.

Brumberg, Abraham, ed. Poland. Genesis of a Revolution. New York: Vintage Books. 1983.

Brus, Wlodzimierz. Socialist Ownership and Political Systems. London: Routledge and Kegan Paul. 1975.

Brzezinski, Zbigniew. The Soviet Bloc. Cambridge: Harvard University Press. 1967.

_____. Between Two Ages. America's Role in the Technotronic Era. New York: Viking Press. 1970.

Churchward, L. C. "Bureaucracy—U.S.A.—U.S.S.R." Co-existence 5. 1968.

_____. The Soviet Intelligentsia. London: Routledge and Kegan Paul. 1973.

Conquest, Robert. Industrial Workers in the USSR. London: Bodley Head. 1967.

Deutsch, K. W. "Social Mobilization and Political Development." American Political Science Review LXV, 3: 493-514. 1961.

_____. "Toward a Cybernetic Model of Man and Society." Modern Systems Research for the Behavioral Scientist, W. Buckley, ed. Chicago: Aldine. 1968.

Drachkovitch, Milorad M., ed. East Central Europe. Yesterday—Today—Tomorrow. Stanford: Hoover Institution Press. 1982.

Eisenstadt, Shmuel N. The Political System of Empires. London: Free Press. 1963.

_____. "Social Change and Development," in Readings in Social Evolution and Development, ed. by S. N. Eisenstadt, Oxford: Pergamon Press. 1970.

Elliott, Florence. A Dictionary of Politics. Harmondsworth: Penguin Books. 1975.

Fainsod, M. How Russia is Ruled. Cambridge: Harvard University Press. 1979.

Friederich, C. J. and Z. K. Brzezinski. Totalitarian Dictatorship and Autocracy. New York: Praeger, 1966.

The Fontana Dictionary of Modern Thought. ed. by Alan Bullock and Oliver Stallybrass. London: Fontana Books. 1977.

Giddens, Anthony. Central Problems in Social Theory. London: Macmillan. 1979.

Goode, W. J. World Revolution and Family Patterns. New York: Free Press, 1963.

Hirszowicz, Maria. The Bureaucratic Leviathan. A Study in the Sociology of Communism. New York: New York University Press. 1980.

Hough, Jerry F. The Soviet Union and Social Science Theory. Cambridge: Harvard University Press. 1977.

Jones, Christopher D. Soviet Influence in Eastern Europe: Political Autonomy and the Warsaw Pact. New York: Praeger. 1981.

Kende, Pierre and Zdenek Striniska, eds. Egalité et Inégalités en Europe de l'Est, Paris: Presses de la Fondation des Sciences Politiques, 1984.

Kiraly, B. K. and P. Jonas, eds. The Hungarian Revolution of 1956 in Retrospect. Boulder: East European Quarterly. 1978.

Kirscht, J. P. and R. C. Dillenay. Dimensions of Authoritarianism. Lexington: University of Kentucky Press. 1967.

Kolakowski, Leszek. Main Currents of Marxism. Vol. 3. Oxford: Clarendon Press. 1978.

Koslow, J. The Despised and the Damned: The Russian Peasant Through the Ages. London: Collier-Macmillan. 1972.

Kuron, J. and K. Modzelewski. "An Open Letter to the Party." Soviet Communism and the Socialist Vision. Julius Jacobson, ed. New Brunswick: Transaction Books. 1972.

Laird, R. Collective Farming in Russia: A Political Study of the Soviet Kolkhozy. Topeka: University Press. 1978.

_____. Future of Agriculture in the Soviet Union and Eastern Europe. Colorado: Westview Press, 1982.

Lane, Davis. The Socialist Industrial State. Towards a Political Sociology of State Socialism. London: Allen and Unwin. 1976.

Male, D. J. Russian Peasant Organization Before Collectivisation: A Study of Commune and Gathering, 1925-1930. Cambridge: Cambridge University Press. 1971.

Matejko, Alexander J. "Some Sociological Problems of Socialist Factories." Social Research 36, 3. 1969.

_____. "Institutional Conditions of Scientific Inquiry." Small Group Behavior 4, 1. 1973.

_____. "Poland's New Social Structure." East Europe 22, 102. 1973.

_____. "The Self-Management Theory of Jan Wolski." International Journal of Contemporary Sociology 10, 1: 66-87. 1973.

_____. Social Change and Stratification in Eastern Europe. New York: Praeger. 1974.

_____. "The Polish Blue Collar Workers." Mens en Onderneming 77, 5. 1977.

_____. "Spontaneity Versus Formalization in East Europe." Nationalities Papers V, 1: 22-66. 1977.

_____. "The Hard Working People: Manual Workers and Farmers in Poland." Solidarity, ed. by Ajit Jain. Baton Rouge: Oracle Press. 1983.

_____. Beyond Bureaucracy?, Cologne: Verlag für Gesellschaftsarchilektur, 1984.

Materialism zum Bericht zur Lage der Nation. Bonn. Federal Government of Germany. 1974.

Matthews, M. Class and Society in Soviet Russia, London. 1972.

Medvedev, Zhores A. Andropov. New York: W. W. Norton. 1984.

Meissner, Boris ed. Social Change in the Soviet Union. Notre Dame: University of Notre Dame Press. 1972.

Mervyn, Matthew. Class and Society in Soviet Russia. Allen Lane: Penguin Press. 1972.

_____. Privilege in the Soviet Union. A Study of Elite Life Styles Under Communism. London: Allen and Unwin. 1978.

Mieczkowski, Bogdan. Social Services for Women in Eastern Europe. ASN Series in Issues Studies (USSR and eastern Europe), No. 3. Charleston: The Association for the Study of Nationalities (USSR and East Europe). 1982.

Moore, Wilbert E. Social Change. Englewood Cliffs: Prentice-Hall. 1964.

Nove, Alec. "History, Hierarchy and Nationalities: Some Observations on the Soviet Social Structure," Soviet Studies XXI, 1. 1970.

_____. "Is There a Ruling Class in the USSR?" Soviet Studies XXVII, 4. 1975.

Osipov, G. V., ed. Industry and Labor in the U.S.S.R. London: Tavistock Publishers. 1966.

Osofsky, S. Soviet Agricultural Policy: Toward the Abolition of Collective Farms. New York: Praeger. 1974.

Peters, B. Guy. The Politics of Bureaucracy. A Comparative Perspective. New York: Longman. 1978.

Pipes, Richard. Russia Under the Old Regime. London: Weidenfeld and Nicolson. 1974.

Podgorecki, Adam. Practical Social Sciences. London: Routledge and Kegan Paul. 1975.

Rakowska-Harmstone, Teresa. "Patterns of Political Change." The Communist States in Disarray, ed. by A. Bromke and T. Rakowska-Harmstone. Minneapolis: University of Minnesota Press. 1972.

_____. "The Dialectics of Nationalism in the USSR." Problems of Communism XXIII, 3. 1974.

Revel, Jean Francois. How Democracies Perish. New York: Doubleday. 1984.

Richman, Barry M. Soviet Management. New York: Prentice-Hall. 1965.

Roberts, P. C. Alienation and the Soviet Economy: Toward a General Theory of Marxian Alienation, Organizational Principles, and the Soviet Economy. Albuquerque: University Press. 1971.

Schapiro, Leonard and Joseph Godson, eds. The Soviet Worker: Illusions and Realities. London: Macmillan. 1982.

Selucky, Radoslav. Czechoslovakia: The Plan That Failed. New York: Nelson. 1970.

_____. Economic Reforms in Eastern Europe. New York: Praeger. 1972.

Siegler, Robert W. The Standing Commissions of the Supreme Soviet. Effective Co-optation. New York: Praeger. 1982.

Sprott, W. J. H. Human Groups. London: Penguin Books. 1958.

Staniszkis, Jadwiga. Pologne. La revolution autolimitee. Paris: Presses Universitaries de France. 1982.

Steven, Stewart. The Poles. New York: Macmillan. 1982.

Stuart, R. C. The Collective Farm in Soviet Agriculture. Lexington: University of Kentucky Press. 1972.

Sulik, B. "Robotnicy." Kultura 349, 10: 65-77. 1976.

SSSR w cifrach 1983, Moscow: Finansy: Statistika, 1984.

Szamuely, Tibor. The Russian Tradition. London: Secker and Warburg. 1974.

Szczepanski, Jan, ed. Przemysl i spoleczenstwo w Polsce Ludowej. Wroclaw: Ossolineum. 1969.

Theodorson, G. A. and A. G. Theodorson. Modern Dictionary of Sociology. New York: Thomas Y. Crowell. 1969.

The U.S.S.R. in Figures for 1981. Moscow: Finansy i Statistika Publ. 1982.

Voslensky, Michael. Nomenklatura: The Soviet Ruling Class. New York: Doubleday. 1984.

Yanowitch, Murray, ed. Soviet Work Attitudes. The Issue of Participation in Management. White Plains: Sharpe. 1979.

Zaslavsky, Victor. The Neo-Stalinist State. Class, Ethnicity and Consensus in Soviet Society. Armonk: Sharpe. 1982.

Zdravomyslow, A. G., V. K. Rozhin, and V. A. Yadov. Man and His Work. White Plains: International Arts and Sciences Press. 1970.

3 BETWEEN EGALITARIANISM AND ELITISM: THE POLISH DRAMA

THE CRISIS

Poland shares, with other countries of the Soviet bloc, several shortcomings of Soviet styled state socialism: central disposition, discouraging local initiatives; artificial price system making cost and profit calculation almost impossible; low wage policy negatively influencing the motivation of people; political factor, contaminating the economic rationality; rigid management, missing many chances; lack of a clear relation between actual labor productivity and material rewards; focus on the needs of the state at the expense of the needs of the population; promotions and bonuses misdirected due to the monoparty system; neglect of agriculture and services for the benefit of heavy industry; and so forth. The attempt of free trade unions to redirect the Polish economic system towards the actual concerns of the population (housing, more food, defense of the natural environment, better services, improved work and safety conditions), has failed due to the armed intervention of the forces loyal to the communist government.

In comparison with the 1970s, the Polish standard of living has diminished considerably during the early 1980s. This is due to the deteriorating market supply of goods, particularly food; drastic cuts of imports; and much lower buying power of wages and salaries, particularly in services and economic branches, which are treated as less important than material production that has strategic importance for the state (i.e., coal, steel, industrial construction, etc.). Living conditions have become more difficult, especially for pensioned people, families with many children, and single mothers. The quality of consumer goods, already inadequate in the 1970s, has further deteriorated;

for example, in the period 1980-83, good products diminished from 25 percent to 16 percent of all market products; in 1983, inadequate quality was evident in 67 percent of chemical products, 63 percent of textiles, 55 percent of furniture, 32 percent of shoes, 30 percent of bakery products and 18 percent of meat products; in general in 1983, 28 percent of market products were definitely defective (60 percent among the durable goods) (Szalajda 1984). When people buy everything because of market shortages, producers do not care what they offer. Polish people spend considerable time and effort in finding goods on the market, and quite often they must resort to bribery on the black market.

TABLE 3.1. Some Data on the Labor Force in Poland

	1970		1983	
The Working Force in Thousands	15,175		17,034	
Wage and salary earners (%)	66		69	
blue-collar workers in the nationalized economy	67[1]		62	
white-collar workers in the nationalized economy	33[1]		38	
Private farmers (%)	29		24	
Others (%)	5		7	
industry	4,453	29%	4,970	29%
construction	1,075	7%	1,219	7%
agriculture	5,210	34%	5,147	30%
forestry	182	1%	158	1%
transport and communication	940	6%	1,058	6%
trade	1,046	7%	1,325	8%
municipal services	252		429	
housing	146		204	
science and technology	72		111	
education	596		861	
culture and fine arts	84	16%	83	19%
health and welfare	424		680	
sport and tourism	27		96	
administration and justice	241		229	
banking and insurance	135		155	

[1]1978.

Source: Maly rocznik statystyczny 1984: Warsaw: GUS, 1984, pp. 38-41.

There is a growing problem of poverty. In 1983 21 percent of wage and salary earners' family members had less than two-thirds of average income per person (17 percent in 1982), and the same was valid for 38 percent of pensioners' family members (18 percent in 1982). In order to cover living costs people take additional duties (moonlighting), cultivate gardens, exchange goods and services on the black market, depend on their better-off relatives living in other countries, and also withdraw their savings; in the period 1980-83, savings, as the percent of total income of the Polish population, diminished from 21 percent to 16 percent. The disporportion of real buying power among the various categories of wage and salary earners has been growing instead of diminishing, despite the official policy for more equality.

The Polish government follows the policy of rewarding primarily those people who are particularly suitable for keeping the system safe (military, police, managers, political functionaries); providing export goods (miners, some branches of manufacturing); and fulfilling tasks of great importance for the state (constructors of priority projects). The rest of the population is vulnerable to deteriorating health services, inadequate housing, irregular market supply, limited chance of advancement, and the difficulty in moving from one place to another (changing jobs and places of living). The young generation is particularly handicapped because they must arrange their life in such unsuitable conditions; young marrieds wait several years for housing space, a telephone, and several gadgets already owned by the older families; there is a great shortage of basic things for babies and children; since both parents are often employed there is a problem of who will take care of the children during their absence; and existing nurseries and kindergartens are in short supply.

The events of the early 1980s constituted a massively negative reaction of Poles, and particularly the blue-collar workers who constitute around 45 percent of the population, against the manipulative model of the mass state socialist society. It was a revolt against the malfunction of the mismanaged system but also against the falsehood of a pseudoideological and pseudopatriotic message, the immorality of social inequalities that were widely practiced under the cover of state socialism, the disorganization tolerated under the disguise of central planning, the impersonality of a bureaucracy pretending to serve social needs. For the ruling elite it was very difficult to suppress the revolt even at its beginning, probably mainly because of the international obligations of Poland. Bloodshed in Poland would cost the elite its credibility in the west, and they wanted to avoid that at any cost. Also the USSR did not want to spoil the growing economic exchange with western Europe.

The temporary introduction of martial law in December 1981

was in reality a "revolution by proxy" and met a very strong criticism in the west, especially in the U.S. (Lewarne, 1984; Perski and Flam, 1984). The situation had become even more dramatic due to the imprisonment of many intellectuals, some of them even Marxists, as well as the leaders of Solidarity. The open question is how the system will function under the new circumstances and who really will gain the upper hand in Poland. The fate of Marxism and Marxists is in this respect particularly vulnerable when considering that the military junta took the upper hand for the first time of the history of eastern Europe under communism.

Due to the growing police repression, the underground Solidarity movement continues its activities only to a limited degree. Some of its activists voluntarily departed from the underground. For example, Alexander Hall, active for several years in the independent student movement, claims in his declaration that Solidarity has outdated itself and it is necessary to look for new alternatives, as well as to use the legalized forms of the struggle. He gives justice to those who still continue the clandestine activity but himself prefers to discontinue to participate in it (Hall 1984, 1). With the relative pacification of the illegal trade union movement, there seems to be less mass interest in public manifestations of the opposition to the existing political status quo. However, the underground press remains quite vital; people do not trust official mass media and read with interest the mimeographed illegal publications. Arrests of underground editors happen from time to time, but others have the will and courage to continue.[1]

The mobilization power of the underground Solidarity has considerably diminished, but this does not mean that the ruling establishment is now necessarily in a much better position. The economic situation has not improved enough to justify any official optimism. The foreign debt remains a heavy burden as long as the Polish export does not have a chance to grow adequately[2] to repay the debt and to satisfy the needs of the population. The growth of income from work (up about 26 percent during 1983) does not go together with an adequate supply of goods and services at the market (the growth of traded goods during 1983 was only about 9 percent). There is a constant shortage of food, household goods, even shoes and clothing. In addition, the Polish economy has increasing difficulties with the supply of labor. In the period 1971-75 labor power grew to 1.8 million, but in the period 1981-85 it was only 0.4 million.

Pluralization of authority in Poland was a fact of life from 1980 until the end of 1981, and the constellation of dialectic relationships between all major centers of power necessitated a new theory and tactics. Solidarity enjoyed mass support, but the defensive nature of the free trade union movement did not allow it to directly confront the most vulnerable and painful present day Polish problems: declining productivity, ossified institutional structure, shortage of food, managerial inefficiency.[3]

Only a major economic reform can rescue the Polish standard of living but in this respect there are great obstacles. The government pays lip service to the autonomy of enterprises and the introduction of market relations (instead of the traditional dependence on the fixed prices and the rationing of scarce resources) but in reality without political liberalization it is difficult to imagine any progress.[4]

In addition, many managers of the nationalized economy prefer to play it safe and feel much more comfortable within the bureaucratic system than in the market situation. They are accustomed to bargaining with higher authorities for various advantages in exchange for the promise that certain quotas of production would be dutifully fulfilled. The give and take exchange of favors is a field well known by executives who have a long experience at hiding the real potential of their enterprises, making a good deal on the target, and afterwards claiming the awards justified by the overfulfillment of production plans. From this perspective the market situation appears to be something much more risky and difficult to manage.

People at the top of the hierarchy have a strong vested interest to keep under control all basic factors of the economy. Several of them pay lip service to autonomy of the enterprises and a flexible price system based on free bargaining, but in reality they want to keep things as they were before. Even the most reasonable reforms become totally unrealistic without institutions willing and able to implement the tasks. It is necessary to consider the impact of harmful vested interests. These institutions whose vested interests introduce a heavy bias to the promotion of goals are useless for a genuine reform. The socialization potential of complex organizations differs widely. Present day Polish society needs a great deal of this potential to channel and adequately use the growing public spirit in Poland. From September 1980 until December 1981 there was a genuine revival of the "public man" whose fall in the capitalist west has been so greatly criticized (Sennett 1978).

Under the current circumstances the underground Solidarity does not have a chance to be officially recognized and return to its previous standing. But the ruling authorities also do not have a chance to mobilize the Polish society to such an effort that would make an evident change in the economy. Paradoxically, in several fields Poland has an important place in the world but remains unable to put her own economy in order. The gap between the ruling and the ruled seems to be larger than before, except under the rule of Stalin. A compromise is improbable due mainly to the Soviet interference. Yet, only such a compromise would create a necessary condition to improve the general climate inside Poland. The conscription army was used as the last chance to "pacify" the nation, but even this army can not be fully relied upon by the rulers. The soldiers obey orders as long as they do not have other alternatives, but their morale seems to be quite low.

For survival Poles have to depend mainly on informal connections because the institutional arrangements remain inefficient. Both public institutions and their clients are evidently hostile toward the other. These institutions are not adequately equipped and staffed to provide services without much strain. On the other hand, the clients have good reasons not to trust institutions and look for informal networks, including bribery, to secure effectiveness of their efforts. For many years the institutions have served the authorities as tools to exercise pressure on citizens rather than tools of the people to help them in their needs. It is very difficult to make any substantial change in this respect, especially when the whole system remains authoritarian and does not tolerate any democratization.

The ruling Polish United Workers' Party (PUWP) together with the members of "allied" political groups constitute together less than 3 million, around 13 percent of the whole population in the production age (males 18-64 and females 18-59). The mobilization power of this "politicized" part of the Poles is limited, much lower now than ever before. The membership of the PUWP has diminished by around 600,000 (in it 405,000 blue-collar workers) since 1978, and the careerist nature of membership is even more pronounced. Activity in the PUWP or allied political groups is mostly a matter of necessity; in order to be promoted to more responsible positions one must belong. Therefore, the interest in joining grows much with the amount of potential rewards.

However, most of these people are far from being enthusiastic for what they are doing politically; especially when the general mood among the population remains bad. The special security troops, ZOMO, established by the authorities to act against strikes and demonstrations are particularly hated and their utilization has a double edge.

Poland is a country with a relatively young population, high concentration of the labor power in the material production, the manual worker stratum dominate in the society and the well-to-do people being in a tiny minority[5] (Maly 1984). In comparison with East Germany and Czechoslovakia, the Polish ruling elite has far fewer resources under disposal to accommodate the dissatisfied population, especially the young people who are in great shortage of housing, career opportunities, and a constructive state ideology. It is the young generation that is the main support group of the political opposition. The educational gap between generations favors the young, but at the same time they have less opportunity to find a satisfactory place for themselves than the older people who have long seniority in their jobs, occupy apartments given them long ago by their employers, and dispose of good connections.

TRANSFORMATIONS OF SOCIETY

The Polish society has changed and this is enough to exercise some pressure. In the society where almost 80 percent of the population maintain themselves by nonagricultural pursuits (only 53 percent in 1950) and where industry supplies one half of the GNP (services excluded) the usefulness of industrialization remains questionable due to the permanent food shortages, limited supply of consumer goods, suppression of several freedoms, and even a limited contact with the rest of the world. In the remaining countries of the Soviet bloc freedoms are so effectively suppressed that the level of mass aspirations does not count much in the political calculations of the ruling elites.

Due to the free religion (21,000 Roman Catholic priests plus as many as 2,000 other religious ministers), relatively liberal education (Rocznik 1983) contacts with other countries[6] and the sociomoral revival related to the phenomenon of Solidarity (Ash 1982; Jain, ed. 1983), Poland becomes more and more difficult for the communist traditionalists to govern in the way expected and accepted by the Kremlin. The economy is obviously sick, and there is not much alternative to abandon rationing of basic food stuffs. The Polish cultural circles are definitely outside the state control even if most of the funds and opportunities are monopolized by the government and the ruling party. Even the members of the apparatus of oppression is not very reliable because they take into consideration the possibility of change of policies and do not want to be made scapegoats.

One of the paradoxes of state socialism is an unsatisfied demand of the labor power,[7] but at the same time it is difficult to find a job that would suit people. With a high number of a relatively well educated men and women,[8] there is strong competition for better jobs. The rise of the educational level among the labor force is a factor that has to be considered as influencing the expectations at the individual as well as collective level. During the slowdown of the economy, rivalry for better jobs manifests itself even more. It is one of the main principles of the Communist Party to allocate all important positions to its members, and not much attraction is left for people who are not in the party ranks. The share of people with at least secondary education is much higher in the ruling party (45 percent) than among the total population (27 percent). This is partly due to the educational advantages given informally to the party members; many of them obtained diplomas in an easy way.

In Poland 17 percent of the population works at private agriculture, and an additional 6.5 percent work in the nationalized agriculture. The population that maintains itself through some pension constitutes 15 percent. The 60 percent or so of the population are mainly blue-collar workers and white-collar workers, as well as people employed in various services.

In the last thirty years the socioeconomic structure of Poland has changed considerably. Of the total working force the number of private farmers has diminished by a half, and the number of wage and salary earners employed mainly in the nationalized economy has grown considerably. In this respect Poland has become closer to East Germany and Czechoslovakia where the labor force consists almost exclusively of wage and salary workers.

The socialist reconstruction of the Polish society obviously altered the relative size of various socioeconomic categories, as happened in other societies in the Soviet bloc.[9] There is in Poland a deeply rooted relationship between the urban population and the countryside. Many Polish towns and cities were populated by people coming from the countryside.[10] On the other side, the countryside is becoming more and more urbanized.[11]

The Polish white-collar groups, as in other state socialist countries of the Soviet bloc, consist to a large extent of uprooted lower class people, and this among other factors explains the relatively high level of their party membership, much above their numerical share in society. To secure enough opportunity within the bureaucratic setup, the party membership card is needed in addition to professional knowledge. With the growing number of well-educated people in Poland, competition for the most attractive jobs grows, and the bargaining power of those outside the ruling party is substantially diminished. However, the party ranks have grown between 1960 and 1978 much faster than the total population: The advantage of being just one of many ruling party members has diminished very substantially, and this partially explains the growing dissatisfaction of members with their own party, as well as the growing internal struggle within the party ranks.

The upgrading of traditionally lower class people to the white-collar positions has been the major attraction of Soviet style state socialism for several years. This attraction depends on the advantages of the white-collar jobs. As the bureaucracy proves to be an inefficient vehicle of modernization, there is less interest in becoming an obedient servant to bureaucratic power. The lower bureaucratic positions are particularly undesirable, and parents try to protect their children from these jobs. On the other hand, the prestige, reward, and working conditions of manual jobs are still not great enough to make these jobs generally attractive. If there is a movement to the blue-collar jobs among the white-collar offspring, it originates mainly from the temporary shortage of better opportunities.

The rapid growth of secondary and post-secondary education led in Poland to the widespread desire to enter the ranks of the intelligentsia. This is seen in the aspirations of lower class parents concerning their children's future (Dyoniziak et al. 1978, 65-67). Members of the intelligentsia do not earn much more than skilled blue-collar workers, but they enjoy a privileged status inherited by intelligentsia descendents of the gentry. Even staying abroad, people like philosopher L. Kolakowski or writer C. Milosz influence the Polish intelligentsia. It seems that the Polish intelligentsia is culturally much more prowestern than the Russian intelligentsia, which while opposed to the political status quo remains nationalistic.

The Polish intelligentsia has influenced the blue-collar workers, and this was particularly evident in 1980-81 when Solidarity had in its ranks blue-collar workers, white-collar workers, artists, and intellectuals all together.

The youth have become more numerous in Poland in absolute as well as relative numbers; their life expectations are definitely growing. They are also more critical than their parents about the status quo, not necessarily because they understand things better but because the fear of Stalinist past is foreign to them. Free education based on selection still remains the vehicle of entering the higher levels of income and privilege that are potentially available to the offspring of blue-collar workers and peasants. But the process is not easy for several objective and subjective reasons (Adamski and Zagorski 1979).

The stratification of working people in Poland according to education, income, and power is quite evident. Distribution of incomes showed much improvement during the 1970s due to the raise of lower-level wages and salaries; however, the actual distribution does not include several fringe benefits limited only to some people. [12] Low-paying branches of the economy are mostly occupied by women, who do not receive an equal share even if formally they are on the equal footing with men. Women dominate the health, education, and culture branches, and these are typically low-paying fields. [13]

The changes in the power equilibrium in Poland due to the political awakening of the blue-collar worker stratum is most clearly seen in the wages and salaries. The relative level of blue-collar worker wages has gone up at the expense of the other categories. In the period 1970-83 in the nationalized industry the ratio of blue-collar incomes to the white-collar incomes changed from 1.0:1.5 to 1.0:.87. Blue-collar workers in the upper 10 percent of incomes have grown from 52 percent to 75 percent. Technical and managerial staff, scientific staff, health services, teachers, and administrators have seen their relative income position deteriorate. The average income of people with higher education is 25 percent lower than the average income of an industrial worker (Zienkowski 1984, 4). This new situation decreases the motivation of people to invest in the higher skills and works as a disincentive. On the other hand, the actual power relations influenced the income position of various groups. Inside the blue-collar worker stratum during the early 1980s the best paid and the worst paid received the greatest raises, at expense of the middle-level workers. These middle-level workers lost because their bargaining power was less than either extreme group.

THE SOURCES OF AN ECONOMIC FAILURE

The basic factor of Polish crisis remains the ailing economy: agriculture is underinvested and underpeopled;[14] industry is not enough efficient and profitable; consumer needs are much neglected; money available to the population is chasing scarce attractive goods; there are serious electric power shortages; business is paralyzed by bureaucracy; opportunities are wasted due to the inadequate technological and organizational background; conflicts occur between various groups of interests,[15] work incomes are not adequately related to the actual performance; managers are dependent on <u>apparatchiks</u>; mutual trust between the decision makers and executors of their will is lacking. Can the ruling communists make things better? Their previous failures and the unpopularity of the current establishment make success of any officially sponsored reform problematic, especially when the evident shortages in all fields limit the scope of available alternatives and make rationing a necessity.[16]

Polish rulers implement economic reform which is supposed to offer more freedom to nationalized enterprises, but there is strong resistance against this, even among the managers themselves. As an obedient hand of the government, the associations of these enterprises are trying to regain their previous high level of control and are using various indirect means to achieve it: directors of enterprises are asked to attend meetings where collective decisions are made, and then are expected to implement these afterwards; and statistical reports are collected, giving the association's bureaucrats the chance to reinforce their informational power. Managers of the enterprises usually take a 'wait and see' stance and do not trust higher authorities as being genuinely dedicated to reform. It seems more convenient to play the traditional game of hiding actual potential at the planning stage in order to gain handsome bonuses from the overfulfillment of production quotas afterward.

It would be almost impossible to promote reform successfully without the encouragement of genuine dedication on the side of managers. Self-governmental bodies (workers' councils) do exist in the majority of enterprises, but their actual functioning is handicapped by the controls and limits imposed from outside (as well as by the ailing economy in general).

Managers of the nationalized economy prefer to play it safe and feel much more comfortable within the bureaucratic system than in the market situation. They are accustomed to bargaining with higher authorities for various advantages in exchange for the promise that certain quotas of production would be dutifully fulfilled. The give and take exchange of favors is a field well known by executives who have a long experience at hiding the real potential of their enterprises, making a good deal on the target, and afterwards claiming the awards justified by the overfulfillment of production plans. From this perspective, the market situation appears to be something much more risky and difficult to manage.

People at the top of the hierarchy have a strong vested interest to keep under control all basic factors of the economy. Several of them pay lip service to autonomy of the enterprises and a flexible price system based on free bargaining, but in reality they want to keep things as they were before.

Even the most reasonable reforms become totally unrealistic without institutions willing and able to implement the tasks. It is necessary to consider the impact of harmful vested interests. These institutions whose vested interests introduce a heavy bias to the promotion of goals, are useless for a genuine reform. The socialization potential of complex organizations differs widely. Present day Polish society needs a great deal of this potential to channel and adequately use the growing public spirit in Poland. From September 1980 until December 1981 there was a genuine revival of the "public man" whose fall in the capitalist west has been criticized (Sennett 1978).

Poland has a very high level of occupational activization (51 percent of the population) and a well-educated labor force, but has a relatively low social productivity of labor: one half of the level in East Germany and Czechoslovakia, and only around 30 percent of the leverage of big industrial democracies taken together. Compared to more effective Western production, Poland must invest too much work and too many raw materials into manufactured products.

> Ninety percent of Polish production is for the domestic
> market and this does not allow enough experience to be
> gained from the more sophisticated foreign industries.
> The whole of Poland's foreign trade is based on only two
> hundred enterprises out of a total of 5405 nationalized
> enterprises existing in Poland. In Polish manufacturing
> industry mass production constitutes only 7 percent (in
> the West, 30 percent and over) and small batch production
> constitutes 51 percent (compared to approximately 20 per-

cent in the West). This is one of the main reasons why it
is still more profitable for Poland to export raw materials
(i.e., coal, sulphur, etc.) than the ready products which
cost too much to be produced. It would be better to buy
several goods outside of Poland, but instead they are produced at great cost at home due to shortages of foreign
currency. Polish import has declined by one half in the
last few years. (Trybuna Ludu, 1985, 1).

The economic position of Poland in the Soviet bloc
has considerably deteriorated. In 1984 exports per capita
of Bulgaria, Hungary, Czechoslovakia and East Germany
were in each case from three to four times better than in
the case of Poland (in 1970 the distance was much shorter);
Romania was much better than Poland (by 65 percent); and
even the USSR had a higher export rate. With the current
debt of Poland at $ U.S. 28 billion owed to the West and close
to $ U.S. 7 billion owed to the Soviet bloc countries, mainly
the USSR, foreign trade badly needs considerable improvement. In the period 1982-84, the positive foreign trade
balance has grown by 58 percent, but this is still far from
being a major improvement. Poland has only 0.6 percent
share in the world export and this is one third lower than
during the interwar period. Without much improvement in
export capacity and ability to import necessary goods,
Poland will not be able to achieve internal peace. The
rigid state socialist system remains a major obstacle
for Poland and without a green light from Moscow the
country will remain in real trouble. However, who of the
powerful in Moscow would be willing and able to permit
Poland to take another road? Of course there may be some
chance that the Soviet masters will tire of Poland's current
economic weakness which does impose some burden on the
USSR and is one of the main sources of internal disturbance
within the Soviet bloc.

Poland's dependence on the import of grain and fodder has
grown instead of diminished, although Poland has improved grain
production in the early 1980s (per capita from 555 kg in 1976-80 to
about 650 kg in 1984). In the period 1970-82 around U.S. $11 billion
were spent on grain import; about 60 percent of all grain in Poland
is consumed by domestic animals and 25 percent is consumed by people. During the early 1980s the shortage of hard currency meant a
decline of fodder imports, contributing to the decline of the meat production per capita from around 75 kg during 1976-80 to 66 kg in 1983;
the absolute amount of meat production declined in that period by 21
percent (Sandomierski 1984, 18).

Between 1960 and 1981 industrial production in Poland grew four times, investments grew three times, the employment directly related to production grew by 57 percent. (Rocznik 1983). These rates of growth were approximately the same as in the USSR. However, the decline of the production rate in the early 1980s, seen in all eastern Europe, was much more dramatic in Poland than in any other country (-5.4 percent during 1979-81). The underutilization of the available production means occurred with the unfavorable balance of payments and the country was unable to buy more necessary western imports. The shortage of electric power has led to several work stoppages in the industrial enterprises. These stoppages have counted much more than strikes.

The difficult economic situation of Poland[17] makes it necessary to mobilize resources, and this is almost impossible as long as a major gap exists between the rulers and the society. From 1950 to 1982 the share of the Polish GDP in the world GDP diminished.[18] This decline was particularly dramatic from 1978 to 1982: from 1.4 percent to 1.0 percent. The Polish GDP per capita compared to the average GDP of the free market European societies declined during 1950-82 from 1:2.3 to 1:3, and compared to the average of the European state socialist societies Polish GDP has declined from 1:1 to 1:1.3 (Wojciechowski 1984, 17, 20).[19]

All these economic facts influence profoundly the situation of working people and particularly blue-collar workers. The average income grew in 1982 by 51 percent but actual buying power has diminished due to rise of the cost of living (it doubled in 1982). The permanent shortage of goods exposes the inequality of additional rationing (distribution of attractive goods and services among the privileged categories of the population), and the black market has grown considerably.[20]

The government hoped the considerable price increases would diminish the pressure of consumer demand and at the same time eliminate the state subsidy of basic food stuffs[21] practiced for many years to keep intact the level of remuneration.[22] This governmental manipulation was particularly painful for the low income families that did not have even enough money to buy their rationed food. Since the radical price increase in 1982, the market situation has not improved considerably and in 1985 further price increases followed. The general decline of output has forced the government to give people more bonuses, especially in mining and other key industries. Workers may have in some cases much more money, but the production of consumer goods remains inadequate and there is not much attraction to buy. In addition, the price increases eliminate the advantages of higher nominal incomes.

Poles improve their households by buying various gadgets. The inadequate supply of them, as well as the high price, is a common complaint. There are great differences in household equipment depending on the income level, especially in the ability to possess automobiles, refrigerators, tape recorders, and other expensive gadgets (Krzeczkowska 1979, 111). Personal cars are not owned by the workers and employees in the low income groups; refrigerators are owned by about half. The same is true for the farmers' households. On the other hand, TV sets, radios, and simple laundry machines are now common in all households.

The technical and economic education are commonplace in Poland. [23] Around 1,000 doctoral degrees in technology and 200 doctoral degrees in economics are awarded every year. Technical courses at the postsecondary level are attended by 120,000 students (in it 28,000 women) and the economics courses are attended by 45,000 students (in it 27,000 women). At the same time the technical and economic progress of the country is obviously inadequate in several fields. In the period 1978-82 the work output of one worker declined in several fields, and the utilization of electric power per one worker has remained at the same level (Rocznik 1983). [24] Power is wasted because of the technical obsolescence of much equipment. In the consumer-oriented industries technical equipment is too old. The transportation cost involved in the process of production in general is too high. Labor costs are excessive even if the incomes of workers remain relatively low compared to western countries.

Poland badly needs technological input from the west but does not have money to buy it (Gruzewski 1984, 17). The close foreign trade ties with the Soviet Union are dictated more by the political dependence than by actual gain. In the ailing economy, Poland becomes even more dependent on the USSR but at the same time has less chance to modernize consumer-oriented production. [25] With the debt over five times higher than the exchange currency yearly incomes from export, Poland is not able to expect more credit from the West.

COMPLEX ORGANIZATION UNDER STATE SOCIALISM

The development of a society, especially under state socialism, is closely related to the growth of complex organizations as factors of role establishment, life perspectives (promotions) and even social stratification (Kolarska and Rychard 1980). For example, in 1979, nationalized enterprises with 5,000 or more workers employed 25 percent of the industrial labor force, and those with fewer than 500 employees accounted for just 13 percent of the labor force (Rocznik 1980, 170). The interests of organizations affects human lives, distances people, and leads to a substantial dependence of people upon their employers. This is particularly true in a society where the choice is limited and political power goes together with the economic power (Rychard 1980). People identify themselves with a specific organization even when they are more or less negatively oriented toward them. They are forced by circumstances to participate in the "games" played within these organizations (Matejko 1984). It is possible to claim that under state socialism the "organizational society" appears even more frequently than under market societies.

The very fast and expensive Soviet-style industrialization of the early 1950s, promoted by the authoritarian bureaucracy, from the beginning led to internal tensions, contradictions, and even open conflicts. Political life became almost exclusively limited to the party members, but among the party intellectuals there was a growing resistance against the ruling apparatchiks. Far from any pluralism, the gap between the wide circles of various experts and the ruling party elite has crystallized. The work councils were spontaneously created in the mid-1950s in various state enterprises by local activists with the tacit consent of management. Local managers were far from happy to play the role of the obedient servants to the bureaucratic power, but being appointed and controlled by the state and party hierarchy they could not revolt. As a new body, the work councils depended neither on the state administration nor the trade union bureaucracy that was subservient to the administration, and, therefore these councils for several months could show some initiative. Eventually, the councils were subordinated directly to the party bureaucracy.

The work councils focused themselves mainly on the economic and organizational improvement of their enterprises, which suffered from red tape imposed from the top. There was a tendency in the second half of the 1950s at the beginning to treat management as the executive body and the council as something as a board of directors elected by the personnel. With the gradual return to power of the state and party bureaucracy, the work council started to play increasingly the role of a consultative body. The factory electorate tended to delegate to the work councils primarily the skilled white-collar workers as better prepared than the unskilled workers to take an active part in the policy matters. The party treated it as a nuisance and started a whole action in favor of giving blue-collar workers a clear priority. It was finally established as a rule that blue-collar workers should constitute at least two-thirds of the work councils.

Already, as still today, Polish intellectuals were unsure and divided regarding the model of democratic socialism to institute in their home country to replace the economy of command. This model in the 1950s was of a crucial importance because on it depended how significant a role would be secured for the works councils. Some Polish economists (Kurowski, Popkiewicz) advocated a free market economy consisting of the autonomous consumers and producers exchanging freely everything with no interference from outside. This approach represented a radical rejection of the rigid state socialism of a Stalinist style directed from the top by the party planners. Other economists, for example Bobrowski, Lange, and Brus, were impressed by Yugoslav experience. They also wanted autonomous enterprises and free exchange, but they were willing to leave substantial power to the state. Even those economists such as Kalecki who wanted to retain the major part of central planning, declared themselves to be in favor of a very considerable democratization of the whole system. The ruling party, PUWP, after a relatively short period of some relaxation decided in the late 1950s to impose a centralism much less oppressive than before but also quite rigid. This policy was adopted against public opinion, and only few economists supported it.

It is clear from the present day perspective that the vested interest of state and party apparatus prevailed over all other considerations and that the rival social powers were too weak, too dispersed, and too divided to be able to provide any substantial challenge to the status quo. The democratic resistance of the mid-1950s was too weak and too short-lived to challenge the ruling bureaucracy. The massive social upgrading of the lower strata during the period of forced industrialization had changed the socioeconomic, cultural, and moral fabric of the society. The democratic ideals were popular mainly among the intelligentsia, which constituted at most 10 percent of the population, and the rest looked mainly for some modest improvement of their very low living standard. When the pressure of the omnipotent state and party bureaucracy relaxed for a while for an internal reshuffle of the ruling elite in the second half of the 1950s, the establishment of work councils was a suitable temporary platform for some local initiatives. However, these councils were concerned almost exclusively with the administrative realm, and the whole problem of a grass-root industrial democracy was almost neglected. Thus, the mass of workers was never mobilized behind the work councils, and this mass remained apathetic when the party decided to tighten bureaucratic control of enterprise.

The abstract reasoning in terms of models of the late 1950s was useful at least to stimulate public interest in the alternatives to the existing state of affairs. Models constructed then still effectively stimulate the imagination of Polish reformers and dissidents. However, not enough attention has been paid to the practical applicability of these models to the Polish sociopolitical and cultural reality. Poles have existed under the bureaucracy for a very long time. Even during 1918 to 1939 the practice of democracy, free enterprise, and entrepreneurship had quite narrow limits. It is necessary to recall that the state was the major employer, agriculture was underdeveloped, and a very considerable part of the labor force suffered unemployment or at least underemployment.

The collective entrepreneurship of the socialized enterprises, i.e., state-owned or coops, may become a reality only on the basis of common interests, strong social cohesion, highly experienced democratic leadership and management, well-functioning autonomous work groups, good channels of communication, high concentration around common tasks, etc. Totalitarianism has been oriented for several decades toward the atomization of society, mutual distrust, dominance of the egoistic preoccupations, general feeling of helplessness, lack of personal responsibility. People have to become effectively socialized under the new socioeconomic models not of an abstract nature but thoroughly well-adapted to the Polish reality.

In the late 1970s the balance of power became much less favorable for the party because of the difficult food situation, a much stronger political opposition, and the internal split within the party ranks. The debates on the new model of organizational society (in distinction to the civil society) have become much more vivid and loaded with content than at anytime before. From contemporary perspective the highly theoretical discussions around the issue of the work councils in the late 1950s look quite naive even if useful and intellectually stimulating.

Polish sociologists take an active part in the discussions on a new model for Polish economy. Their names often appear in the mass media. Even before 1980 there were sociologists who made a meaningful contribution. For example, Kaminski (1979) criticized a nondialectic, mechanistic concept of planning with the center of domination external to the society. He emphasized that

> under the conditions of centralized control the most rational strategy for subordinate levels is to play against the planning center, since the central decisions become for them the major source of uncertainty. This effort toward the reduction of uncertainty, typical of every organization, takes on the form of strategies aimed at neutralizing and obstructing initiatives of the center. . . . As the object of the internal rivalry is to gain better access to resources of the society, and as success in this rivalry depends on the bargaining power of the parties involved, which in turn depends upon the amount of resources an organization unit already has at its disposal, the net result will be the growing rigidity of the system (Kaminski 1979, 9).

The power game between the planning center and lower organizational units is based on mutual distrust and opposed vested interests. Resources are hidden, information is distorted, efficiency is diminished, waste is encouraged, particularistic interests gain priority under the guise of public interest; there appears an informal "reprivatization" of political sphere.

An effective articulation of various group interests, their mutual reconciliation, and aggregation are necessary to achieve some internal equilibrium in the society. This must be done in a flexible manner as "a continuous, mutual interaction of incomplete programs and prognoses, containing social and physical limitation" (Lipinski 1969, 144). Even under the rigid centralized planning the planning center is in fact under the constant pressure of various conflicting vested interests, and the planners have to accommodate them by constantly improvising some corrections dictated by changing circumstances.

The variety of particularistic interests conflicting with central planning under state socialism was revealed in the writings of Narojek (1974, 1975) and Staniszkis (1972). Narojek took for granted that "the economy is an extensive area of various interweaving types of social bonds: relations of superiority and subordination, relations of friendship, relations of competition, etc." (Narojek et al. 1975, 58). It is up to the social scientists to pay attention to these bonds and relate them to the performance of a planned economy. This looks like a self-evident truth, but in the early 1970s it was received by local Marxists as a novelty.

In the Polish sociology of complex organizations efforts have been directed toward using relationships as steering mechanisms of society—neglecting the participatory needs and aspirations of the rank and file and giving priority to the managerial point of view (e.g., see Morawski, ed. 1976). Some sociologists recognize that promoting the managerial perspective is not limited to western social scientists appearing as "servants of power" but also is seen in socialist Poland as well (see Kuczynski 1980, 266-67). There is a growing interest in the mutual relationships between technology and society. Several sociologists take active part in the international or local conferences in this field, as well as do research (Zacher 1981, 143).

In the sociology of complex organizations the pathology of organizational structures has been studied by Staniszkis (1972, 1982) since the 1960s, but the later studies are mostly of a more abstract character: the degree of coherence and mechanisms of transformation of organizational structures (Mrela and Staniszkis 1977), formalization, standardization, and centralization (Kolarska 1977).

The constitutive role of work places in the urban surrounding has been of great concern to sociologists. For example, Nowakowski (1980) shows the differences in this respect under capitalism and under socialism and especially the role of socialized enterprises as sponsors of local services, main employers, factors of stratification and mobility. He also provides an insight into the conflicts appearing in all these fields.

Managers remain in Poland a noncohesive category due mostly to the dependence in their appointment on the PUWP (ruling party), the variety of professional and educational backgrounds, and their frequent transfers from one position to another. On the other hand, around 60 percent of the managers identify themselves with the "profession" of a manager (Kostecki 1977, 93), and this happens more often at the higher ranks than at the lower ranks. "There are objective mechanisms which speed up the process of transferring the management from an aggregate of individuals distinguishing themselves thanks to similarities of their actual position into an integrated category" (Kostecki 1977, 94). With the growing practice of hiring managers on the basis of an open competition and the declining dominance of PUWP over the recruitment procedure, Polish managers may become more autonomous as a group.

Most managers have a technical education and are not well-enough acquainted with the economic, organizational, human, and social aspects of decision making. Their ability to make decisions of an innovative nature that would recognize the whole variety of involved problems has been negatively affected (Zacher 1981, 139).

Since the 1960s the selection of candidates to the executive positions has become much stricter concerning the degree of higher education (Kostecki 1977, 87). Yet, at the same time it appears that it has become more common for party candidates to high positions to obtain diplomas without much effort. Technical education prevails,[26] but in the 1960s a trend started to allow people with an economic education to be promoted to executive positions. For years Polish executives have needed more freedom of decision (Kostecki 1979, 90). They have been overly restricted by the bureaucratic rigidity of a highly centralized planning and looked for some relaxation of the internal discipline within the managerial ranks. The top level expected local managers to blindly obey and interfered constantly with the duties of their subordinates. This has led to a considerable bureaucratization of the managerial ranks (Kostecki 1977, 93).

Recruitment policies to the executive positions have promoted party members. For example, in the chemical industry during the period 1945-52 the share of party members among executives grew from 28 percent to 85 percent and the share of executives with higher education diminished from 84 percent to 20 percent. In 1974, 78 percent of executives were party members and 60 percent of them performed some political functions some time in their career. Among executives there were over eight times more party members than among the average adult citizens (Kostecki 1979, 23). Due to the careful selection of executives (PUWP has a list of suitable candidates for these positions) and their circulation between various posts, executives represent a relatively homogeneous category of people totally dependent on PUWP politically, disposable, tough in their execution of orders coming from above, and very pragmatic.

To be a party or state executive in Poland is not very secure to be sure, but it is profitable. Many and varied are the privileges that fall to people appointed by the party to responsible positions: apartments, cars (for the use on duty or for private purchase at a discount), expense-paid holidays in Poland and abroad, etc. A person who enters the executive circle remains in it permanently and is simply transferred from one management position to another that is no less profitable. Polish intellectuals, however, need not envy these executives. To rule the society, the party has created a body of totally dedicated management personnel and has given it certain privileges in return for loyalty, although these remain far below what executives in the west have.

In return for permanent employment and certain privileges, the executives must give the party their souls and their bodies—something not demanded of the intelligentsia. They often work a dozen or so hours daily, they are always on call, and they have to beware of internal office politics and of being replaced by somebody else (there are always a number of people just itching for the chance at every executive's position). The numbers of executive personnel are actually rather small, for the generally badly paid lower-rank managers can hardly be included.

An executive is not supposed to benefit from the pleasures of life because people may think he or she has been stealing or because such luxury damages the authority of the party (this is especially true for an executive working in the countryside). An executive should not have a clear-cut, personal opinion, because the party may change its dogma, and the loyalty of a dedicated party member is primarily expressed through the resignation of one's own ego. The family of an executive is also continually on show, and must behave in such a way as not to draw the slightest criticism.

In actual fact, therefore, the executive is considerably more restricted than anybody else and particularly more so than the intellectual. The boring official newspaper of the party is everyday reading material for the executive (reading it regularly is in itself a hardship), together with various immensely monotonous party periodicals and materials. If an executive dares to read other things (and one is not likely to have much desire or time for it), then they too must in some way be connected to the professional responsibilities. There always exists a suspicion that reading nonparty, and even more so anti-Party, material can give an executive ideas and lead him or her to some sort of activity that while perhaps not fractional, is at least not directly related to the realization of the party's current goals.

It is the duty of the executive to love the Soviet Union, which is, however, a very unattractive proposition in view of the propaganistic nature of the lectures and speeches about that country, infrequency of trips to the USSR (even among party functionaries), and the experiences and material goods that acquaintances (very often not party members) bring back with them from trips to the west. The snobbery of the intelligentsia is transferred to the executives to some extent and effectively keeps them from proclaiming love for the USSR. The leisure of executives is also connected with the intelligentsia. But at the same time the latter is a constant sore spot; it is the intellectual, not the party organizer, who travels to the west, shamelessly turns on Radio Free Europe, reads the emigrant magazines, chatters away in cafes, and makes fun of the "ignoramuses." Sometimes the executive manages to catch an intellectual out and tries to make life thoroughly unpleasant for him/her but the result somehow turns out awkwardly and ends up in loss of face for the party. The punished intellectual cries out for revenge to the whole world and makes a virtue of his clumsiness, solidifying his position all the more.

Thus, it is better for the party executive to limit oneself to minor skirmishes with intellectuals in the privacy of one's own office: to play cat-and-mouse with them in the matter of a profitable trip abroad ("We well know what sort of 'learning' they are after with all these trips!"), to tempt them with an apartment ("Why are these intellectuals so constantly moving or getting divorced?"), to sympathize disgustingly with creative torments or marital problems, or, finally, to quite brutally refuse the allocation of attractive goods ("We cannot, comrades, diminish the possessions of the workers in that way!"). The intellectual stops being flattering and starts being unpleasant, and probably runs to a cafe to vocalize the series of unending complaints.

LIMITS OF AN ENFORCED SOCIALIZATION

The highly bureaucratized model of state socialism imposed by force was oriented mainly to external control of Polish life through the network of institutions infiltrated by people totally subservient first to the ruling Polish Workers' Party (PWP) and afterwards to the Polish United Workers' Party (PUWP) (Polonsky and Drukier, eds. 1980).

This institutional network was handicapped not only by the centralization of actual power and the red tape related to any bureaucracy but also by the full concentration of the economy on heavy industry. In the period 1950-78 accumulation within the GNP grew 12 times, consumption grew only six times, and investments grew 16 times. During the 1950s and the 1960s consumption was kept at the level of around 75 percent of GNP, (material production only) and during the 1970s it was lowered to around 65 percent. In the period 1965-79 the total private consumption more than doubled, but industrial investments have more than tripled (Rocznik 1980, XXXV). Only since 1981 has accumulation declined to around 20 percent.

The organizational structure of Polish society remains a "foreign body," and a considerable vacuum exists between the primary group commitment and the national commitment. "While nation stands for a kind of a moral community of all Poles and has an autotelic value, state is viewed as merely a system of a top level organization" (Nowak 1980, 8). None of the secondary bonds seems to evoke a mass-scale identification, except the Catholic Church (which has remained independent of the state and party) and Solidarity in the early 1980s.

The general feeling that the existing organizational framework is just a nuisance seems to be widespread in Poland, and this impairs the functioning of society. The distinction between "we" (family members, friends, decent people) and "they" (bureaucrats, imposed masters, troublemakers, lazy bums, incompetent and cynical careerists) is evident and makes any improvement of the situation very difficult.

Nowak writes about the gap between the "world of people" and the "world of institutions" (1980, 10). Friendship ties are commonly treated as the only way to "soften" the world of institutions, make it personally useful, humanize it. "Personal contacts appease institutional rules, render the institution understanding, sometimes even helpful" (Nowak 1980, 10). Friendship and bribery go quite often together. "The factor of interpersonal bonds modifies the functioning of the configurations, softens the stiffness of institutional structure and often makes it function more effectively, though not always according to formal rules" (Nowak 1980, 10).

Since 1980 the question remains open how much Polish people are really interested in the state socialist model as applied in Poland since the late 1940s. On the basis of research data, Nowak claims that Poles in reality accept the system but would like it to be more attentive and efficient. "People accept the situation in which most aspects of their lives depend more on the functioning of centrally managed institutions and on political decisions than on their own decisions and acts. . . . The concept of national economy and central planning has taken a strong root in the minds of the Poles" (Nowak 1980, 11). However, the distinction in Poland between "us" and "them" goes so far that it creates a barrier that is very harmful to any meaningful communication between the state institutions and the majority of society. Common people often have quite unrealistic expectations of the state and become very dissatisfied when it is unwilling or unable to satisfy them. On the other hand the state institutions follow their own rules of existence, more or less ignoring the demands and expectations of people. The difficulties that grew between PUWP and Solidarity originated from

this deep gap between the masses and the institutions that under socialism are supposed to serve common people but in reality remain primarily the obedient servants of the ruling power.

There is some confusion in Polish minds. The commitment to
equal opportunities for everybody is widespread among the population,
but at the same time people are not ready to share the cost of that
commitment. The state is expected to take care of people in need (for
example, the idea of a social minimum is very popular), but there is
a great reservation against any further state interference into private
affairs. Egalitarianism is popular, but many Poles show rigidity and
even authoritarianism. "People seem to see the need for 'democratization' of the system without having a clear idea what democracy means
in practice and how it should be realized" (Nowak 1980, 14). People
are frustrated with the inefficiencies of state socialism, but there is
a clear conflict between the democratic ideals professed by the majority of citizens "and their psychological predispositions to their own
democratic functioning within the society" (Nowak 1980, 15).

There is a double standard between the rules for oneself and
rules for others. For example, "The average Pole does not believe
himself to be bound by any moral norms in his interactions with institutions, yet he applies univocal moral criteria to representatives,
particularly to executives in these institutions. . . . The Poles do
not consider telling the truth an important value in interpersonal relations. . . . On the other hand, the Polish society is very sensitive
indeed to what it considers to be untrue in official enunciations of the
mass media" (Nowak 1980, 16). Poles are not consistent but expect
consistency from the people who rule the country. The commitment
to personal freedom is very strong among the people, but it does not
mean that the freedom of others is always recognized. Religiosity
manifests itself in the churches full of people attending Sunday masses,
but the implementation of Catholic morality is very liberal.

The emphasis on survival is strong, and this explains why in
Poland "there is absence of both antagonistic or at least strongly differentiated group value systems, and also absence of consistence in
themselves yet mutually opposed life, ideological and moral orientations on the individual level" (Nowak 1980, 19). Religiosity is a matter
of private philosophy; there is strong mutual tolerance in many spheres
even if debates and antagonisms are heated. The pressure exercised
on Poles by the state socialist institutions has created several defense
mechanisms rooted in primary bonds that allow people to help each
other survive across the existing ideological and cultural divisions.

VALUES AND MORALITY

According to the official doctrine, people in Poland were supposed to become much more socially oriented than when under conditions of a market economy. Taking into consideration hardships of rapid industrialization and the heavy burden imposed on society (low wages and very modest housing conditions), it would be reasonable to expect at least some sociomoral advantages of socialism. There are several sociological studies that shed some light on this important issue.

In Poland before World War II sociocultural and economic stratification was very evident in daily life. Better-off people were proud of their superior origin, literary language (instead of local dialects typical for lower classes), better life opportunities, better clothing, etc. In socialist Poland acquired skills, occupations, and educational levels started to dominate value systems (Koralewicz-Zebik 1979, 178). Work and effort have become publicly recognized as the basic factors of success, and this is the altruistic orientation expected from others. However, instead of treating hard work and effort as virtues, individuals very often use them as token manipulatory devices to exercise moral pressure on others to behave according to the vested interests of a given individual (Koralewicz-Zebik 1979, 181).

Poland under state socialism does not differ much from the societies to which Poles are inclined to compare themselves—the western societies where a considerable number of Polish emigrants have settled. As in the west, Poles are preoccupied with themselves, their families, friends, and colleagues (Nowak 1980, 6), but the state controls the implementation of personal goals. The fact that the state and PUWP priorities for many years pushed aside the personal priorities of many Poles has become a source of irritation and frustration. A permanent housing shortage, irregular delivery of food, economic hardships, bureaucratic inefficiency, etc., have created a general feeling that the state is unable or unwilling to bother about people, except a small category of specially privileged people.

The surveys have found that disparities in income and wealth are primary sources of social tensions, especially among the blue-collar workers. "Those who had higher income and privileges had a much higher understanding of the necessity for differentiation in income and privileges than those who did not. . . . The higher up the social ladder the respondents were, the more democratic and the less egalitarian they were" (Nowak 1981, 52).

The summary by Nowak (1981) of more than 150 surveys conducted in Poland since 1956 of standards by which Poles judge or evaluate both themselves and the world shows the homogenization of values and attitudes (due partly to the grinding mill of Stalinism), commitment to the equality of life opportunities (but the majority still accepts some income inequality), expectation of an active role of the state in providing the general welfare, lack of interest in Marxism, and religious beliefs persisting. The social structure of Polish society in the subjective vision of its members appears "to be a 'federation' of primary groups united in a national community" (Nowak 1981, 51). There is a notable lack of cohesive social institutions between the circle of friends and that of the nation. This gap seemed to have been filled at least temporarily by "the spontaneous development of the Independent Free Trade Unions, called Solidarity" (Nowak 1981, 52).

Even more than in Russia (Smith 1977) friendship ties in Poland have become a mechanism of gaining security and satisfaction, as well as vehicles to solve many daily problems that in the market societies are usually dealt with by the specialized formal organizations. "We turn to our friends for help in difficult situations and feel obliged to be of help to them," states Nowak (1980, 8). Because of the general shortage and the red tape there are usually so many "difficult" situations that friends are constantly needed. Conformism within the circle of friends is the price that people are willing to pay to maintain psychological and material support the circles offer.

Primary bonds are treated in general much more seriously than formal obligations, particularly work obligations, and the practice of informal deals is common. Neither the existing labor relations system, which does not adequately reward good work and a creative attitude toward it, nor the value system informally prevailing in the society give praise to the work performance (Koralewicz-Zebik 1979, 182). Material stability, family happiness, future of children, and clear conscience are in general much more appreciated than any risk-taking, big effort, ambition, etc. It is significant that Poles show a very limited interest in advancing to the positions of power (Koralewicz-Zebik 1979, 186), and this seems to be related to the politicization of these positions, long hours of work, and the high turnover among the managerial personnel.

The utilitarian, nonromantic orientation among contemporary Poles has become considerably reinforced by the massive advancement of traditional lower classes, a gradual decline of the old intelligentsia tradition (Gella 1971), the shift in the professional structure from the humanistic intelligentsia to the technical experts, and the growth of mass consumption, until the late 1970s. There is a strong preoccupation with status as well as with material well-being, and these characteristics are in general typical for the status-seekers who just recently managed to make an upward career move (Koralewicz-Zebik 1979, 190; Narojek 1975). The mass upgrading of lower classes during the period of rapid industrialization has brought to towns many people of peasant origin. Koralewicz-Zebik also mentions the impact of petty bourgeoisie mentality, conformistic school model, and malfunctioning of bureaucratic institutions (1979: 185).

Studies of the young generation done in the early 1970s show that good friends, family life, and good health take priority among them. Young people do not want to hurt anyone and are not ready to sacrifice their lives unless beloved ones or the country were in an ultimate danger. They are not eager to take risks and get involved in problems that do not concern them personally (Smola 1977, 133). In most aspects there is a clear similarity between the values of the adult generations and the values dominating among the young. The problem is that this relative model of a quiet and secure life is almost unobtainable for the people who face a shortage of housing, low incomes, and since the late 1970s a permanent shortage of food. Virtues popular among the youth such as amiability, benevolence, helpfulness, honesty, industriousness, reliability, sincerity, and tolerance (Smola 1977, 135) do not fit very well into the situation dominated by the struggle for survival. Therefore, "the model favoured by young people is internally inconsequent" (Smola 1977, 135). Egoism is reinforced by the tough life circumstances and the competition for scarce resources. Yet, an altruistic and friendly attitude toward others is a respected value. Lack of consequence forms a common escape. "There is a wide gap between the claims young people formulate towards other members of the society and those which they formulate for their own sake" (Smola 1977, 136).

Young people are patriotic and do not show such an inferiority feeling toward western nations as is typical among the older generation (Smola 1977, 138). They are also very sensitive to human dignity.

In spite of the Catholic majority, the existence of truly Christian spirit in Poland should not be overestimated. As Maria Ossowska rightly underlines, the model of a knight, the model of a gentleman, and even the model of a courtier, which are so attractive to the Poles, are in many aspects contrary to the Christian spirit. "The ideal of a gentleman is not moral virtue but honour. . . . Anything that speaks highly in social sense about the man is an asset for him. It is not, therefore, a set of Christian characteristics" (Ossowska 1973, 171).

Contemporary Poles' sense of honor is probably not less significant than in previous generations, and possibly even more important because of urbanization and the filling of ranks of intelligentsia by peasant elements that had advanced through education, jobs outside agriculture, and the ruling apparatus. However, the meaning of honor has considerably deviated from its original understanding; it now often means freedom from all outside criticism, or even any critical allusion. Care is taken not to allow others to perform or say anything offending, which eliminates in advance a much more important question, that of what one is really like. The sense of honor understood in this way can exist very well side by side with dishonesty in public, or even in family matters, or affairs between friends. It is a manipulation of the world through silencing everybody else regarding the fact that, possibly, the king—in this case me—might be naked.

This kind of manipulation is often used by bureaucrats who, as opposed to institutions that have to compete in a free market, obtain great gains from their monopoly. The dream of being the only one, of being indispensable within an area, and being able to silence all others is, probably, not foreign to any of us.

The gentry tradition and the postfeudal heritage of Poland seem to be particularly strongly accentuated, especially compared to North American mass societies. The massive social upgrading of people from the traditionally lower classes under the communist rule has substantially contributed to a move toward a mass society model. However, the social attractiveness of the intelligentsia, which inherited directly from the gentry the "governance of souls," has not yet diminished. The dissemination of culture and mass education and the numerical growth of the white-collar workers from 16 percent of the total population before World War II to 25 percent now have contributed to a widespread acceptance of the preferences and values typical of the intelligentsia.

Of course, contrary to the situation before the World War II, the intelligentsia does not rule anymore. In fact it is subdued to the rule exercised by the party and state functionaries and must obey them. Still, it is practically impossible for functionaries to govern without making use of all kinds of experts who bring with them to the ranks of decision makers the values and aspirations traditionally common among intelligentsia.

THE LIFE-STYLES

Poland is a fascinating country, among others, due to the coexistence of various life-styles—modernized as well as traditional (Los 1977, 1979). The sociocultural heritage of intelligentsia (Gella 1971) is intact, although, according to sociologists (Sicinski 1978), there is a progressing unification of life-styles typical for mass societies. Life-styles characteristic for such strata as urban blue-collar workers, village peasants, urban white collars, etc. still coexist. Some new life-styles became products of socioeconomic transformations in the country. The facts that mass media represent to a very large extent the taste and preferences of intelligentsia and that the upgrading to the cultural level of professional intellectuals or artists remains highly attractive play a major role in the cultural image of society.

Even though in communist Poland the Polish nobility ceased finally to exist, and therefore ceased to influence the national character, state socialism model (as opposed to the libertarian socialism) tends toward elitist models in social and private life. Just as the existence of a knight depended on privileges and the ability to pass on the yoke of work to people deprived of these privileges, so it is in Soviet-style state socialism; privileges are the principle of life.

Poland never really experienced her own capitalism, and therefore never had an occasion to consolidate the bourgeois morality in the society, but instead made a leap from a national character formed mainly by the feudal system to a mentality formed by Soviet-style state socialism. Both systems are similar in at least some important aspects. In the first system as well as in the second, the great majority of the people have no privileges of importance, and the most they can ever hope to achieve is to get some privileges illegally. In both these systems the value of man is measured mainly by his unlimited loyalty and availability to the actual ruling elite. An ordinary citizen, just by virtue of existence, is indebted to the establishment until death; this debt is expected to continually be paid by personal sacrifice for the system's good. Whatever the official doctrine, it is always interpreted in such a manner so as to enhance the cult of power, curb individual thinking and creativity, and rely on ritual rather than intellectual thinking and moral ferment.

Leisure activities and preoccupations play a growing role in eastern European societies and in the long run they may have some major impact on the life-style and thoughts of the population. In the field of leisure some new social distinctions develop, and new vested interests are established. The shortening of the work day, improved standard of living, higher educational level, and broader availability of public leisure facilities affect the satisfaction of the population and its sociocultural aspirations. The goods and services produced under state socialism do not match the general acceptance by the public of what is offered. The new leisure patterns quite often develop very fast, and the egalitarian trends within the state socialist societies stimulate this process very much. Within the framework of the state socialist leisure institutions, people of various sociocultural backgrounds mix with one another and easily acquire some new needs that afterwards become articulated as mass demands.

Even in the period 1918-39 Poland was largely an agricultural society in which annual leave and the travel related to it were limited to a few members of the privileged strata. In the Polish territory before the World War I the right of annual leave was limited to civil servants, officials of local government, administrators in trade, and academic workers. In 1922 the Polish parliament enacted one of the first laws in the world on the annual leave for all nonagricultural employees: for white-collar workers, 15 days after 6 months of work and afterwards one month per year; for blue-collar workers, 8 days after one year of work and 15 days after three years of work. Some categories of employees—the supervisors, salespeople, among others—managed to include themselves into the category of white-collar workers for leave rights. By the 1920s the rail workers and some categories of blue collars who worked under particularly difficult conditions gained 14 days of leave after just one year of employment, 21 days after three years of employment, 28 days after 10 years of employment, and 35 days after 20 years of employment.

Although paid annual leave was a legal right of manual workers, in fact many of them were not able to take advantage of it. It was convenient for the employers to release the worker before he gained the right for the annual leave and to hire him again a few months later. Manual workers also used to sell their leave. Only a few percent enjoyed real leisure during their leave instead of moonlighting, helping their peasant relatives in the countryside or wasting time drinking and playing cards. The white-collar workers had an entirely different pattern. They used to go for a few weeks to the resorts or other scenic places, staying in the pensions, manors (it became quite common among the landlords during 1930s to offer room and board), or at least peasant homes. The summer drive to the countryside became a mass white-collar movement even before World War I. In the middle 1920s the socialist leader Kazimir Kornilowicz started to develop on a small, experimental scale group holidays among the manual workers. This action was discontinued during the big crisis, but in the middle 1930s it was revived, extended, and generously supported by the government (it was thought that in that time the annual leave of the manual workers could be used to give them the paramilitary training).

Wages and salaries were kept low in the 1940s and 1950s to have more for investment. The communist government from the beginning decided to sponsor the yearly holidays for working people to offer them some relaxation as well as to take them out of the traditional family bonds to some extent. The privately owned pensions, inns and hotels were taken over by the central leisure fund (FWP) or by individual state enterprises to accommodate the new kind of guests. Food, accommodation, and services were generously subsidized by the state.

This arrangement became burdensome to the state and therefore gradually the fees workers had to pay grew. In the 1950s the workers' fee was about 33 percent of the total cost. That covered 80 percent of the food cost, but food constituted only a half of the total cost (Wzory 1971, 1: 163). Starting from the early 1960s the fees became dependent on the level of incomes earned by clients.

Simultaneously with changes in financing the holiday hostels, the relative number of wage and salary earners utilizing them started to diminish. During the 1950s use of the FWP during a given year declined from 10 percent to below 6 percent of all employees, and from 40 to about 10 percent of the blue collars. Restrictions were imposed to limit the number of people who utilized the government sponsored holidays. The priority was given, especially for family holidays, to highly productive and innovative manual workers. Special mother and child holidays were limited to highly productive female workers and to single mothers. The family members of the employees were able to take part in the holidays if they paid in full.

The demand of subsidized holidays among white-collar workers was very strong, and they managed to dominate the FWP facilities even if this was against the governmental policy. In the late 1950s they constituted 90 percent of all the guests. Although the much stricter policy of distribution of the holiday places led to the decline of this share in 1964 to 56 percent, white-collar workers still dominated in the best season and in the locations of high demand. The survey done in the late 1950s in two very attractive resorts showed that half of the inhabitants of the holiday hostels took three or more government sponsored holidays, and 16.5 percent of them even six or more subsidized holidays, when in general old employees took holidays two or three times in a lifetime, and younger employees got just one holiday (Wzory 1971, 1: 155). In 1958 every sixth white-collar worker utilized the FWP but only every 96th blue collar worker did so. In the first half of the 1960s the participation of lower income employees had even diminished (Wzory 1971, 1: 194, 196).

A survey done in the early 1960s in several attractive government sponsored holiday hostels located along the seashore and the lakes has shown that white-collar workers participated there three times more often than would be expected from their actual share in the urban population (Wzory 1971, 2: 20, 25, 36-39).

The much higher demand of government sponsored holidays among white-collar workers in comparison with the blue-collar workers may be explained by several factors. One of them is the difference in life-style. Manual workers are traditionally much less mobile, especially when the family is not able to join them on holidays. Personal cars are still relatively rare in Poland (73 cars per 1,000 population in 1981 compared to 168 in East Germany and 155 in Czechoslovakia), especially among the blue-collar workers. On the other hand, the equipment of the household is sufficient to feel comfortable at home, especially if the dwelling is not too congested.

The social gap between blue and white-collar workers played, until the late 1960s, a very important role in resistance of the former to utilize to the full extent the government sponsored holiday facilities. A few hundred interviews done by sociologists with the manual workers in the holiday hotels in 1949-50 showed that interviewees had difficulty enjoying holidays to the full extent because of the dominating white collar style and pattern of vacations. Manual workers were the worst dressed, found more difficulty to converse, had some inferior feelings that prevented them from having an equal footing with the white-collar workers that numerically dominate the holiday hostel (Dobrowolska 1963; Morawska-Pankiewicz 1961).

In the 1970s the situation changed thanks to the equalization of blue and white collar annual leave rights, incomes, and the growing opportunities for manual workers to have their holidays in Poland or even outside of the country. By the end of the 1960s the length of the annual leave began to depend on the length of employment, not the manual or mental nature of work: 14 days after one year of work, 17 days after three years of work, 20 days after six years of work, 26 days after ten years of work. All education above the elementary level was added to the length of work. Miners, fishermen, sailors, teachers, and academic workers have longer leaves than the above mentioned. Seasonal employees have on the other hand shorter leaves (Wzory 1971, 1: 42-57). This new arrangement means an improvement in the social status of the manual worker.

The growth of the government sponsored facilities has been just enough to increase opportunities not only for the white-collar workers but also to a growing extent for the blue-collar workers. By the early 1960s the holidays sponsored by the individual work places and trade unions outnumbered the FWP holidays. In the period 1958-64 use of the non-FWP facilities jumped from 1 to 7 percent of all employees while FWP facilities saw a constant 6 percent (Wzory 1971, 1: 199). The number of working people who stayed in hostels centrally administered and practically fully controled by the state has grown from 455,000 in 1955 to 545,000 in 1965 and 650,000 in 1975, but it declined to 365,000 in 1982.

Since the mid-1960s several forms of holidays have been introduced: skiing, bridge playing, foreign language education, sailing, tourism in the countryside or in the cities, health spas, foreign travel. In the period 1949-58, only 4 percent of all holidays were arranged for employees' families or single mothers with children, but now the new holiday hostels sponsored by the individual enterprises admit employees together with their families. In 1982 2.7 million people took advantage of the holiday hostels administered by individual enterprises.

The governmental facilities have been attractive mainly to people with little leisure experience (as the first step). Persons with a higher level of experience and aspirations look for something more private or at least different. By the early 1960s, only 33 percent of the Polish people spent their vacations in any organized form. Interesting are the survey data from the same period of time that deal with summer vacationers at the Baltic shore and the Mazury lakes. Almost a half of the people surveyed would like to spend their annual leave somewhere outside Poland, and only 6 percent had managed to fulfill this dream before. The number of those who spent their last vacations in the government sponsored holiday hostels (52 percent) was greater than the number of those who would like to continue it in the future (44 percent). There was a very clear relationship between the level of holiday aspirations and the educational level. With the progress of the educational level, the desire to arrange holidays in a private way as well as to go abroad grew (Wzory 1971, 1).

Some interesting insight is also available from the 1960 survey of the urban population regarding holiday preferences. Vacations privately arranged in the rented rooms were fairly popular among the professionals (16 percent), but much less among the lower rank of white-collar workers (9 percent). Also there was a clear gradation of the opportunity to take advantage of the government sponsored holidays: among the college educated white-collar workers, 33 percent took holidays; among the remaining white-collar workers, 20 percent took holidays; among skilled blue-collar workers, 14 percent; and among unskilled blue-collar workers, 8 percent.

Significantly, the hierarchy of aspirations was opposite to the actual fulfillment of them. Among the college educated white-collar workers who desired to spend their annual leave in the government sponsored holiday hostel only 6 percent took those holidays; among the remaining white-collar workers, 14 percent; but among the unskilled blue-collar workers, 25 percent to 33 percent. Tourism was popular among 33 percent of the students (20 percent of them actually traveled); 20 percent of the white-collar workers (10 percent actually traveled); 16 percent of the skilled workers; and 10 percent of the unskilled workers (Wzory 1971, 1: 213-15).

In the period 1960-75, tourism in Poland grew six times, particularly excursions rather than stays based more or less permanently in one place. Full-scale tourism grew in that period five times, as did the annual number of various tourist awards. The number of people who annually left Poland for holiday grew from 216,000 to 8,151,000 (of this number, 5,657,000 went to East Germany). In the same period 1960-75 the population of Poland grew only 15 percent. From 1960 until 1978 the number of people per 1,000 population taking advantage of the holiday hostels and other leisure facilities has grown from 24 to 128, but it has declined to 102 in 1983 (Maly 1984, XLVII). In the period 1975-82 the tourist traffic outside Poland declined very considerably from 8.2 million to 1.0 million (in 1983, 1.75 million), due to currency restraints and the hesitancy of East Germany, Czechoslovakia, and the USSR to welcome Polish tourists.

Poles currently look more and more for privacy. In the period 1975-82 organized tourism declined by a half (Rocznik 1983, 460). Blue-collar workers prefer over the FWP facilities that allow them to spend holidays together with their own families. White-collar workers have become bored and tired with the FWP holiday hostels that have been used by them for many years. The dream of owning a private car

is very common in all strata of the Polish society, especially among
the young. The fulfillment of this dream is much beyond the financial
capacity of most Poles, but the demand is there. According to 1975
data, the average Polish industrial blue-collar worker had to work
almost 8,000 hours to earn enough to buy a subcompact car with 45-
50 hp, compared to 5,000 hours in the case of an East German worker
and 1,200 hours in the case of a West German worker (Matejko 1977).
More realistic is the purchase of a motorcycle and this is very popular
in some eastern European countries including Poland (in 1983 there
were 2,813,000 private cars and 1,616,000 motorcycles in Poland).
Travels to foreign countries by car, mostly to other east European
countries, are very popular especially among the owners of private
cars, but a considerable number of people take part in the group excursions to foreign countries arranged by the state travel agency Orbis.
Rationing of gas has much limited the leisure application of private
cars.

The dominant leisure patterns of vacations are further and further from the doctrinaire state socialism based on equality, collectiv-
ity, and social utility. By enjoying themselves in a similar manner to
the western countries, or at least by trying to do it with the available
financial and other facilities, the Polish people clearly show their
present day preferences, and these are very far from what would be
expected from more than 30 years of Soviet-style communism. Take
the case of the movie-going public. In 1982 only 9 percent of the regular
films shown in the Polish movie houses were from the U.S., Great
Britain, France, and Italy, but they were seen by 45 percent of the
public, while the Soviet films were seen only by 7 percent of the public, although they constituted 31 percent of all films shown (Rocznik
1984, 443).

This is not just a problem of a prowestern traditional orientation
of Poles, which is more clearly seen in the young, but it is also the
issue of the great attractiveness of consumer-oriented societies over
the production-oriented state socialist systems of eastern Europe. [27]

The consumer appetites of Poles have grown even under conditions of a highly inadequate market supply, the necessity of spending
much more on food than in the west, and the low quality of products.
According to 1982 data, food constitutes 49 percent of expenditures in
the budgets of blue-collar worker households, the same in the farm
households, 58 percent in the pensioner households, and 44 percent
in the white-collar worker households (Maly, 1984, 111). The total
consumption of food has grown in the period 1980-82 from 31 percent
to 38 percent, and alcohol has remained at the level of 12 percent.

Annual holidays during the summertime in Poland are the major
leisure, as in many other European countries. People save money for
these holidays and make plans well in advance. The difficulties which

they meet in this respect are a considerable nuisance. Overcrowding
of the public transportation during the summer time, difficulty with
the tourist facilities the capacity of which is highly inadequate, and
seasonal shortages of food and other goods in several tourist centers,
all sources of constant irritation for many Poles. Especially during
the summertime in recent years people commonly spend whole nights
waiting in line to make a train reservation for ordinary seats or for
the sleeping car when they want to secure a comfortable travel for
their families. In the mountains ski lifts are constantly heavily overcrowded and skiers have a very hard time getting up the mountain.
During the summertime all around the country it is difficult to find
overnight facilities. In the restaurants and cafeterias the service is
quite often highly inadequate, and guests waste their time waiting for
service. These inadequacies are blamed on the rigid state socialist
system that does not allow private and cooperative initiative to take
over from the state tasks that the latter is not willing or able to fulfill.
Frustrations experienced by vacationing Poles undermine their trust
in the system and in the long run contribute to the gap between the
masses and the ruling elite.

Not all Poles experience these frustrations to the same degree.
There is a whole gradation of privileges and informal dealings that
provide several people with some cushions on their annual leave. The
most influential occupational groups and institutions have their own
exclusive recreational facilities that are generously subsidized from
the recreation funds under their disposal. These people and institutions
sometimes have also their own channels to the travel agencies, which
saves them from having to wait in line like everybody else. Scientists,
writers, party bureaucrats, military, police, state functionaries,
movie stars, stage theater actors etc., have their own elitist holiday
facilities (hostels, sport clubs, social clubs, restaurants, libraries),
in which they can enjoy themselves in isolation from the hardships
experienced by the average worker. Rich enterprises are able to provide for their employees much better vacations in their recreational
facilities than the poorer enterprises. The distribution of all attractive
recreational facilities is under the constant pressure of people who
compete with one another for them. The informal grapevine plays a
very important role in this distribution, and some people obtain year
after year attractive holidays when others do not obtain them at all or
have to accept much less desirable options.

The social stratification based only partially on wealth but mainly
on power and privilege is particularly evident in the availability of the
recreational facilities compared to the annual leave among various
categories of the population. It is enough to compare the guests of the
most attractive resorts with the guests of the least attractive tourist
places. I have here in mind mostly the middle-age and older portions

of the population because the young, as in the west, to a large extent prefer to spend annual holidays their own way.

CONCLUSIONS

The promotion of economic and social modernization in Poland has led to the growing mass articulation of complaints and reformistic demands in various fields, primarily in the labor relations field. The rapidly growing number of industrial personnel has been frustrated by the limits imposed by a rigid system unable to establish its own feedback mechanism. Even the lower party ranks have had more and more reason to express their discontentment with the status quo. The developmental discrepancies of Poland and the pressure of growing consumer demands have substantially undermined the power exercised by the political establishment.

Since the fall of 1980 blue-collar workers and farmers have become a major factor in Poland, and PUWP has practically lost the possibility of formally representing them without asking for their consent. Both of these classes, by organizing themselves, have also become independent partners of the intelligentsia, which traditionally has dominated them, especially in the sphere of educational opportunities.

Poles now less than ever before have reasons to be proud of the system in which they live. The traditional animosity to Russians and Germans justified by atrocities committed especially during World War II (Zawodny 1980; Kulski 1979) contributes to the unpopularity of the Soviet system imposed upon Poles and ensured by the military power of the neighbors, particularly of the USSR, East Germany, and Czechoslovakia.

The future events in Poland will probably be dominated by the unavoidable struggle between authoritarianism and liberalism, elitism and egalitarianism, command economy and market economy, central ism and decentralization, political dogmatism and enlightenment. This struggle is long overdue in the Soviet bloc, and the ruling establishment only with great hesitancy is willing to admit the appearance of injustice, inequality, corruption, and exploitation. On the other hand, even in the USSR "the increasing accessibility and variety of consumer goods, housing facilities, and 'cultural' goods have created new opportunities for social differentiation, opportunities for translating even reduced inequalities in monetary rewards and substantial differences in educational levels and 'value orientations' (to use a favorite Soviet term) into distinct modes of life" (Yanowitch 1978, 47).

The social liberation of the Polish blue-collar workers did not last very long, but it was strong enough to mobilize the world attention.

It seems improbable that the current communist establishment will be successful in its attempts to suppress this new historical trend. In the case of the government being pushed by circumstances to accept a real marketization of the economy, there will be much more room in Poland for cultural and political pluralism. The ruling communists would like to have a better economy, but they do not want to limit their own power and control. Without relaxation of this control the spirit of entrepreneurship will not grow and the situation will not change.

The lack of actual economic improvement is there. People have more money due to the improvement of incomes, but the production of consumer goods remains much behind, leading to an unavoidable inflation. Only a genuine reform could improve things. However, such reform is impossible without democratization, and this is what the authorities are most afraid of. I agree with Timothy G. Ash (1984) that from the beginning there was no goodwill on the side of the authorities concerning the democratization started by Solidarity. However, it is in the common interest of all Poles, those who rule and those who are ruled, to reconstruct the economy of the country. The Hungarian positive experience is encouraging in this respect. Yet, the Romanian economic failure shows that even under considerable freedom from the direct Soviet interference, the society can suffer greatly under communism.

Are there any real chances for a climate of cooperation between main rivals in Poland at least in the program of economic recovery? A much higher stake is involved in this respect than just the matter of free or regulated prices, more or less freedom of decision taken by managers, or even the union-management relationships. The communists have to learn how to tolerate free people; the opposition must learn the political art of achieving under given circumstances what is realistically possible. Sometimes it is better not to act than to inspire false expectations among people who afterwards become disillusioned when the action fails.

In the terms of sociocultural consciousness, Poland is probably much more western now than before the communist seizure of power. The educational and cultural progress has been a substantial factor in this respect. The Soviet version of Marxism has not established itself in Poland due to the religiosity of the population, traditional animosity between Poles and Russians, major cultural differences, the feeling of superiority among Poles, enforced propagation of the unpopular doctrine, and the corrupt nature of communist promoters. Identification of Marxism with careerism and subservience to Soviet interests has made it difficult, especially for the young generation, to take this doctrine seriously enough. In addition, Marxism has become an obligatory part of the school curriculum, and this has worked against it.

The social organization of Poles emphasizes family and friendships much more than in the developed societies where the secondary ties of a formalized nature predominate. The basic asset of the anti-governmental forces in Poland is the informal network of relationships based on mutual trust and help. The friendship ties are difficult to penetrate by the state security forces. This network may be much activated under any future suitable circumstances to revive the Solidarity action.

NOTES

1. There is an underground action to discourage people from taking part in the official elections for the following reasons: the parliament remains a body totally subservient to the ruling authorities, the municipal authorities depend fully on the higher administration, the nomination of the candidate is decided by the ruling Communist Party, and secrecy of voting is not safeguarded. "A repressive legislation is in force, paralysing social life. It is impossible to establish organizations and to conduct an electoral campaign independent of state control. The legislative competence of the People's Councils does not enable these bodies to function as genuine self-governing territories. Electoral regulations are unquestionably undemocratic. Society's answer to such elections can only be a complete boycott." "Why We Should Boycott the Elections," News Solidarnosc (Brussels) 1984, 22, 2.

2. In the period 1980-83 the Polish export beyond the Soviet bloc diminished by 13 percent, and the import diminished by 45 percent (in stable prices). Stanislaw Gruzewski, "Liczyc, liczyc, i jeszcze raz liczyc," Polityka-Eksport-Import 1984, 4: 17.

3. Only because of governmental ineffectiveness in this field, Solidarity had shown during 1981 increased involvement in the fields of workers' self-government and in the economic reforms. This involvement led to more and more confrontation with the government and the ruling PUWP, and finally to the imposition of martial law in December 1981, which lasted until the end of 1982.

4. It is significant that even the new "trade unions" sponsored by the government to replace the banned Solidarity are against marketization. To appeal to the widespread feeling of insecurity, these "unions" exercise pressure to fix prices, suppress private business, and spend more public money on welfare. The defenders of reform claim that such pressures may lead to ossification of the economy and hand it over to conservative forces within the ruling establishment.

5. Thirty-two percent of Poles are 18 years old or younger, in comparison with 25 percent in West Germany and 26 percent in East Germany. Ten percent of Poles are 65 years old and over in compari-

son with 16 percent in West Germany and East Germany (Rocznik 1983, 495). Eighty-four percent of the labor power in Poland is involved in material production (30 percent in agriculture and forestry), in comparison with 80 percent in East Germany, 71 percent in West Germany, 56 percent in Canada (Rocznik, 1983, 497, 498). In the structure of the gainfully employed population, blue-collar workers constitute about 45 percent, the white-collar workers 23 percent, and private farmers 27 percent. Private business, mostly craftsmen, account for 4 percent of the working population (1982 data) (Rocznik 51). In 1982 only 10 percent of the Polish population earned more than 150 percent of average income (zl 11,575); 8 percent among white-collar workers (34 percent of all employed), and 11 percent among blue-collar workers (66 percent of all employed). In January 1983 among employees with postsecondary education, 11 percent earned more than 150 percent of average income (zl 10,784); 17 percent among engineers (but 61 percent among mining engineers), 14 percent among medical specialists, 13 percent among political scientists, lawyers, and economists, 4 percent among teachers, 7 percent among specialists in culture, 1 percent among librarians (Rocznik 1983, 147).

Incomes in the nationalized economy differ now even more than before depending on the branch. In 1982 the average industrial income directly from production was zl 12,400 per month for blue-collar workers, zl 14,600 for technical staff, and zl 10,600 for administrative staff. However, if compared to an average production income of 100, industrial income was: 204 in the coal industry, 179 in power industry, 78 in light industry (textile, clothing, leather), 90 in the food industry, 80 in science, 78 in trade, 73 in education, 76 in health care, etc. (Rocznik 1983, 205, 143). In 1983 the average monthly income in the nationalized economy was around zl 14,000; more than 150 percent of what was earned by only 10 percent of blue-collar workers and even fewer white-collar workers. Among the population 15 years old and up, the share of those with at least secondary education grew in the period 1970-82 from 16 percent to 27.5 percent (Rocznik 1983, 38).

6. In the late 1970s close to 8 million people went to other countries, mostly to East Germany and Czechoslovakia. In 1981 more than 1,300,000 Poles went outside the Soviet bloc. Later on, due to the external and internal restrictions, Poles' travels outside Poland considerably diminished.

7. Women are almost as active in the job market as men. In the nonagricultural activities in Poland, among employment-age people 86 percent of the male population (age 18-64) and 69 percent of the female population (age 18-59) work. The birth rate of urban women 15-49 has declined in the period 1950-1981 from 99 to 65 percent (in the rural areas only from 116 to 92) and this is probably mainly due to the high employment rate.

8. In 1981 among the working people 8 percent had higher education (up from 5 percent in 1970), 21 percent had secondary professional education (14 percent in 1970), 6 percent had secondary general education (also 6 percent in 1970), and 25 percent had basic vocational education (17 percent in 1970). This means a continuation of the trend to upgrade continuously the educational level of all employed people, including the blue-collar workers. In the total Polish population over 15 the percent of those with at least secondary education has grown in the period 1970-81 from 16 percent to 27 percent; from 16 percent to 23 percent among men and from 15 percent to 29 percent among women. All these more educated people push for a better living standard and more freedom under the system that shows a definitely conservative bias and does not want to change.

9. Within the labor force in the period 1960-72, blue-collar workers have increased from 34 percent (in 1931, 26 percent) to 42 percent, while the share of private farmers has diminished from 44 percent to 32 percent. At the same time the share of white-collar workers has grown from 18 percent to 23 percent (Zagorski 1976, 30). The growth of wage and salary workers was even more pronounced among close neighbors of Poland: Hungary, Czechoslovakia, and East Germany.

10. According to 1972 data, among the urban nonagricultural employees 33 percent were born in the rural areas (among the executives, 25 percent). Among the manual workers 25 percent had peasant fathers or mothers. On the other hand, among white-collar workers 40 percent had manual worker fathers and 27 percent had peasant fathers (Zagorski 1976, 189). In Hungary the level of social mobility appears to be even higher than in Poland (Andorka and Zagorski 1980, 61). Among Poles and Hungarians in the early 1970s in each case about 20 percent worked as white-collar workers but only 10 percent were of white collar origin (Andorka and Zagorski 1980, 24). In both cases about half of all nonagricultural workers and employees are from the peasantry.

11. About 60 percent of all private farms have less than five hectares and 40 percent of farmers' income comes from nonagricultural sources (20 percent among all farmers). According to the expert estimate, only farms with 12-13 hectares or more are able to be fully productive and offer an adequate living standard for their occupants, but in Poland only 15 percent of all farms are 10 hectares or more (they occupy 41 percent of the total agricultural area). Under such conditions the dependence of a considerable part of the rural population gainful employment outside their farms is a matter of necessity.

12. In Poland as in the other state socialist countries there is a tendency to supplement incomes by various social benefits. During the 1970s benefits have grown from 18 percent to 22 percent of total income.

However, the fact that these social benefits are under the disposal of state bureaucracy does not secure the state's effectiveness. With the general relaxation of political pressure in 1980, public criticism started to grow of the bureaucratic malfunctioning.

13. The employment of women is common in Poland: It has more than doubled in the period 1955-77 (among men it has grown by 45 percent), while the development of services was relatively slow. Women are concentrated in office work, retail trade, health, and education, as well as in agriculture; in all these branches women constitute more than half of the labor force. Still, women are greatly underrepresented among the executives (30 percent) and technical specialists (23 percent). The educational level of female population over 15 years of age is now equal to or even better than that of the male population; in the period 1960-76 the percentage of females with at least secondary education has grown from 11 percent to 23 percent (14 percent to 21 percent for males) (Krzeczkowska, 1979, 146). All these factors lead to rising expectations that do not correspond to the reality of a country in which the distribution of basic goods is clearly inadequate; part-time jobs are available only to a very limited extent, shopping is very time consuming and frustrating.

14. Thirty-four percent of all labor power is in food production, but for several structural and policy reasons this is not enough to feed the nation. The average age of the farmer is very high because young people prefer to move to gainful employment outside private agriculture. Farmers have great difficulties buying what they need to keep farms in good shape. Governmental services in agricultural areas are inefficient and corrupted. Poland has to import food (17 percent of the total import in 1982), while the export of food items remains relatively insignificant (7 percent in 1982) (Rocznik 1983, 330-34).

15. During the 1970s the number of scientific workers grew from 40,000 to 70,000, but the effort put into research does not contribute enough to the actual well-being of the nation. According to Pawlowski, research has become in several instances mainly the art of making a career and earning money. Insignificant and noncumulative efforts done by individuals or teams waste the resources without improving the state of economy.

16. Particularly drastic is the housing shortage. So far the government seems to be helpless in dealing with this vital issue. In 1982 2 million people who had payed in advance for their apartments were on the waiting list, of those 400,000 had waited for seven years and more (Rocznik 1983, 400).

17. The neglect of consumer-oriented branches of industry (food, clothing, shoes, textile) for the sake of heavy industry is now one of the main reasons why Poland is in trouble. In the period 1960-81 the food industry has diminished from 30 percent to 18 percent of total

industrial production, while the share of the metallurgical and machine building industry has grown from 14 percent to 31 percent. The consumer-oriented industry in general has diminished from 42 percent to 36 percent of total industrial production. It would make sense in the case of heavy industry playing a constructive role in the long run. However, the building of industrial might at the expense of the national well-being sooner or later has to lead to the evident negative results.

18. Poland's gross national income declined in the period 1978-82 by 25 percent; the volume of production diminished in the period 1979-82 by 16 percent; in the same period the production per one employee diminished by 10 percent; investments diminished by 48 percent; in construction the production diminished by 34 percent (by 23 percent if taking the production per one employee); the export of coal diminished by 38 percent; employment declined by 9 percent (although the population has grown by 3 percent) mainly due to the 1982 transfer of almost 800,000 employees to an early retirement or pension.

19. The industrial potential puts Poland in the second place within the Soviet bloc after the USSR, but since 1977 Poland's share of the total production of the bloc has diminished from 10 percent to 8 percent. Comparing production per capita in 1980 within the bloc countries, Poland (100 percent) is below the average (115 percent), much lower than GDR (188 percent) and Czechoslovakia (161 percent), even lower the USSR (113 percent) (Paradysz 1983).

20. People have become accustomed to buying everything available and this has accelerated demand. The total personal expenditure of the population has grown in 1982 by 67 percent. But the supply of goods on the market has diminished by 10 percent, some merchandise much more.

Food sales have grown from 29 percent to 35 percent of total sales, and alcohol sales have grown from 12 percent to 15 percent of total sales. This shows the progressing impoverishment of the population and at the same time the lack of choice. People becoming poorer have to concentrate primarily on buying food. On the other hand, when there is not another choice people buy more alcohol because it is easily available.

21. Since the late 1970s the shortage of food has become the basic problem in Poland. Food remains a very important item in total expenditures (34 percent in 1981 and 45 percent in 1970), and this is related mainly to the low standard of living in Poland in comparison with Hungary (29 percent on food in 1979) or East Germany (26 percent on food in 1979). The neglect of local agriculture and the shortage of hard currency to import food have led to the critical situation—especially, when the yearly food consumption per capita has grown in the period 1960-79 quite considerably in several quality items: from 14 kilograms to 21 kilograms in fat, from 28 kilograms to 44 kilograms in sugar, from 0.1 kilograms to 0.6 kilograms in tea.

22. The short supply of food is particularly dramatic for the lower income people, who spend proportionally more on basic items. According to the 1974 data, among the households of peasants, worker-peasants, unskilled workers, and pensioners, who together constitute a very considerable part of the population, food expenditures were relatively much higher than among the well-paid engineers, administrators, even teachers (Kudrycka 1979, 262). The below-average income was shared by well over half of all employed people, and food constituted among them about half of all household expenditures, while only 25 percent to 33 percent of well-paid employees' incomes (graduate engineers, miners, managers). It is worth mentioning that the employment of both husbands and wives was more common among these better-off categories and contributed to their relative well-being. These people had also much better housing conditions; for example, 71 percent of engineers and 50 percent of administrators lived in the well-equipped dwellings, compared to only 26 percent of unskilled workers (Kudrycka 1979, 268). The manual workers at the low level of skill and education are particularly handicapped in their housing conditions. It is not uncommon for two or more of these workers households to share a dwelling (Zarski 1982).

23. In the period 1970-82 the membership of professional technical associations grew from 313,000 to 486,000. The Polish Association of Economists has about 60,000 members (Rocznik 1983, 408, 409).

24. In 1981 the use of electrical energy in industry and construction in Poland in thousand kilowatts was 12, in comparison with 17 in West Germany, 33 in Sweden, 49 in Canada, 31 in the U.S. (Rocznik 1983, 527).

25. This production needs much modernization also in the USSR.

26. In general, the technical education is the most numerous in the higher education. Among people finishing postsecondary studies in Poland, from one fifth to one fourth are in the technical field (agriculture not included). In the USSR, over 40 percent of the graduates are in the technical field.

27. Under the pressure of the growing consumer demands, the Polish government was forced to develop a new wage and salary policy in the first half of the 1970s that led to the current imbalance between the buying power of the population and the supply of several most attractive goods (meat, sugar, dwellings) and services (public transportation, recreational facilities).

REFERENCES

Adamski, W. and K. Zagorski. Szanse zdobywania wyksztalcenia w Polsce. Warsaw: The Polish Academy of Sciences. 1979.

Andorka, Rudolf and Krzysztof Zagorski. Socio-Occupational Mobility in Hungary and Poland. Comparative Analysis of Surveys 1972-1973. Budapest-Warsaw: Central Statistical Offices. 1980.

Ash, Timothy Gordon. "The Significance of Solidarity." Survey. 1982, 26, 1-2, 3-4.

_____. The Polish Revolution. New York: Charles Scribner's Sons. 1984.

Baka, Stanislaw. Interview Polityka. 1984, XXVIII, 16: 5.

Dobrowolska, Danuta, ed. Robotnicy na wczasach w pierwszych latach Polski Ludowej. Wroclaw: Ossolineum. 1963.

Dyonizia K. R. et al. Wspolczesne spoleczenstwo polskie. Warsaw: PWN. 1978.

Drygas, M. and P. Wiatrak. "Obszar gospodarstwa a dochody ludnosci chlopskiej." Wiadomosci Statystyczne. 1983. 3: 7-8.

Gella, Alexander. "The Life and Death of the Old Polish Intelligentsia." Slavic Review. 1971. 30: 1-27.

Hall, Alexander. "Nadszedl czas aby isc wlasna droga." Mysl Polska 1984, XLII: 5/6, 1.

Jain, A. ed. Solidarity. Baton Rouge: Oracle Press. 1983.

Kaminski, Antoni Z. "General Public Interest in the Non-Dialectic Theory of Planning, and Obstacles to Participation." The Polish Sociological Bulletin. 1979, 4: 5-20.

Kolarska, Lena. "Formalization, Standardization and Centralization. A Critical Analysis of Selected Research." The Polish Sociological Bulletin. 1977, 2: 63-74.

_____. "The Functioning of Voice in the Polish Economy." The Polish Sociological Bulletin. 1980, 1: 39-47.

Kolarska, Lena and Andrzej Rychard. "Wplyw organizacji przemyslowych na strukture spoleczenstwa socjalistycznego." ("Influence of Industrial Organizations on the Structure of a Socialist Society) Studia Socjologiczne. 1980, 2: 155-171.

Koralewicz-Zebik, J. "Niektore przemiany systemu wartosci, celow i orientacji zyciowych spoleczenstwa polskiego." (Some Transformations of the Value Systems, Goals and Life Orientation in the Polish Society) Studia Socjologiczne. 1979, 4: 175-190.

Kostecki, Marian J. "The Managerial Cadres of the Polish Industry: Research Report." The Polish Sociological Bulletin. 1977, 2: 85-96.

_____. "Managers of Business Organizations in a Socialist Society: Political Aspects of Their Functioning." The Polish Sociological Bulletin. 1979, 4: 21-28.

Krzeczkowska, E. et al., eds. Tendencje Rozwoju Spolecznego. Warsaw: Central Statistical Office. 1979.

Kuczynski, Pawel. "Spoleczne uwarunkowania wiedzy o organizacjach formalnych." ("Social Conditioning of the Knowledge of Formal Organizations"), Studia Socjologiczne. 1980, 1: 257-79.

Kudrycka, Izabella. "Zroznicowanie wydatkow konsumpcyjnych w grupach spolecznoekonomiczych i zawodowych" in Tendencje rozwoju spolecznego, E. Krzeczkowska et al. ed., Warsaw: Central Statistical Office. 1979.

Kulski, J. E. Dying, We Live. New York: Holt, Rinehart, Winston. 1979.

Lewarne, Stephen. "Sociotechnics and the Implementation of Martial Law in Poland: A Sociological Perspective of Political Realities." Newsletter of the Research Committee on Sociotechnics I.S.A. 1984, 6: 36-66.

Los, Maria. "Group Ethoses in the View of Polish Empirical Researchers." The Polish Sociological Bulletin. 1977, 3-4: 113-130.

_____. "Class Ethos" in Multi-Dimensional Sociology. A. Podgorecki and M. Los, eds. London: Routledge and Kegan Paul. 1979.

Maly, Rocznik Statystyczny, 1984, Warsaw: GUS, 1984.

Matejko, A. Social Change and Stratification in Eastern Europe. An Interpretive Analysis of Poland and Her Neighbors. New York: Praeger. 1974.

_____. "The Hard Working People: Manual Workers and Farmers" in: Solidarity. The Origins and Implications of Polish Trade Unions, A. Jain, ed. Baton Rouge: Oracle Press. 1983.

_____. Beyond Bureaucracy? Cologne: Verlag fur Gesellschaftsarchitektur. 1984.

Morawska-Pankiewicz, W. Zagadnienia dystansu spolecznego w swietle materialow dotyczacych wczasow. Warsaw: PWN. 1961.

Morawski, Witold, ed. Organizacja strucktur, procesow i rol (Organization of structures, processes and roles), Warsaw: PWN. 1976.

Mrela, Krzysztof and Jadwiga Staniszkis. "Degree of Coherence and Mechanisms of Transformation of Organizational Structures." The Polish Sociological Bulletin. 1977, 2: 49-62.

Narojek, Winicjusz, et al. "The Planned Society—Discussion." The Polish Sociological Bulletin. 1974, 2: 39-59.

_____. "Przeobrazenia spoleczne z perspektywy losu jednostki" (Social transformations from the perspective of individual life) Studia Socjologiczne. 1975, 3.

Nowak, Stefan. "Value Systems of the Polish Society." The Polish Sociological Bulletin. 1980, 2: 5-20.

_____. "Values and Attitudes of the Polish People." Scientific American. 1981, 245, 1: 45-53.

Nowakowski, Stefan. "Zaklad pracy a miasto w systemie socjalistycznym" (Workplace and town in the socialist system) Kultura i Spoleczenstwo. 1980, XXIV, 1-2: 77-87.

Ossowska, Maria. Ethos rycerski i jego odmiany. Warsaw: Panstwowe Wydawnictwo Naukowe. 1973.

Pawlowski, Lucjan. "Konta i tytuly." Polityka 1984, XXVIII, 19: 11.

Paradysz, S. "Rozwoj i przemiany strukturaine przemyslu europejskich krajow R.W.P.G." Wiadomosci Statystyczne. 1983, 2: 1-6.

Perski, Stan and Henry Flam, eds. The Solidarity Sourcebook. Vancouver: New Star Books. 1984.

Polonsky, Anthony and Boleslaw Drukier, eds. The Beginnings of Communist Rule in Poland (December 1943-June 1945). London: Routledge and Kegan Paul. 1980.

Rocznik Statystyczny. 1980, 1983. Warsaw: Central Statistical Office (published annually).

Rychard, Andrzej. "Interakcje polityki i gospodarki" (Interactions of politics and economy) Studia Socjologiczne. 1980, 1: 301-18.

Sandomierski, Tomasz. "Urodzaj w witrynie handlu" (A good crop in the shop window) Polityka. 1984, XXVIII, 47: 1.

Sennett, R. The Fall of Public Man. New York: Vintage Books. 1978.

Sicinski, Andrzej, ed. Styl zycia. Przemiany we wspolczesnej Polsce. Warsaw: PWN. 1978.

Skorzynski Z. and A. Ziemilski, eds. Wzory spoleczne wakacji na wsi. Warsaw: Scientific Institute of Physical Culture. 1971.

Slomczynski, K. and T. Krause, eds. Class Structure and Social Mobility in Poland. White Plains: M. E. Sharpe. 1978.

Smith, H. The Russians. New York: Ballantine Books. 1977.

Smola, Maria. "The Ethos of Young Poles." The Polish Sociological Bulletin. 1977, 3-4: 131-44.

Staniszkis, Jadwiga. Patologie struktur organizacyjnych. Proba podejscia systemowego. Wroclaw: Ossolineum. 1972.

_____. Pologne. La revolution autolimitee. Paris: Presses Universitaries de France. 1982.

Szalajda, Zbigniew. Polityka. 1984, XXVIII, 16: 5.

Wojciechowski, B. Interview. "Przeciw statystycznym mitom." Polityka. 1984, 8: 17-20.

Yanowitch, W. Social and Economic Inequality in the Soviet Union. New York: M. E. Sharpe. 1978.

Zacher, Lech. "Technika i spoleczenstwo jako przedmiot badan w Polsce" (Technology and society as research subjects in Poland). Studia Filozoficzne. 1981, 1: 137-47.

Zagorski, Krzysztof. "Changes of Social Structure and Social Mobility in Poland" in Transformations of Social Structure in the USSR and Poland, ed. M. N. Rutkevitch, et al., Moscow-Warsaw. PWN. 1974.

_____. "Changes of Socio-Occupational Mobility in Poland, The Polish Sociological Bulletin. 1976a, 2: 17-30.

_____. Zmiany struktury i ruchliwosc spoleczno-zawodowa w Polsce. Warsaw: GUS. 1976b.

Zarski, T. "Zmiany w zaludnieniu i wyposazeniu mieszkan w miastach, w podziale wedlug grup spolecznych" Praca i zabezpieczenie spoleczne. 1982, 8-9.

Zawodny, J. K. Death in the Forest. The Story of Katyn Forest Massacre. South Bend, Indiana: University of Notre Dame Press. 1980.

Zienkowski, Leszek. "Rownosc w biedzie" (Equality in poverty) Polityka. 1984, 47: 1, 4.

4 THE WORKING PEOPLE AND THE MYTH OF A KNIGHT

The Communist-sponsored industrial revolution in eastern Europe created a large nonagricultural labor force in some countries and substantially transformed this labor force in others. Workers in industry constituted, in 1982, 29 percent in the USSR, 30 percent in cent in East Germany, 36 percent in Romania, and 36 percent in Bulgaria of the working force (Maly 1984, 327). By claiming the dictatorship of the proletariat as justification of their rule, the east European communists have become victims of their own myth as it may be seen in any serious clash between the workers and the omnipotent state employer. The events in Poland in 1980-81 were very significant in this respect and signaled much more trouble for the east European governments in the future.

The growth of the wage and salary earners in eastern Europe and the inability of Soviet-style state socialism to satisfy the rising material and social aspirations of those workers will probably lead in the long run to gradually aggravating tension between various working strata and the ruling class. This tension, contrary to expectations of the east European rulers, as well as even some western experts of east European affairs, becomes more acute with the economic progress. The reason of it is clear when recognizing that the traditional Soviet model is not sensitive enough to the exigencies of a sophisticated developed society, particularly in mass consumption (Matejko 1974, 1979).

THE BLUE-COLLAR WORKER'S CAUSE

To understand the situation of blue-collar workers in the Soviet bloc, one must look into the Soviet planning system that allows and encourages the predominance of the command principle, an unplanned labor supply, a ubiquitous system of targets, unequal priority to certain sectors of the economy at the expense of others, lack of elasticity in planning, lack of any meaningful economic pluralization, great losses in labor productivity due to mismanagement and bureaucratization, an "underground" economy, and political pressure and organized rate-busting as traditional measures of labor policy. According to D. A. Dyker, "The kind of political stability produced by accommodation of apparatchik vested interest and shop-floor complacency must continue to have strong attraction for the regime and society that has good enough reason to fear instability. On the other hand, extrapolation of existing trend can only mean a continued downward trend in growth rates, an ever tighter macro-economic balance and continued failure to 'intensify' the economy, except in patches" (Schapiro and Godson, eds. 1982, 71).

The role of the official trade unions is to keep workers under state control. According to Godson, "Any hope of establishing an association of workers for the free collective action that goes against the principle of having a prior party acceptance is, for the immediate future at least, totally unrealistic" (Schapiro and Godson, eds. 1982, 128). The existing unions remain totally subordinated to the state and party authorities and function mainly to encourage workers to remain loyal and work hard. Loyal service in the trade union administration is seen as a qualification for trade union leadership. Every trade union body is infiltrated by the party in an organized way. Strikes are practically excluded.

The fact that trade unions administer several public funds and facilities does not provide union leadership with influence and independence. On the contrary, the administrative duties exercised by unions on behalf of the state make them even more dependent on the ruling party.

It is necessary to remember that public welfare available to workers is a substitution of low wages. According to the calculation of the buying power of Soviet incomes by K. Bush (Schapiro and Godson, eds. 1982), the same "shopping basket" that required a person to work 12 to 21 hours in the west, required over 42 hours of work time in Moscow in 1979. The average Russian spends eight times as many hours working to buy a color television set or a small car than a western counterpart. Rent is relatively lower, but the housing conditions in the USSR remain very bad.

The blue-collar worker stratum is deprived in eastern Europe of its own institutions and remains subdued by control from outside, which prevents the workers from defending their joint interests and developing a collective consciousness (Bahro 1978). The ruling communist parties have a monopoly on this consciousness and are the only representatives allowed into the field. As long as the blue-collar worker stratum consisted mainly of people who had moved recently from the farm to nonagricultural occupations, the dominance of the party over blue-collar workers was relatively safe and unshaken. However, the progressing adaptation of newcomers to the industrial-urban setting, the growing level of education and sophistication, and especially the arrival of a new generation has led to the transformation of the blue-collar workers' consciousness. These workers have become—particularly in Poland—much more aware of their collective power and available opportunities to use it to defend their claims. In contrast to the white-collar workers, they can move with relative ease from one employer to another without too much fear of negative consequences for themselves. They have less to lose, and within a full employment economy there is always a need for their work. For example, in Poland, around one-fifth of wage and salary workers per year change their employer. In Polish industry, stoppages among production workers have declined in 1983 to one third of the 1981 level[1] (Maly 1984, 50, 51).

The communist one-party systems probably will face more and more often the demands to bargain with blue-collar workers who act in a collective manner: formulate their joint demands, reject their traditional docility, bargain through their own elected bodies, utilize experts as their professional consultants, sign the labor-management contracts, and enforce the contract through their own stewards and other trade union officials. It is not easy for the communist authorities to prevent workers from exerting pressure for their demands because there are many informal ways of undermining the work discipline: absenteeism, labor turnover, slowdown of production, some local, spontaneous small-scale work stoppages, etc. Any major difficulty in the labor field may have serious consequences for the planned central economy, and, so far, the communist systems have been unable to establish peaceful ways of problem solving in this sensitive field. The brutal actions by police when dealing with Russian, Romanian, German, and Polish workers in the past may be explained to some extent by the rigidity of systems that claim to offer a "workers' paradise" but in reality remain insensitive to the basic needs of workers. State and party authorities see the use of brutal force looks as the only answer. On the other hand the brutality of the authorities unifies blue-collar workers against the political system that provides only token freedom and well-being. The moderate response to striking workers in Poland in 1980 was met with disbelief or even scorn by other communist parties in eastern Europe, and their growing pressure on Polish authorities was mainly responsible for the brutal repression practiced under martial law in December 1981.

Blue-collar workers in eastern Europe are in a great need of an economically viable system with an adequate ideological and administrative superstructure. From this perspective, the issue of civil rights is of importance to them as long as it is related to the improvements of the total socioeconomic system. On the other hand the tiny groups of intellectuals who constitute the backbone of political opposition in eastern Europe commit themselves primarily to freedoms of a more general and abstract character. The Polish case of strikes for free trade unions in 1980 was particularly interesting and important because of its potential for gaining significance all across eastern Europe.

There is an obvious status incongruence among Polish blue-collar workers, especially among the younger generation. By pushing forward with industrialization and egalitarianism in at least some areas and by generating great expectations regarding the general improvement of working-class conditions, the communist establishment paved the way for dissatisfaction. There was a too great discrepancy between the growing aspirations of blue-collar workers and the reality of low wages, limited opportunities for promotion, poor working conditions, and ineffective management. The mass demonstrations, strikes, and struggles of 1980-81 in Poland were the outcome of these growing contradictions.

The growth of social aspirations may lead either to social conflicts or to constructive reforms. The new technocratically oriented Polish elite had the opportunity to institute real reforms. It seemed necessary not only to considerably improve the ossified and inefficient managerial system but also to give workers more of a chance to practice real, not merely token, industrial democracy. However, is such industrial democracy imaginable without allowing basic political freedoms? The blue-collar workers who demonstrated in 1956, 1970, 1976, and 1980-81 talked not only about prices and wages but also about freedom of speech. It seems quite improbable that it would be possible to substantially improve the economy of Poland without instituting basic political reforms. However, such reforms depend not only on what happens in Poland but also upon the internal policy of the Soviet bloc.

Common sense tells the blue-collar workers that the highly bureaucratized economic system of Soviet-type communism does not function effectively enough. Blue-collar workers blame the current organizational and managerial setup for the existing low efficiency and inadequate wages. The fact that an average industrial blue-collar worker wastes 25 percent of his working time is not due to his laziness but to the paradoxically chaotic state of a "planned" and centrally steered communist economy. Alongside the rising expectations of blue-collar masses, the conservative stabilization of the existing system becomes unacceptable. The young generation of blue-collar workers is aware that without basic reforms, further modernization is impossible. The questions are which regime, how, and when will have the courage and power to introduce any far-reaching reforms.

Egalitarian feelings are widespread in Poland, particularly among blue-collar workers. Many have achieved social and educational upgrading under the communist system. They have moved from poor villages to towns, industrial establishments, and even leading positions. The urban areas have already had since the 1950s a considerable migration surplus at the expense of rural areas (plus only two million migrants during the 1970s). Many of the party and state officials, executives, and a large proportion of the intelligentsia are of a blue-collar background. The appearance of egalitarian aspirations within this group does not mean, of course, that people are satisfied with the status quo. Egalitarian aspirations are even stronger in the traditionally lower strata than among the intelligentsia. Unskilled workers and people with less education often feel they are deprived of status. However, during the period 1980-83 the percentage of blue-collar workers earning below the average income for the whole nationalized economy has declined from 58 percent to 42 percent, and the percentage of white-collar workers earning above average has remained at the level below 40 percent (Maly 1984, 101).

A high percentage of wage-earning workers covered by the quota sample of the total male urban population studied by Stefan Nowak (1964) defined their social status as lower than average: 66 percent among unskilled workers and 45 percent among skilled workers. The lower the educational level and the income of a blue-collar respondent, the more unfavorable his/her evaluation of his/her social status. Wage-earning workers, especially unskilled ones, were less optimistic than members of higher social strata regarding the decrease of distinctions between members of different social groups in Poland. Income, education, and managerial or nonmanagerial positions were perceived by blue-collar workers as primary sources of division in society.

Egalitarian postulates among blue-collar workers are related, among other things, to their great dependence on decisions of somebody at the top who is out of touch with reality. People at the bottom take full responsibility for the final outcome of their work, but the "cream and sugar" will be consumed at higher levels of authority. According to the above-mentioned research by Stefan Nowak, even in 1961, 53 percent of skilled wage-earning workers and 44 percent of unskilled wage-earning workers wanted to see the social differences disappear entirely in the future, compared to 38 percent of the creative intelligentsia (Nowak 1964). It does not mean, however, that the blue-collar workers were in favor of the full equalization of incomes. Research done in Poland in 1959 by Adam Sarapata showed that the Polish people universally regarded the differentiation of earnings as normal and that different occupational groups formed different wage hierarchies. The steelworkers, miners' wives, and various manual workers surveyed by Sarapata ranked university professor, cabinet minister, mechanical engineer, and physician among the top four occupations (there was relatively little difference in that respect in the opinions of wage-earning workers and representatives of other occupational groups). Such professions as actor, priest, construction laborer, nurse, spinner, and recreationist (a community social worker in the field of recreation) did not receive a consistent ranking (Sarapata 1963).

The same research showed that the level of earnings claimed by blue-collar workers as desirable for their own groups did not greatly exceed the level of actual earnings. Respondents were realistic enough to demand no more than 20-25 percent increases over their actual incomes. At the same time they were interested in limiting the highest possible incomes to the wage typical for the highest paid wage-earning workers. Quite different were the opinions of highly qualified professionals. Their level of a reasonable income was much higher. There were several reasons: the incomes of these professionals often were higher before the war, there was a tendency (much stronger than among the blue-collar workers) to compare one's own income with salaries paid in other countries, and there was a conviction that one's real contribution was much greater than real income (Sarapata 1963).

Relatively light work, good working conditions, opportunity for advancement, permissive discipline, and a standard of living much higher than that of one's parents are the values for which the young generation of workers strive. For the past generations of blue-collar workers, particularly those who had experienced the unemployment of the interwar period, the war, and the German occupation, it was satisfactory just to get steady work in state-sponsored industry and a place to live in the town. During 1950-60, the number of people employed in industry and construction per 1,000 population had grown in Poland from 105 to 134 and afterwards 190 in 1978 (169 in 1983) (Maly 1984, XLI). The social aspirations of people looking for job advancement were gratified to a large extent, and their hopes were more easily transferred to their children. The old generation's hope was that the young generation would advance further up the social ladder and would obtain better conditions of work, finally ceasing hard physical labor.

Already by the late 1950s several values very attractive to the old generation were no longer exciting their offspring. What had been considered a real achievement by people deprived of social facilities in the past was taken for granted. For example, the son of a blue-collar worker was not satisfied just to find a job. If he was still willing to become an industrial wage-earning worker, he wanted to work in relative comfort and to take full advantage of all opportunities for promotion.

The younger generation of blue-collar workers take for granted improvements in economic and health conditions achieved by the older generation. Their sociocultural aspirations have been stimulated by the rapid development of the mass media, which are sponsored by the state and, therefore, are relatively inexpensive. Fewer and fewer young people are inclined to follow their parents' way of life: to accept heavy physical work, poor living conditions, restrictions on where to spend their leisure time, and to exhibit passive attitudes toward short-comings at the workplace. The expectations of younger blue-collar workers are growing even faster than the effective progress in technology, the improved organization of work, knowledge, the social culture of people occupying supervisory positions, the average income level, the supply of material goods, and the real decrease of differences between blue-collar workers and the intelligentsia (Jarosz 1984).

In principle the full-employment policy of the government guarantees younger people a place to work and live; however, this place is quite often not up to their aspirations and expectations. The transition from a permissive school environment to the average work environment is not easy. The young people have to overcome the negativism and defensiveness of the older generation, which feels endangered by their less-experienced but better-educated younger colleagues.

With their improved educational and cultural level, new generations of blue-collar workers expect not only a higher degree of social egalitarianism but also a considerable reduction of physical effort and better operation of the enterprises. There is a growing recognition of shortcomings in the organization of work, in the interdepartmental and extradepartmental economic cooperation, and in the management. For example, the absence of wage and salary earners due to sickness and accidents has grown from 1300 days to 1950 days during the period between 1970 and 1983 per 100 people employed per year (Maly 1984, 301). The question is how much room there will be in the political arena to accept the blue-collar workers' criticism as a constructive social force that will help to improve the total economic system. This is the problem of the autonomy of an enterprise as an economic and social subject able to engage the forces that originate in the growing social consciousness of the blue-collar and white-collar workers. It is also a problem of internal democracy at the workplace (Matejko 1981).

The wage-earning workers expect better treatment, higher wages, and better opportunities for their children. The prospect of social advancement opened within the communist system was at first very attractive for the lower class people; but with the passing of time blue-collar workers have come to view the new rights less as privileges and more as self-evident facts of their daily life.

The political and social advancement of the blue-collar workers is another factor that stimulated their aspirations. Many industrial executives are of worker or peasant origin. The promotion to executive positions is tightly related to party membership as a necessary first step to any administrative career. It is worth mentioning here that the administration in the ruling party differs in various categories of workers. Party membership is relatively much more common among male blue-collar workers than female blue-collar workers, among skilled workers than among unskilled workers, and among people with seniority than among people without seniority (Bauman 1962).

The participation of workers in party organizations increases with occupational status, and in this respect the unskilled workers are handicapped in comparison with their more skilled colleagues. Political activity is seen in 30 percent of the technical staff; 20 percent of the foremen; 14 percent of the clerical staff; 9 percent of the skilled blue-collar workers; and 4 percent of the unskilled blue-collar workers (Krall 1970).

OFFICE WORKERS

Communism is primarily in need of personnel for the bureaucracy, the military, and the police force. All the other strata of white-collar workers are of secondary importance. The state machine tends to give a bureaucratic content to every kind of job. Also, the party shows deep appreciation for technology, not so much because of its crucial importance for party ideology as because of its contribution to the fulfillment of party goals. For example, the utilization of electric power in industry (an indicator of technical modernization) has grown 3.6 times between 1960 and 1983, but there was very little progress in the housing space per capita (15.5 m^2 in 1983 in comparison with 12.6 m^2 in 1970) (Maly 1984, XXIII, XLVII).

Immediately after World War II in Poland white-collar workers were in such demand (22 percent of the total population was killed by the Nazis, and the victims were mostly Jews and intelligentsia) that all sorts of candidates were admitted to salaried posts. The party felt it was in its interest to have loyal and reliable people socially advanced from lower ranks in industry.

The social position of the office worker is relatively low because of the traditional red tape associated with the job, the low educational level, the emphasis placed on production, and a general underestimation of the social and economic importance of administrative work. According to a public opinion survey conducted in Warsaw in 1958, the office clerk was placed in one of the lowest positions, based on social prestige, job security, and material rewards—much lower than the average skilled blue-collar worker (Sarapata and Wesolowski 1961).

Office workers are quite aware of the relatively low level of their profession. "A view particularly common among office workers is that their work, that is, office work, is not a skilled job, and that they are not skilled workers. For many of them this is the cause of much disappointment and dislike for their work. Many of them feel underprivileged and wronged, and have an inferiority complex with regard to other comparable occupations" (Lutynska 1964, 81).

In Polish society there is a common distaste for clerks as the bulwark of the highly bureaucratized state machine. "Lower-echelon employees become the scapegoats of any and all shortcomings and deficiencies in the present order. They are blamed for 'bureaucratic' distortions, and the populace very often holds them responsible for any inconveniences, shortages of goods, and so forth" (Szczepanski 1970, 123). Therefore, movement into the clerical ranks is no longer attractive for the young generation of blue-collar descent. Clerical occupations have become more distasteful to blue-collar workers than to the intelligentsia. This fact contributes substantially to the general dissatisfaction of clerks with their professional image.

The clerical staff is to a large extent made responsible for the inefficiency and inhumanity of bureaucracy. However, most clerical workers do not really have anything to say. Low-paid women occupy 70 percent of lower and middle clerical positions, even in industry. A considerable percentage of clerks have relatively low education levels and are of manual-worker descent. Their incomes are much lower than those of technicians and quite often below the wages of workers. In 1982 the administrative and clerical staff working for nationalized industry, including managers, averaged 10,600 zloty per month, less than blue-collar workers (12,100 zlotys), and much less than the 14,600 zlotys of the technical personnel.

The clerical staff in industry and in other branches feel that their position is inferior, that they are grossly underpaid, and that it is not worthwhile to be a clerk. For example, of the trade employees (sale clerks as well as store managers) surveyed by Jerzy Altkorn, about 70 percent did not want their children to enter the same profession; this was true in almost the same degree for their sons as for their daughters. Only 24 percent of sale clerks and 33 percent of store managers said that they would choose the same profession if they had another chance (Altkorn 1963, 29, 37).

For clerks and even more so for their supervisors the practical solution is to strengthen their position by joining the party. Therefore, people from the clerical and administrative ranks are eager to be accepted into the party. However, the Polish United Workers' Party is endangered by this inflow from the bureaucracy, which is widely disliked or even hated by the masses. Thus, from time to time there is a purge of party ranks in which mostly clerks suffer by being fired and losing their privileges.

TEACHERS

Status incongruity appears in several other white-collar professions, especially in those whose occupants only recently entered the ranks of the intelligentsia. The profession of primary school teacher is a case in point because it has changed considerably since the end of World War II. The rapid development of a free education system has created a great demand for teaching personnel. The number of teachers in primary schools increased from 66,600 in 1946-47 to 270,000 in 1983-84. But the increased opportunities to enter other occupations have considerably diminished the attractiveness of the teaching profession; in addition, salaries are relatively low and the responsibilities disproportionately large.

During the interwar period the majority of teachers were recruited from the urban population, but now many of them are of peasant background. There is also an increasing number of women among teachers. Both these facts mean that currently the primary school teacher occupation is attractive primarily to those social groups with limited opportunities to obtain better-paying jobs. "New opportunities whereby people can gain an education and fulfill their ambitions and the relatively easy entrance into other more attractive occupations have led to a situation where relatively few pupils attending the primary and secondary schools at present choose teaching as a profession" (Woskowski 1964).

Programs of additional education and involvement in political activity give primary school teachers an opportunity to improve their status, which is declining relative to professions that are growing in importance as industrialization continues. Many teachers try to supplement their education by taking training courses.

The political participation of primary school teachers is relatively higher than in many other professions. Many teachers take active part in local government and in various social, cultural, and athletic associations. The percentage of religious believers seems to be lower than in other professions. The primary school teacher is expected to represent the official doctrine, especially in the countryside where there are relatively few government officials and where the teacher is predisposed to be a member of the local elite. However, teachers are simultaneously in a relatively worse social and material position than many professions that are growing very rapidly both in the towns and in the countryside. There are also controversial issues on which the primary school teacher has to take a stand, risking the goodwill of either a considerable part of the population or the authorities.

Given the framework of official goals and principles sponsored by the party, Polish teachers, as agents of socialization, represent a particularly interesting and illuminating case of status incongruence, as well as cognitive dissonance. Because religion in Poland is at odds with the official ideology, and yet most of the Polish population believes in God, teachers are pressured from both sides. They are expected by their employer to conform to official policy, but at the same time they do not want to alienate the parents of their pupils.

While the general public in Poland still holds teachers in high esteem, their position in the local community is at least ambiguous, if not unfavorable. Even within the larger professional-educational establishment the teacher is in a much more inferior position than before World War II. Secondary school teachers in interwar Poland were relatively well paid. Some of them were very active in the intellectual and political life of the country. There was some advancement from their ranks into the ranks of the academic staff. Some university teachers originally used to work as secondary school instructors and gained an academic chance due to talent and hard work. Today the differences in credentials, institutional affiliation, geographical locations, income, and degree of freedom from external pressures are greater than before. Concentrated in large cities, the academic staff in general enjoys more freedom from local interferences of a political nature than do the elementary and secondary school teachers, who are widely dispersed in rural and urban communities. Between 1970 and 1983 the number of secondary general school teachers has grown from 19,000 to 23,000 and has grown from 29,000 to 49,000 in the vocational secondary schools (Maly 1984, 280-81).

The recruitment process for the teaching profession is far from being satisfactory. A substantial portion of the candidates for the teaching profession are young people who failed to achieve something more socially attractive, such as a professional career based on academic credentials. The prestige of teachers in the local community is not sufficiently high to impress pupils or their parents. The majority of teachers in Poland feel inferior. Many among them think of themselves as "professional failures, since they do not possess the credentials which lead to greater professional recognition" (Fiszman 1972, 318).

TECHNICAL CADRES

In the period 1958-82 the number of people with higher education employed in the Polish nationalized economy grew from 240,000 to 973,000 (women from 67,000 to 450,000), and the number of people with a secondary professional education doubled in the period 1970-82. Many are engineers and technicians. From a small privileged group during the interwar period (5,000 in 1921 and less than 15,000 in 1939), engineers have become very numerous. Employment of engineering and technical personnel in the nationalized industry doubled in the period 1960-71, and the membership of technical professional associations more than doubled. In 1982 there were in Poland 356,000 employed engineers with a postsecondary diploma, among them 80,000 women.

Engineers prefer design bureaus of research and development institutes over employment in industry. In the case of a sample studied by Anna Grzelak (1965), 66 percent of the surveyed engineers mentioned poor human relations and 50 percent mentioned poor work organization as serious shortcomings of their work places. This was so characteristic of the political and managerial system that engineers felt helpless in dealing with such problems. In Zdzislaw Kowalewski's study (1962) of chemical engineers, 50 percent did not believe that they could improve the situation by their own actions or did not want to act, and only 10 percent felt personally responsible for what happened in their work place. A survey of engineers employed in heavy industry in Warsaw showed a very high level of dissatisfaction with the organization of work (81 percent), with salaries (77 percent), with the employer's attention to the interests of his subordinates (72 percent), with prospects for promotion (60 percent), and with the atmosphere (51 percent). Among engineers, those wanting to change their jobs numbered 70 percent in enterprises, 62 percent in design bureaus, and 58 percent in research institutes. A negative evaluation of work organization was given by 81 percent of engineers in industrial enterprises and 68.5 percent of engineers in design offices and institutes. A very positive opinion about organization was expressed only by 3 percent of the engineers in enterprises and 4 percent of the engineers in bureaus and institutes. By comparison, the climate of human relations was evaluated more favorably. The formal organization imposed by the higher authorities was the primary cause of dissatisfaction (Hozer 1970, 156).

In the circumstances of constantly being pressured by an ossified and dehumanized formal organization imposed arbitrarily from outside of one's own work place, the only rescue may be provided by friends. Engineers surveyed by Jan Hozer were asked who would defend their interests if necessary. Twelve percent said the management of their factories, 10 percent said the party (or other political institutions managed by it), 16 percent said professional associations, 18 percent said that nobody would help them, and 41 percent, the largest portion, said their friends. This means that informal ties play a much more important role than any formalized safeguards (Hozer 1969, 119).

It is significant that dissatisfaction with the formal organization existed even among engineers in managerial positions. Dissatisfaction was reduced somewhat higher up the hierarchy, but the drop did not seem large enough to change the picture greatly. Under the highly centralized system of management, all engineers in work places, whether occupying managerial positions or not, felt dissatisfied.

A study of engineers in the electrotechnical industry done by L. Pasieczny led him to conclude that the currently applied "system of financial rewards in general does not stimulate a motivation which would favour technical progress" (Pasieczny 1968, 352).

The dissatisfaction among engineers does not mean, however, that they necessarily withdraw from commitment to the party. Many of them have advanced socially under the new regime, and they have to pay in a political sense for their promotion. People educated under the rule of the present regime are less reluctant than their forefathers to join the party and to gain concrete advantages from it. As recently as the late 1970s the percentage of young people ideologically committed to religion was decreasing and the number of people not concerned about any ideology was growing. There was no reservation about becoming active in the party, especially if it seemed necessary to support one's professional career. This explains why already in the early 1960s the percentage of party militants "was highest among comparatively young engineers and technicians, who had been party members for 6 to 10 years and who had been working for 3 to 5 years in the same place of employment and who had a fairly high level of education (Bauman 1962, 64).

It seems possible to generalize that the evident growth of importance in Polish society of specialists such as graduate engineers has a very substantial impact on the changes in its ethos. People become more practical, less vulnerable to ideological manipulation, much more utilitarian and task-oriented. Joining the party ranks becomes a purely practical issue with no substantial ideological consequences. By entering the party ranks, engineers strengthen the party's economic and administrative power but also contribute to the progressive dilution of its doctrinal content.

ARCHITECTS

The principal outlet for architectural activity in Poland is within the framework of the 270 designing agencies, which employed a total of 72,000 people in 1983 (Maly 1984, 160). It is common knowledge that these agencies—to a great extent subordinated to the construction industry's rigorous demands—have brought a methodology to the field of architecture considerably different from the traditional one. An effective harmonizing of the construction bureaucracy's requirements with the creative demands of architectural designing has become particularly important. The construction sector, being significantly limited in its resources and rather conservative, forces the designing agencies "to treat designing as if it were production. From this arises the inappropriate application of the same yardsticks to the organization of designing as are applied to industrial production" (Buszko 1967, 21). As a result, designing agencies limit the creative aptitude of designers much more than they facilitate the development of such aptitude.

> The material stimuli applied in designing agencies do not
> encourage designers to seek innovative solutions. . . .
> The lack of suitably high rewards for innovative solutions,
> the tension of design deadlines, the endlessness of design
> outline approval, the difficulties of overcoming resistance
> to novelties, and the heavy work load, incommensurately
> rewarded, connected with the constant quest for remunera-
> ative, all discourage the designer from introducing tech-
> nological and economic advances (Pirog 1966, 64).

There is comparatively little room in the Polish economy for consciously undertaken, calculated risk; many errors result from the lack of opportunity to gain experience from small mistakes. Designing agencies have no resources, no suitable legal framework, nor even a sufficiently wide margin of freedom in self-initiative and so are neither capable of nor prone to experimentation.

Architectural design, as practiced by existing design agencies, is becoming more and more anonymous; the creator is losing control over the product. Architect's supervision is turning into more or less of an illusion. The most important reason is the decline of construction investments for the period between 1978 to 1983 from 10 times the 1960 level to 2.5 times the 1968 level (Maly 1984, XXXIII). The situation is also partly connected with the change in the architect's role from a patron to a coordinator of the activities of various specialists in modern construction. There is a peculiar institutionalization of an architect's work, which makes it an impersonal product of agency X and not the product of a particular person or a particular group of people.

The engineering and technical personnel work in studios that usually have quite a bit of independence as far as taking on contracts and settling accounts are concerned. Employees' remuneration is tied to the type of contract that the studio obtains. Much depends on the astuteness of the studio's director and on the extent of his or her personal contacts. As a result, there are often considerable differences between particular studios in the average employee compensation.

Within particular studios there is a differentiation of social positions that is not necessarily linked to the differentiation of rank because in a creative milieu professional criteria are usually placed above administrative and institutional criteria. The director, especially in larger studios, does not occupy the highest position socially. In fact, because the director does not participate directly in the designing, subordinates often consider him or her to be less important than the senior designers. The director's domain is the drawing up of contracts, the evaluation of documentation costs, deadlines, and bargaining for the studio's design projects with the agency management.

Professional authority is always controlled by the senior designers—the team leaders. Teams that collaborate to produce a design are usually found in larger studios and consist of one or two designers, some assistants, and a draftsman in addition to the senior designer.

The team leaders or principal designers are the hub of the studio; they establish its work trends, inform the studio director about production quotas and how many contracts the group can take on (contracts that the studio director then must find), divide bonuses among the group members, and make recommendations for promotion.

The collaboration of designers and constructors demands a good employment atmosphere. That atmosphere greatly depends on the management, which can to a greater or lesser extent make allowances for the needs and ambitions of particular subordinates that are employed in creative work.

As is well known, the prevailing system of work and remuneration in a given organizational unit has an important effect on the formation of co-workers' friendships. Such bonds between colleagues are also undoubtedly strengthened by everyday contact when working together. The basis of such contact is either a common task so involving that it actually helps to bring people together, or a common hobby that gives the opportunity for finding a mutually agreeable level of personal communication.

Professional bonds among groups of designers or technical consultants are found not only within a given studio but also between studios because of the necessity for collaboration among experts representing complementary specializations. Both formal and informal bonds enhance the collaboration. For example, any fundamental changes in a design, which are very troublesome to effect through formal channels, can be made with comparative ease and rapidity in an informal way if the professionals involved are good friends.

In studios substantial antagonism is connected with differences of privilege and, thus, the possibility of raising one's income. Distances between particular ranks and conflicts arising from them seem to manifest themselves in studios with greater distinction than, for example, in scientific research groups. The amount of actual remuneration is known and is an important criterion of prestige—much more so than in academic circles. Ill feelings between group members are fed not only by differences of privilege but also by the restricted office space and tense work situations. In both these respects, the average engineer and technician are worse than scientists.

The prevailing concept of designing agencies shows a clear preference of productive qualifications over creative qualifications. Agencies are not interested in the creative stimulation of designers, and this is manifested by the dearth of organized exchanges of experiences (in Poland and abroad), by the lack of education for the novice and re-education of older personnel, and by the lack of stimuli for creative pursuits.

The internal organization of designing agencies is based on administrative and bureaucratic criteria and necessarily bypasses professional criteria. Creative needs by no means influence the structure and personnel of the studios, for the sole considerations are the needs of the current administration. This gives rise to organizational rigidity, overgrowth of personnel beyond reasonable bounds, poor morale of the administrative support personnel, and the impossibility for designers to answer the dynamics of changing creative tasks. As a result, the organization instead of serving the creative needs of architecture suppresses them by isolating itself from them and by coming to be an end in itself.

In the concept of designing agencies, institutional loyalty is far more important than professional loyalty. However, in their aspirations and values architects and designers always remain professionals and do not become members of institutions. Preservation of this attitude is in the interest of designing agencies because an ambitious architect-creator will always design better than an architect-bureaucrat, even if the former is not sufficiently subordinated.

The role of architectural coordinator and director requires a suitable level of autonomy and necessitates protecting him or her from pressure and giving the director enough leeway to take responsibility for the work. In the final analysis, the designing agency as an institution is not capable of completely meeting the architect's professional needs. The responsibility for architectural bungling is diluted in impersonal institutional responsibility. Whenever no one takes responsibility for a given piece of work from beginning to end, and exerts proper influence on the work, undesirable results are inevitable.

There is considerable truth in the universal grumbling of architect-designers that designing agencies are too conservative. This conservatism results from these agencies being adjuncts to the construction industry. Instead of a creative interchange between architectural concepts, investment needs, and construction requirements, the latter has all the say. And in the designing agencies there are insufficient resources for propagating novelties and putting them into practice. Efforts aimed at preserving the status quo reign supreme.

JOURNALISTS

Polish journalists consider themselves to be members of the intelligentsia (Kupis 1966; Dziecielska 1967). They are connected by social and cultural ties with other members of this social stratum, and they are extremely interested in showing that they share the traditional social values held by the intelligentsia. The freedom of self-expression, the opportunity to achieve something socially valuable, professional autonomy, and the opportunity to travel abroad and learn something about the world are much valued by journalists.

Journalists are encouraged by their environment to accept the values mentioned above. A journalist does not want to be ashamed when comparing his or her own professional conduct with the conduct of the sociocultural reference group (spouse, friends, and acquaintances). A journalist's professional activity is under constant scrutiny by these people who read his or her articles, are critical of them, and expect the journalist not to be opportunistic, narrow-minded, or too materialistic. The fear of not being sufficiently appreciated by members of one's own social circle plays an important role in a Polish journalist's motivation.

The reporter is continually under stress. Sometimes the journalist needs the opinion of a reliable professional colleague. Other people's opinions of the journalist's work are only relative and are not always convincing. The effects a journalist achieves are ephemeral. It is not surprising, therefore, that the reporter's moods sometimes change from one extreme to another: from an irritating nonchalance to complete discouragement. This fluctuation of mood is very characteristic of newspaper staffs; periods of great enthusiasm alternate with periods of apathy.

A pleasant atmosphere among the staff, inspired by the behavior of the editors, is therefore of particular importance. A friendly atmosphere in the office is an effective antidote to depression. The understanding and help of other people on the staff neutralize the stresses caused by the very character of the job and may help restore emotional balance.

The confidence felt by the staff in the assessment of their work by superiors who enjoy all-round authority (professional, administrative, and personal) facilitates self-analysis and helps people take a balanced view of their work. When a person knows that his or her actions and words affect the situation in the office, it is easier to find a firm foothold both on the paper and in this occupation as a whole. Freedom in the office encourages people to take a positive attitude toward their work and attach appropriate weight to its ethical aspect.

A study of the staffs of two prominent Polish journals and two well-known newspapers, made in 1963 (Matejko 1970), showed that the attractiveness of a particular working environment is evaluated by journalists and reporters not only on the basis of material reward but also according to the possibility of maintaining the intellectual, moral, and social standards held by the intelligentsia. The management of a newspaper, magazine, or journal has to take this into consideration if it wants to keep its employees and promote a climate favorable to creativity. The employees expect their supervisors to protect the freedom of the editorial staff from external pressures, to maintain high professional standards, and to take care of the basic material needs of the personnel. They also expect to have an opportunity to participate in important decisions.

Effective management of a magazine, journal, or newspaper in Poland consists, according to the survey mentioned above, of effectively counterbalancing the external pressures with the professional and social aspirations of the personnel. In this respect the most effective managers are those with strong political positions who spend most of their time and effort making the external authorities as predisposed as possible toward the publication. However, they have to simultaneously recognize the professional aspirations of their subordinates' to allow room for expression, not take their own power too seriously, and be friendly with publicists who enjoy high professional prestige.

The publicists form the professional elite in the best Polish newspapers and journals. They feel responsible for the good name of the journal or newspaper; they have a decisive voice in many internal and external affairs; they are the intermediaries between journalists and other professions; they also have many connections with important political pressure groups. A good management is eager to cooperate with publicists, thus establishing its own power and avoiding unnecessary tensions. The alliance of management and the publicists was typical for the journalistic teams studied, which showed very high indexes of work satisfaction and professional creativity (Matejko 1970).

The journalistic team has been mentioned to emphasize two characteristics of Polish professionals. One of them is shared with professionals everywhere, and especially in the west: a strong predilection for professional autonomy. The other is much more unusual, although not unique to Poland. It deals with the specific social role of the profession as a link between the individual and the intelligentsia, which has a specific tradition and myth of being the moral leader of the nation. In this last respect Polish journalists differ greatly from, for example, American journalists, whose frame of reference is in general much narrower, limited to their own profession or even to their own newsroom (Breed 1955).

On the four Polish papers studied, the staff members had very strong social and professional ambitions. They tended to look on journalism as a job calling for boldness, a job in which they should put forward and submit for public discussion such issues that lead to wide controversy and would inspire and compel others to revise their stereotyped ways of thinking and acting. It is not surprising that several journalists abandoned their profession after the introduction of martial law at the end of 1981.

On the papers in our study the journalist occupied the dominant role on the staff. On both dailies journalists constituted a majority of the editorial staff, and on both weeklies they formed a very pronounced majority. Journalists set the tone of the paper, it is their opinions that count, and their values and aspirations as professionals count the most. As a result, all four papers are quality publications.

It often happens that reporters' ambitions extend beyond journalism to the creative, literary sphere as well. There is a fairly sharp difference here between the reporters studied by us and the American reporters studied by W. Breed. The Americans live in a homogeneous circle that restricts their ambitions. The Poles live in a professionally mixed environment of intelligentsia and are under the pressure of its traditional values, norms, and patterns. Polish journalists want to raise their prestige to the level of the intelligentsia, and, therefore, try to make their work as creative as possible. They specialize and try to secure a stable position not only in their own world of the press but also in the particular environment—artistic, legal, political—in which they are professionally interested. Contacts with these other professions enable journalists to keep introducing new subjects that will be of interest to the public and that will bring public approval not only to the paper but also to themselves.

Many factors—the authorities' approval or disapproval of the ideas put forward by the paper, limitations of space, the editor's encouraging or discouraging attitude toward the ideas submitted, commendation or lack of commendation by colleagues, the habits of readers—all affect the creative atmosphere in the newspaper office and determine which new topics will be given space. In the case of the two weeklies in the survey, these factors had an inspiring effect; and the same was true of the two daily papers to a lesser extent.

In all four cases, however, the staffs' considerations did not influence editorial decisions. Finding space for articles, being able to execute bold new plans, finding access to material (for example, through foreign travel), or reporting an interesting subject were restricted, mostly by external considerations independent of the paper. Both the editors in charge and the journalists were well aware of the necessity of accepting restrictions from outside, and this awareness formed one of the strong bonds between them.

THE DILEMMAS OF SCIENTISTS

In a society that becomes more and more sophisticated, as is happening in Polish society, there is a growing demand for research and development. The relativistic and skeptical orientation among scientific workers reflects the dominant tendencies among the youth. Among adults this orientation also is becoming dominant as the number of skilled specialists increases, scientific reading increases, political cynicism progresses, disillusionment with Marxism and other current ideologies grows, utilitarian orientation spreads and mass involvement of a technocratic nature grows. It is significant that in the period 1970-82 the total membership in the techno-scientific professional associations grew by 55 percent (almost three times in the period 1960-76), while, the government-sponsored Association for the Promotion of Atheistic Culture declined in its membership by 24 percent.

Scientific workers are beneficiaries of the rapid industrial growth promoted within the Polish state socialism by the ruling party, but at the same time they are also particularly vulnerable to the inefficiencies of the socioeconomic system based on primacy of politics, monopoly of power by one party, and the following of a specific ideology imposed on the population without asking for its consent. The Polish scientists have a long tradition of contacts with the western world, and their commitment to the cosmopolitan culture is in general higher than in the USSR. The party has tried hard to put scientists under control. The bureaucratization of all research, technical development, and the higher education teaching for the young generation have achieved this control.

It is obvious to many Polish scientists that the rule of bureaucrats in the institutions of the research, development, and specialized training is to a large extent harmful, leading to waste, protectionism, and low motivation. Membership in the party is much more common among the current generation of Polish scientists than in the 1960s, but it is commonly treated as a utilitarian safeguard and not an ideological matter. The trend toward political opportunism is very common, but at the same time a growing number of individuals are ready to manifest their rejection of official slogans and myths or even openly oppose Marxism-Leninism, party rule, and subservience to the Soviet Union.

The main weakness of applied research in Poland is directly related to the nature of a highly centralized economy. All enterprises are just units of a bureaucratic hierarchy that are busy overfulfilling their quotas to gain bonuses (Brus 1975). The risk-taking related to any innovations, particularly to those based on applied research, is against the long-range interests of the enterprise and its crew. By hiding resources and bargaining with the higher authorities for the relaxed production quotas, the enterprises are able to secure for themselves some attractive bonuses (Richman 1965).

Although the whole system of higher education is centralized, the members of the teaching staff enjoy relative freedom in planning and performing their work. Course curricula have to be approved by the educational authorities, but it is up to the individual teachers to prepare and eventually change the detailed syllabuses. The contents of lectures, seminars, and tutorial classes are left almost entirely to the initiative of heads of institutes who differ in the degree to which they are personally inclined to control their subordinates within the institute. Being busy with their own research work or writing, in most cases the heads leave much freedom to the staff. For the most part, teachers in Polish universities are content with such a situation because it permits them to concentrate their time and energy and get on with their "own work," by which they mean research. By and large, the Polish academic system, despite the centralized control and the alertness of the ruling party to deviant opinions, does allow the university teacher to get on with "his or her work."

Traditionalism and modern red tape (Matejko 1969) taken together make the organization of research too rigid and hamper the development of new initiatives, especially those related to the interdisciplinary approach. Research institutions have their own vested interests, which are not necessarily the same as interests and aspirations of researchers (Matejko 1976).

Two fundamental trends collide with each other. The first finds its expression in the progressing institutionalization of scientific activity, which implies the subordination to requirements of a bureaucratic nature and thus enhances the danger of ossification. The second trend represents professionalization, meaning that scientific workers are deeply concerned with the values, patterns, and standards of their professional setting. This trend, in turn, threatens to alienate the sciences from the essential social needs and to limit the sciences to particularistic values. Domination by either trend leads to the degeneration of science (Matejko 1969).

Both trends are seen in Poland, although not equally. The administration striving to subordinate the scientists to bureaucratic order, does not have enough foresight, does not provide enough real help, and sometimes even stands in the way of research. There are many bureau-

cratic obstacles that appear almost every time when people who belong
to various organizational units try to do something together or even
only to communicate with one another (Matejko 1973). Any such unit
has its own range of decisions and its own interests. The academic
staff members are cut off from one another by the bureaucratic boundaries between various institutions.

It is one of the paradoxes of centralized planning in Poland that
to fulfill the ambitious official tasks it is necessary for the researcher
to be an informal entrepreneur, knowing how to exploit the network of
human relations, various loopholes of the bureaucratic structure, and
even some antagonisms and rivalries among various institutions. For
example, it is the rivalry among the state-owned publishing houses
that allows the scientists to publish, at least from time to time, some
nonconformist writings in social sciences.

Informal pressures and counter-pressures have greatly influenced the development of Polish science and scholarship in the last
few decades. Centralization versus autonomy, elitist ambitions of the
senior staff versus the official egalitarian ethos of a socialist society,
fragmentation of organizational units versus the integration of interdisciplinary research, political conformity versus the traditional individualism of the intelligentsia—all such contradictions are evident
in the growth of higher education and academic research in Poland
(Matejko 1969). The considerable progress that has been achieved is
because, to a great extent, of the fierce and unyielding attachment of
many Polish academics to the universal tradition of learning and to
the international academic community that affirms those traditions.
It is the quality of the people and of their academic ethos that has been
the decisive factor.

THE CULTURAL ELITE

When considering the intelligentsia in eastern Europe, and particularly in Poland, one should remember the relative value of such
terms as "intelligentsia" and its traditional elitist social position. As
members of the educated stratum of society "who have an interest in
ideas and a certain degree of consciousness of themselves as a social
stratum" (Theodorson and Theodorson 1969, 210), the intelligentsia
shares with the ruling establishment a concern for major problems
of society. It is especially valid for the intellectuals who are or who
pretend to be creative, and for the leaders of the class as a whole.

One has to agree with Alexander Hertz (1951) when he says that
the term intelligentsia, and by the same token the subject it describes,
fits better in Slavic civilizations than Anglo-Saxon civilizations. The
traditional, relatively high social status of people accepted as mem-

bers of the intelligentsia has its source in European societies with their strong feudal background, their economic backwardness that lasted until the recent period of Communist industrialization, and the privileges derived from possessing any education beyond the elementary level (Hertz 1942). The gradual disappearance of some of those factors tends to make some Marxist-oriented sociologists conclude that the intelligentsia as a distinct social stratum is gradually declining. J. J. Waitr says, "The very notion of 'intelligentsia,' currently in the under-developed countries but somewhat alien to the speech habits of the western nations, becomes increasingly nebulous in Poland of the second half of the 20th century; and it is more than probable that the type of stratification in which the 'intelligentsia' has occupied a specified position will slowly disappear" (Wiatr 1962, 14).

When considering the future of the intelligentsia as a separate social stratum, its traditional functions and social position must be considered. In both those respects the Polish intelligentsia has some unique features that justify its relatively high social esteem, an active or even leading role in the nation, and a special sociopolitical respon-sibility. Szczepanski points out that by

> remaining closely linked with the nobility and the upper classes, who comprised the repository of the traditional values, the Polish intelligentsia was not alienated cultur-ally from the nation, as was the Russian, since it culti-vated values accepted by the whole nation. . . . It fulfilled an important social role which it regarded as a national duty, viz., to keep alive the national traditions, to develop the values of the national culture, to educate the new gen-erations, for the struggle for national goals. It maintained and developed the language, literature, arts and science, it created social and political ideas, it searched for pos-sibilities and analyzed social forces within the nation which would be decisive for regaining political indepen-dence (Szczepanski 1969, 34-35; see also Szczepanski 1962; Pipes 1961).

All these circumstances are crucially important for understanding the social situation of the intelligentsia in contemporary Polish society; thus, it seems premature to assume that the intelligentsia as a social stratum is close to social decline.

The fact that so many members of the intelligentsia originally came from the gentry has far-reaching implications. Of professionals who were born in the period 1760-1880 and who are mentioned in bio-graphical dictionaries, 60 percent were from the gentry and only 10 percent from the bourgeoisie, the remaining were from the lower classes. Most were intellectual professionals—scientists (21 percent), writers and journalists (18 percent), or artists (14 percent)—and only a few were practical professionals—physicians (10 percent), engineers (3 percent), or lawyers (3 percent). The remaining were in other professions. About 90 percent were Catholic; conservatives and democratic liberals were equally represented. Half took active part in national insurrections and conspiracies that resulted in repression. A great majority traveled to other countries, many were forced to leave the country, and 20 percent died outside of Polish territory (Szczepanski 1960, 133-39). [2]

Poland's oppression at the hands of Russian and Prussian expansion since the 18th century to a large extent shaped the mentality of the Polish intelligentsia. As Adam Bromke sees it:

> The discrepancy between Poland's potential and actual
> position in the international sphere has generated a ten-
> sion between the political order as people think it ought
> to be and as it is. In short, Poles have been divided into
> political idealists and political realists. . . . Romanti-
> cism and positivism are both self-defeating if pushed to
> their extremes. The end of the moderate versions of both
> programs is essentially the same: to cope with the secur-
> ity dilemma by advancing Poland's interests vis-a-vis
> its more powerful neighbors. . . . Each of them repre-
> sents values which in the long run are indispensable for
> the survival of a nation—particularly a nation placed in
> as difficult a position as Poland. Political idealism em-
> phasizes the need for cultivating the high morale of the
> people, while political realism stresses the necessity of
> developing the human and material resources of the coun-
> try. As such, in the long run, romanticism and positivism
> are not only compatible but actually largely complementary
> (Bromke 1967, 2, 253).

However, it seems that the tradition of the Polish intelligentsia was not oriented toward a skillful oscillation between moderate versions of political idealism and political realism but, rather, to romanticism. The idea of shaking off the yoke of the east or of the west, regardless of human costs, was always very tempting for the young generation of the gentry or intelligentsia, especially if a feeling of strength predominated. Alexander Gella points out that "The championing of social freedom and national independence became not only a basic characteristic of the Polish intelligentsia but also helped to determine its character and destiny. In a nation without institutions of formal political leadership, the intelligentsia acquired an actual, though informal, position of national leadership and strong charismatic feelings" (Gella 1971, 13).

The idea of honor, inherited from the gentry (Keen 1984), stimulated personal and social aspirations among the intelligentsia that were very difficult, if not impossible, to fulfill under foreign rule and the change from feudalism to capitalism. Furthermore, as Andrzej Zajaczkowski says, "The member of the intelligentsia defends himself against the inferiority complex, and the concomitant passivity, by trying to assure himself how good he is, by promoting the affectionate style of life, showing broad socio-political and cultural interests, by suggesting that exactly he only is really well-mannered, cultured and patriotic" (Zajaczkowski 1962, 26; see also Zajaczkowski 1961). Such pretensions saved the intelligentsia from social, economic, and moral hardships. On the other hand, they led to snobbishness. In Poland the cultural elite has traditionally enjoyed a social esteem often greater than the real social contribution of its individual members (Rawin 1968, 362). However, elegance, refinement, and good manners were not enough to bring success in the new capitalist world. People who possessed entirely new qualifications, and in addition often did not have much in common with the Polish noble heritage, managed to gain power.

Social revolution, independence, or preferably both became the common dream of the intelligentsia. World War I provided the opportunity to pursue these dreams to an unexpected extent. As Solomon Rawin explains, "It was only in independent Poland that conditions arose for crystallization of the intelligentsia identity as the nation's new elite. . . . Throughout the interwar period, the special right of the intelligentsia to shape the new nationhood was hardly challenged. . . . Poland became 'an intelligentsia-dominated society' and there was hardly an area of public endeavor which did not bear the imprint of the intelligentsia's presence" (Rawin 1968, 362).

Many new employment opportunities that had previously been limited to foreigners (mostly Russians and Germans) became available to members of the intelligentsia, who had aspirations and pretensions inherited from the gentry. "The ideal of the intelligentsia was not a competent professional man, but a 'cultured man' participating widely in the nation's cultural heritage, a man with knowledge of history, literature, the arts, and good manners" (Szczepanski 1962, 408). This does not mean, however, that the general educational level of white-collar workers grew adequately during the interwar period. In 1931 (the second and last Polish interwar census) only 55 percent of non-manual workers had at least a high school diploma (Bartnicki and Czajkowski 1936). On the other hand, many graduates found it very difficult to obtain gainful employment. Therefore, the frustration of a considerable portion of the young intelligentsia led them either to servility toward the establishment or to radical orientations, both left and right (Blit 1965).

The "governance of souls" belonged in the period 1918-39 primarily to that part of the intelligentsia in public service, education, and culture. The nucleus of the intelligentsia, the professionals, constituted only 2 percent of the total population. Only 10 percent of white-collar workers had higher education, but in the institutions of higher education there were 7.5 times more students of white-collar descent than would be justified by their portion of the total population. Between 20 and 25 percent of white-collar workers came from lower classes; the rest either originated from the white-collar class or came from other privileged groups (Zarnowski 1973). The dependence of more than 50 percent of the intelligentsia on the state led to discrimination. Among the professionals, Jews represented over 50 percent, but among white-collar workers in general only 14 percent—little more than in the total population. There was a tendency to employ very few Jews in the civil service (Zarnowski 1973, 189-227).

The Polish intelligentsia maintained social aspirations relatively higher than the intelligentsia in several other Slavic countries—such as Bohemia, Slovakia, Bulgaria—where the intelligentsia came mostly from the countryside and claimed to be related predominantly to the peasantry and its folk culture. The Polish intelligentsia has played an exceptionally active role in social, cultural, and political fields. There were practically no Nazi supporters among the Polish intelligentsia; and the left-wing orientation of a considerable part of the intelligentsia was another reason the Nazis decided to adopt an extermination policy to prevent the intelligentsia from reviving and reassuming the leading position in Polish society.

The close traditional relationship of the Polish intelligentsia to the gentry and the attractiveness of the social pattern of the nobility transformed into intellectuals have been emphasized and vividly criticized by those intellectuals who have wanted to associate the intelligentsia with the lower strata. Jozef Chalasinski argued that the identification of the intelligentsia with the gentry has considerably weakened its interest in economic problems, and this has had unfortunate repercussions on the total life of the nation. The intelligentsia's admiration of the societal patterns created by the gentry and the simulation of its way of thinking have, as Chalasinski (1946) maintained, directed the attention of the intelligentsia more toward responsible social activity.

THE POLISH ETHOS

Many elements of the gentry ethos still exist in the Polish national character. "On the one hand, cautiousness; on the other hand, risk and gesture, well known from the Polish saying 'zastaw sie, a postaw sie' which, translated, means something like this: 'pawn yourself, but keep your status.' On the one hand, industriousness, on the other, contempt for work for profit, especially physical work; on the one hand desire for fame, on the other, desire for security" (Ossowska 1973, 216). The politics of the Polish emigres, cultivated mostly in the Polish ethnic community in Great Britain and to some extent also in Canada, seems to be closely related to the gentry ethos.

The above-mentioned ethos, historically speaking, takes its roots in the social role of a knight (Keen 1984). We can find the first elements of the prototype of a knight in old Greece. This legendary figure reached its peak importance in the Middle Ages in Europe. The heroic type can, however, also be found in Japan (Samurai), India, and even in the years much closer to our times, in the prototype of an English gentleman. In Poland heroism has become the matter of historical necessity dictated by the history of partitions, struggle for independence without much chance to achieve a victory, and adversary conditions inside the country (poor living conditions, a chronically bad economic situation, and even poor public health).[3] Poles individually and collectively have achieved much quite often against all odds, and therefore romanticism has a very strong public appeal (Lepkowski 1985, 2). Even leading Polish positivistic philosophers, basically dedicated to realism and cold calculation, have sometimes shown a definitely romantic orientation. For example, Tadeusz Kotarbinski (1965), a well known philosopher and the creator of the praxiologic school,[4] propagated a moral model of a reliable guardian, which is closely related to the prototype of a knight in the best sense of the word.

To understand the knight of the Middle Ages, we must realize what the life in the Middle Ages was like. It has been well described to us, especially by Marc Bloch (1961), a French historian who lost his life at the hands of the Nazis. People in the Middle Ages lived for only a short time, were faced with many dangers and deprivations; the poor were greatly dependent on the more powerful and rich. Common people had no significance whatsoever. The heroic ethos was, to a degree, a challenge directed at this harsh reality. It was something greater than life, where great achievements were attempted without much consideration of the realistic possibilities. Without this model, it would have been easy to become unmotivated and despondent; it would have been easy to let fear dominate.

Exaggerated care for one's honor and fear of ridicule was a cover-up for the constant feeling of insecurity. Hospitality and generosity assured reciprocity, or at least the right to it, in case of need. Courtesy between adversaries curbed, at least to a degree, the generally practiced cruelty. Considering oneself worthy of great deeds and having the moral right to perform them gave courage to act. A knight was to be "rightly proud," finding in his way a happy medium between modesty and conceit. "The most important possession of a 'rightly proud' man is his honour. But he is content in a moderate manner—only when his honour is recognized by honourable people. . . . 'Rightly proud' is generous, he is ashamed if he experiences generosity from others. He always tries to repay more than he had received, because he desires to be always superior" (Ossowska 1973, 49-50).

It should be mentioned that working for a living was below the knight's dignity because he was destined for higher deeds. Besides, every act of a knight was considered from the point of view of personal honor, and reaching one's material goal was not all that important. "It was expected that a knight be constantly preoccupied with his own fame" (Ossowska 1973, 94). Of course, whatever was undertaken had to be fulfilled, but only in relation to one's equals. Every insult had to be avenged, so as not to leave the slightest blemish on the knight's honor. Death was not feared, but it had to come under praiseworthy circumstances. The spirit of Christianity only superficially touched the knight. His characteristics were: "Pride instead of humility, vindictiveness instead of pardon, complete lack of respect for human life, the element of unreality clearly noticeable in the ease with which a travelling knight chopped off the heads of all encountered adversaries" (Ossowska 1973, 110).

The Polish nobility, which formed an exceptionally large percentage of the population (12 to 15 percent), was so influential that it can still be traced in the collective character of the Polish nation today. Although in communist Poland the Polish nobility finally ceased to exist, and therefore to influence the national character, Polish state socialism (as opposed to libertarian socialism) still tends toward mythological models in social and private life. Just as the existence of a knight depended on privileges and the ability to pass the yoke of work on to people deprived of these privileges, so it is in Soviet state socialism; privileges are the principle of life (Matejko 1974).

Poland really never had the extensive experience of its own capitalism, and therefore never had an occasion to consolidate the bourgeois morality in the society. Rather, Poland made a leap from a national character formed mainly by the feudal system to a mentality formed by the Soviet style state socialism. The systems of transformation are similar in several important aspects. In both most people have no rights of importance and the most they can ever hope to achieve is to get some privileges illegally. In both systems the value of an individual is measured mainly by his or her unlimited loyalty and availability to the actual ruling elite. Ordinary citizens, by virtue of their existence, are indebted to the establishment until death. The debt is continually being paid through personal sacrifice for the system's good. Whatever the universal obligatory doctrine, it is always interpreted to enhance the cult of power, curb individual thinking and creativity, and rely on ritual rather than intellectual and moral ferment.

The Protestant revolution hardly touched Poland, and, beginning with the eighteenth century, the issue of keeping alive the national identity eclipsed all other aspects of social awareness of the ruling classes. Soviet communism was forced on Poland already after it had become ideologically sterile. Thus, communism played the role of a cap covering bureaucracy with imperialistic tendencies of the Soviet state, and its chauvinistic attitude toward everything non-Soviet. In addition, the version of communism forced on Poland easily absorbed many elements of traditional Polish ethos that could be treated as harmless ornaments: emphasis on military rather than civilian glory, pretense, cult of ritual and all kinds of trinkets (medals, distinctions, etc.), an ostentatious pathos regarding "sacred things." It is not by chance that these and other similar elements are part of the traditional model of a knight or a courtier. Under state socialism in force in Poland, the modern work morality has had no chance to establish itself. This kind of socialism stresses the high tempo of social-industrial growth. How is it possible, though, to reach the higher stages of economic development without the support of honest working people rather than crooks, brawlers, and charmers?

Soviet-style bureaucracy in its very foundations requires blind obedience, even if only in appearance. Thus, bureaucracy restrains the appearance of all virtues but loyalty. The endless argument between the experts and the apparatchiks must finally be won by the latter if the model of state socialism and monopartyism is to remain in force.

The reconciliation of the individual good with the common welfare is an essential question in all social systems. Depending on the model adopted, one or the other is emphasized. There is no room in a state socialist system that considers individual good to be only a derivative of common welfare for a gentleman whose characteristics are "stateliness and security of an independent person" who is trustworthy and inspires trust (Ossowska 1973, 170).

In the meantime, however, the people in Poland are more and more charmed by the model of a perfect gentleman. This is not solely infatuation with all that comes from the west but probably a historical discouragement, firmly embedded in the Polish national character, over the uncompromising loyalty required by bureaucratic institutions, institutions that in present day Poland usually function poorly, disappoint the citizens, and have no consideration for public good. Bureaucratic Polish organizations are used by preying cliques for their own particular goals. And above all, bureaucratic institutions have proved to be historically unstable. Thus it is necessary to rely on oneself only and to try not to become too involved in something that might disappear from the scene tomorrow.

Out of different possible attitudes, the Polish young prefer the attitude of a gentleman who keeps distance from all that surrounds him rather than that of a party agitator or an ardent revolutionary.

The clumsiness and conservatism that characterize Soviet-style state socialism are the most important obstacles to the formation of a national ethos that would assist the ruling communist elite in Poland. Existing within the stiff framework of bureaucracy and facing the many inconsistencies in everyday life have led to a widespread criticism in Poland of the state socialist model. The rulers of the country accuse the population occasionally that it is succumbing to western influences and tastes. However, the real ethos of contemporary Poland results from the escape to slightly updated traditional models or to models that are quite foreign to Poles, like that of a gentleman. But at least for the time being, these models offer a psychological shelter—to wait it all out.

The heirs of yesterday's knights strive to get privileges under any pretext and try to find a good position for themselves at the cost of the rest of the population, pointing to their actual or feigned services rendered to the ruling system. Thus play is mandatory in all three directions: toward the elite, toward their own social group, and even toward themselves.

Every authoritative system with centralized power favors the "court" institution, which is explained by Ossowska as "a group of people dependent upon a given dispenser of power and money" (Ossowska 1973, 129). Charm and nonchalance secure success in the court. It is essential to know how to present oneself, to call the attention of influential people to oneself, to sell one's talents for the best price. People connected with courtlike institutions become servile and at the same time falsely proud; lazy and, at the same time, occupied with the time-consuming task of securing favors from the powerful. They flatter the people higher in hierarchy and are contemptuous toward those lower than they.

Bureaucracy, which in the state socialist system grows to a monstrous size, has many characteristics of the court tradition. The morality of the bourgeoisie, is undoubtedly based on a calculated personal effort impersonally oriented. This orientation toward a goal opposes the "heroic" orientation of a knight or courtier, which is first of all directed toward his social status.

NOTES

1. Calculated in hours per year per 100 production workers.
2. All these data were collected in the 1950s on the basis of historical research.

3. In the period 1970-1982 there was a considerable growth of sick and accident leaves among Polish working people. The governmental Report on the Demographic Situation of Poland in 1983 relates the deteriorating health conditions due to environmental pollution, inadequate working and living conditions, and other factors mostly rooted in the ailing economy and administrative negligence. In Poland in 1982 among 10,000 people there were 18 physicians and 70 hospital beds in comparison with 29 and 100 in Czechoslovakia and 21 and 103 in East Germany (Maly 1984, 377). In Poland in addition there is a great shortage of medical drugs and other facilities. For the above mentioned Report see Podwysocki (1985).

4. The books and lectures of the late Professor Kotarbinski are oriented to the ideal of a quality work done heroically by individuals mainly because of their sense of public duty. This is in a country where still, now manual work is treated as something inferior and for many people to do nothing is the best possible deal in a life time! Being one of the students of Professor Kotarbinski I was impressed by his personal consistency in the implementation of his duty against all odds.

REFERENCES

Altkorn, Jerzy. "Identifikacja pracownikow handlu z zawodem" (Identification of trade employees with their profession) Handel Wewnetrzny. 1963, 5.

Bahro, Rudolf. The Alternative for Eastern Europe. London: New Left Books. 1978.

Bartnicki, T. and T. Czajkowski. Struktura zatrudnienia i zarobki pracownikow umyslowych (Structure of employment and salaries of white-collar workers). Warsaw. 1936.

Bauman, Z. "Social Structure of the Party Organization in Industrial Works." Polish Sociological Bulletin. 1962, 3-4.

Blit, Lucjan. The Eastern Pretender. London: 1965.

Bloch, Marc. The Feudal Society. London: Routledge. 1961.

Breed, W. "Social Control in the Newsroom. A Functional Analysis." Social Forces. 1955, 33.

Bromke, Adam. Poland's Politics. Idealism versus Realism. Cambridge, Massachusetts: Harvard University Press. 1967.

Brus, Wlodzimierz. Socialist Ownership and Political Systems. London: Routledge and Kegan Paul. 1975.

Buszko, Henryk. Proba oceny aktualnej sytuacji architektury polskiej i zawodu architekta. (Evaluation of the current situation of Polish architecture and of the architectural profession). Warsaw: SARP. 1967.

Chalasinski, Jozef. Spoleczna genealogia inteligencji polskiej. (Social origin of the Polish intelligentsia). Lodz: Czytelnik. 1946.

Dziecielska, Stefania. Sytuacja spoleczna dziennikarzy polskich. (The social situation of Polish journalists). Wroclaw: Ossolineum. 1967.

Fiszman, Joseph R. Revolution and Tradition in People's Poland. Education and Socialization. Princeton, N.J.: Princeton University Press. 1972.

Gella, Aleksander. "The Life and Death of the Old Polish Intelligentsia." Slavic Review. 1971, 30: 1-27.

Grzelak, Anna. "Problemy adaptacji mlodych inzynierow" (Adaptation problems of young engineers) in Problemy kadry przemyslowej, Maria Hirszowicz, ed. Warsaw: Wydawnictwo Zwiazkowe CRZZ. 1965.

Hertz, Alexander. "The Social Background of the Pre-War Polish Political Structure." Journal of Central European Affairs. (July 1942): 145-60.

_____. "The Case of an Eastern European Intelligentsia." Journal of Central European Affairs. 1951, 11 (1).

Hozer, Jan. "Inzynierowie w przemysle" (Engineers in industry) in Przemysl i spoleczenstwo w Polsce Ludowej, Jan Szczepanski, ed. Wroclaw: Ossolineum. 1969.

_____. Zawod i praca inzyniera. (Profession and work of an engineer). Wroclaw: Ossolineum. 1970.

Jarosz, Maria. Nierownosc spoleczna. Warsaw: Ksiazka i Wiedza. 1984.

Keen, Maurice. Chivalry. New Haven: Yale University Press. 1984.

Kotarbinski, T. Praxiology. Oxford: Pergamon Press. 1965.

Kowalewski, Zdzislaw. Chemicy w Polskiej rzeczypospolitej ludowej. (Chemists in People's Poland). Wroclaw: Ossolineum. 1962.

Krall, Hanna. "Pobiezny szkic do portretu klasy" (Essay on the working class). Polityka-Statystyka. 1970, 5.

Kupis, Tadeusz. Zawod dziennikarza w Polsce ludowej (The journalistic profession in People's Poland). Warsaw. KIW. 1966.

Lepkowski, Tadeusz. Opolskim charakterze narodonym (On the Polish National Character). Zwiazkowiec (Toronto), 1985, 21: 2.

Lutynska, Krystyna. "Office Workers' Views on Their Social Position." Polish Sociological Bulletin. 1964, 1: 79-83.

_____. Pozycja spoleczna urzednikow w Polsce Ludowej (Social position of clerks in People's Poland). Wroclaw: Ossolineum. 1965.

Matejko, Alexander J. "Planning and Tradition in Polish Higher Education." Minerva. 1969, 42: 621-48.

_____. "Newspaper Staff as a Social System" in Media Sociology, J. Tunstall, ed. London: Constable: 1970.

_____. "Institutional Conditions of Scientific Inquiry." Small Group Behavior. 1973, 4, 1.

_____. Social Change and Stratification in Eastern Europe. New York: Praeger. 1974.

_____. "Recherche scientifique contre bureaucratisme en Pologne." Revue d'Etudes Comparatives Est-Quest. 1976, 7, 1: 185-210.

_____. "Basis and Superstructure in Poland." Nationalities Papers. 1979, VI, 1: 79-93.

_____. "Les ouvriers polonais: Une classe qui s'eveille." Revue d'Etudes Comparatives Est-Quest. 1981, 12, 4: 133-62.

Nowak, Stefan. "Changes of Social Structure in Social Consciousness." Polish Sociological Bulletin. 1964: 2.

Ossowska, Maria. Ethos rycerski i jego odmiany (Heroic ethos of knights and varieties thereof). Warsaw: Panstwowe Wydawnictwo Naukowe. 1973.

Pasieczny, Leszek. Inzynier w przemysle (The engineer in industry). Warsaw: PWE, 1968.

Pipes, Richard, ed. The Russian Intelligentsia. New York: Columbia University Press, 1961.

Pirog, Stanislawa. Bodzce materialnego zainteresowania w opiniach pracownikow biur projektow. Warsaw: PWE, 1966.

Podwysocki, Tadeusz. Biologiczne zagrozenie (Biological Danger), Nowy Dziennik (New York), 1985, XIV, 3572: 2, 3573: 2, 10 (Reprint from Veto appearing in Warsaw).

Rawin, Solomon J. "The Polish Intelligentsia and the Socialist Order. Elements of Ideological Compatibility." Political Science Quarterly. 1968, 83 (3).

Richman, Barry M. Soviet Management. New York: Prentice-Hall. 1965.

Sarapata, Adam. "Iustum Pretium." Polish Sociological Bulletin. 1963, 1: 41-56.

Sarapata, A. and W. Wesolowski. "The Evaluation Occupations by Warsaw Inhabitants." The American Journal of Sociology. May 1961.

Schapiro, Leonard and Joseph Godson, eds. The Soviet Worker: Illusions and Realities. London: Macmillan. 1982.

Theodorson, G. A. and A. G. Theodorson. Modern Dictionary of Sociology. New York: Thomas Y. Crowell. 1969.

Szczepanski, Jan. "Z badan nad inteligencja polska XIX wieku." (Studies on the 19th century Polish intelligentsia) Kultura i spoleczenstwo. 1960, 4 (3).

_____. "Pracownicy administracyjno-biurowi" (The clerical staff) in Przemysl i spoleczenstwo w Polsce Ludowej, Jan Szczepanski, ed. Wroclaw: Ossolineum. 1969.

_____. Polish Society. New York: Random House. 1970.

Wiatr, Jerzy J. "Stratification and Egalitarianism." Polish Perspectives. 1962, 12.

Woskowski, Jan. "Primary School Teachers and Their Social Position in People's Poland." Polish Sociological Bulletin. 1964, 1.

Zajaczkowski, Andrzej. Glowne elementy kultury szlacheckiej w Polsce (Basic characteristics of the gentry culture in Poland). Wroclaw: Ossolineum. 1961.

_____. Z dziejow inteligencji polskiej (On the history of the Polish of the Polish intelligentsia). Wroclaw: Ossolineum. 1962.

Zarnowski, Janusz. Spoleczenstwo Drugiej rzeczpospolitej 1918-1939. (Society of the second commonwealth 1918-1939). Warsaw: Panstwowe Wydawnictwo Naukowe. 1973.

5 THE SOCIOLOGICAL REFLECTION OF REALITY

THE UNEXPECTED CHAIN OF EVENTS

The complicated dialectics of socioeconomic and political transformations in Poland during the early 1980s has brought to question the predictive power of sociological diagnosis. The numerous and selectively financed empirical studies of the Polish working class, and especially the blue-collar workers (see the review of these studies in Jarosinska and Kulpinska 1978), did not provide any significant evidence suggesting that workers would organize themselves into an independent power, start mass strikes, bargain successfully with the government, challenge the ruling Polish United Workers' Party (PUWP), abandon the party-controlled progovernmental trade unions, etc. According to the officially supported sociological studies of the blue-collar worker class published in Poland, there was a constant improvement of the situation of workers (see, among others Sufin 1979a and 1979b). Some shortcomings and inadequacies (housing shortage, high labor turnover, etc.) were registered, but they were treated as being of only a transitory character, and they were not supposed to spoil the generally rosy picture of the Marxist synthesis. For the official sociological establishment, what happened in 1980 and afterward was as unexpected and shocking as for the ruling communist politicians and even to the managerial ranks. Several sociologists outside the official establishment took a much more independent and critical perspective, but their opportunities to express themselves in public were quite limited until the fall of 1980 and are even more restricted since the end of 1981.

Only a limited success has been achieved by the ruling elite in the control of sociology by the government's selective granting of "positive" research and "reliable" sociologists or because of the censorship that prevented critical studies from being published. Sociology and sociologists have enjoyed relative freedom since the late 1950s, and an atmosphere of open intellectual exchange, including debates between Marxists and non-Marxists, has been maintained in Poland without much difficulty. During the late 1950s and the early 1960s several prominent independent sociologists involved themselves in the public debates with the representatives of the official Marxist-Leninist doctrine. Beginning in the mid-1960s, the ruling party, with rekindled vigor, promoted political loyalists to the top administrative positions in sociology and actively discouraged any promotion to these positions of people who remained independently minded. Under the pretention of Zionism, in 1968 several politically influencial Marxist sociologists were eliminated because they refused to follow blindly the orders coming from the highest party ranks. These sociologists also intended to use their influence to pursue a different political line of thinking.

Until the early 1980s the sociological analysis of socialist industrialization in Poland took for granted that the official goals of reshaping the whole country according to the Soviet pattern were beneficial for the nation. This is now widely questioned because Poland's difficult internal economic situation shows faults that were allowed to accumulate throughout the period of socialist industrialization. Among these faults it is necessary to mention the promotion of grandiose industrial and construction projects (in total investments the production investments have grown between 1960 and 1978 from 64 percent to 76 percent) without promise of a long-term return, neglect of agriculture (in 1975, in comparison with 1970, investment into nationalized industry had grown by 160 percent, but only by 59 percent in private agriculture), neglect of basic material needs of the population, enforced urbanization leading to the uprooting of people and the deterioration of the countryside, dependence on imports without the possibility of balancing them with adequate exports, neglect of transportation, public health, education, and other fields of vital importance. The Polish experience shows clearly that the socialist industrialization does not eliminate the negative side-effects nor recognizes them early enough to deal with them. The secret rules of the Polish state censorship revealed by a censor who fled Poland show the very systematic suppression of any information about negative phenomena that in any democratic society are treated as deserving public attention (Raina 1981, Blazynski 1979, Singer 1981).

Even before 1980 some Polish sociologists suggested that problems were behind such symptoms as the decline of interest among the young peasant population to remain on the land and to become farmers, the dissatisfaction of blue-collar workers with the inadequate working conditions and the organizational disorder at the work places, the feeling of social degradation among clerks, the great adaptational problems among people starting their first job, the appearance at the work places of delinquent gangs that used the public facilities for the promotion of their own interest, the disregard of central bureaucratic bodies for the local needs and initiatives, the dilution of the feeling of responsibility among people who were supposed to serve the public, the excessive waste of human resources in several fields, and the excessive formalization of several administrative procedures (see Studia Socjologiczne). However, the authorities were neither willing nor able to pay attention to these signals and make practical conclusions out of them.

The sociological expertise of a new kind was started in the late 1970s by the informal group of Polish intellectuals and professional managers named Experience and Progress without any public funds or even governmental consent. The advice given by sociological centers was quite critical of the existing regime and its policies and showed that sociologists under the existing conditions were anxious to preserve and strengthen their independent judgment. This could make, in the long run, the sociological expertise more and more anti-establishment oriented; especially if the government remained idle and defensive instead of becoming energetic in facing the urgent social needs. On the other hand how the ruling elite would regain control of institutions that produced the socioeconomic expertise potentially harmful to the vested interests of current rulers posed an interesting question.

Within the system based on the concentration of power at the top and relying on suppression of all criticism by the official censorship, the global analysis of society promoted by the underground dissident groups functioned as a correction of the official image (Simon and Kanet 1981). The global analysis developed by dissidents (Kuron, Modzelewski, Michnik, Moczulski and others) had focused mainly on the failures, contradictions, shortcomings, and falsifications of truth originating at the top. The rejection of the status quo had become the rallying point of all dissidents even though they widely differed among themselves and quite often accused each other of being too soft on communism. Under the circumstances that existed in Poland until September 1980 (the contract between government and Solidarity was signed at the end of August 1980), there was not much room for a well-balanced diagnosis of Polish society (Raina 1981). Both sides, the ruling party and dissidents, were so much apart from each other that the moderately oriented sociologists had either to commit themselves decisively on the side of the dissidents and suffer the persecution by the government or claim their full loyalty to the party or at least pretend full allegiance with the regime.

As long as the ruling establishment was not challenged by another independent social power, there was no incentive for the rulers to pay genuine attention to the sociological experts (another question, how valid was what these experts said). Therefore, a very considerable amount of sociological information, financially sponsored by the government, was actually wasted, and preference was given to the propagandistic version of sociological studies oriented toward either the glorification of Poland's socialist achievements or the Marxist condemnation of the "bourgeois" west.

The progressing dominance of loyalists (and simultaneously careerists) as the holders of all strategic positions in Polish sociology during the 1970s led to a substantial influx of government grants, a gradual elimination of what were considered the politically unreliable personnel, and a considerable institutional development in terms of new research centers, departments, etc. Polish sociology reformed by new masters could gain materially much more than under the previous leadership of such independent-minded scholars as Ossowski, Chalasinski, Nowakowski, and others. However, the growing involvement of sociologists in the support of the current party line had reinforced very considerable opportunism hidden under the disguise of pragmatism, realism, and the practical applicability of sociological research. The Polish Sociological Association had grown to more than 1,000 in 1979 and had preserved its autonomy. Its activity was mainly oriented to sponsoring public lectures, conferences, etc. It has remained independent and has allowed interested sociologists to develop their own spheres of interest. The growth of sociotechnics, sociology of law, and sociology of organizations were probably the most significant phenomena in this respect.

In the second half of the 1970s the average number of students of sociology was around 1,500 each year, and the average yearly number of graduates was 165. People who finished sociological studies quite often faced a gap between what they had learned and what they were expected to do afterward in research institutes (about 20 percent) and practical institutions of various kinds (about 50 percent). In this respect the Polish situation did not differ much from other parts of the world. "Many institutions offer a job to a sociologist without really knowing how to use him; they expect from sociologists that they would define their responsibilities themselves. . . . Many employers become convinced that sociology and sociologists can be of little use to the solving of their particular problems" (Lifsches 1979, 86-87). What to do with young sociologists after graduation remains a problem, even if the enrollment is normally limited and only few candidates are accepted on the basis of an entrance exam.

The establishment of Solidarity and the relaxation of censorship changed this situation between the second half of 1980 and December

1981, offering sociologists the opportunity to take a much more independent position. The messy side of current Polish society could be described and analyzed much more critically. There were studies on widespread alcoholism, growing delinquency, great material hardships of the population, difficulties encountered by working women, social inequality in various fields, and even the authoritarian tradition of political life under state socialism in Poland. The ruling political elite had a vested interest in documenting the shortcomings and hardships to show how much cooperation and dedication was needed from everyone to improve life in the country. Before August 1980 the emphasis was on minor changes; from 1980 to December 1981 the emphasis was on showing how difficult it was to govern Poland and gain some results.

THE CURRENT STATE OF AFFAIRS

Polish sociologists currently suffer several difficulties experienced by other disciplines: drastic cutbacks of foreign books and imported equipment; decline of the buying power in comparison with such privileged occupations as miners, police, etc.; shortage of funds for the attendance of conferences; shortage of research funds. The relative position of academics in the income hierarchy has considerably deteriorated in comparison with the 1970s and this is felt by sociologists. However, politics forms a much more painful problem. The ruling authorities are attempting to reinforce the role of official Marxism. On one hand it was decided to get rid of those Marxists who for a variety of reasons looked unreliable. The most important act in this respect was the elimination from the party ranks of Adam Schaff after the Viennese publication of his book (Schaff 1982) in which he claimed that Marxism has to suffer in its humanitarian aspirations as long as the economic basis in the socialist countries remains inadequate. In early December, 1984, a big party conference of social sciences postulated the reinforcement of the leading role of party activists in Polish social sciences.

However, in reality the situation is not conducive to infiltrating sociology with party doctrine. Books and articles published in this field in Poland show that politicization on the side of the ruling authorities remains quite modest. Most of the publishing sociologists want to remain independent and to not appear loyalistic. In the underground press unfavorable analyses of the authorities appear quite often and many are probably written by people with at least some sociology education. The underground book on participation by Stefan Bratkowski, the past president of the Polish Association of Journalists, claims the need to create in Poland an informal "participatory society" independent of the authorities.

With little hope that the bad economic situation will improve, there are many opportunities for social conflicts of various kinds, and sociologists are needed to analyze them. In comparison with all remaining countries of the Soviet bloc, in Poland sociology has been tolerated as a scientific discipline that should not be overly politicized. Of course, Marxism remains privileged, and the leading sociologists from time to time at least pay lip service to it.

One of the current problems is the progressing proletarianization of the intelligentsia; a very sensitive issue in the country where traditionally members of intelligentsia have the leadership aspirations. The Marxist class differentiation does not help to understand conflictual problems in a state socialist country that at least formally follows the Marxist developmental perspective. How to explain the fact that among the best paid people two-thirds are blue-collar workers but at the same time manual work is commonly treated as inferior? How to reconcile the "leading" role of manual workers with their actual paralysis as a social category devoid of its own institutions? How to explain the growing gap between the well-to-do and the quite poor (Jarosz 1984) in a society claiming social equality as it's highest aim?

Polish sociologists, together with other social scientists, are professionally in the center of the major contradictions and inconsistencies of the system that is supposed to solve or at least alleviate social problems instead of multiply them. With the government sacrificing the material privilege of scientists to calm down manual workers by offering them more premiums, sociologists themselves are vulnerable to the feeling of injustice and discrimination. As long as they remained relatively privileged, it was much easier for at least some of them to play the role of the obedient servants of political power.

Employed sociologists by Polish standards constitute 4 percent of all social scientists. At the end of 1984 there were 631 employed sociologists in comparison with 3,117 economists, 3,305 philologists, 1,416 historians, 1,149 law specialists, 749 psychologists, 467 political scientists. It is significant that the ruling party affiliation is much less common among sociologists (20 percent) than among social scientists on average (40 percent) and even less common than among law specialists (80 percent) (Polityka, 1984, XXVIII, 50, 5). This means that the bargaining power of sociologists within the diminishing state expenditures of the science[1] is far from being strong. Social scientists, including sociologists, are young,[2] and their living conditions are far from being satisfactory.[3] From 1979 until the end of 1984 the average income of the young academic workers (assistants, etc.) compared to the average income in the nationalized Polish economy diminished from 1.36:1.0 to .74:1.0 (Polityka, 1984, XXVIII, 42, 11).

Dealing directly with grave social problems facing the Polish society, sociologists are perhaps less willing than other social scientists to orient themselves opportunistically. Under the current difficult conditions the authorities have lost interest in sociology, especially because other social scientists are much more willing to serve obediently; for example every second philosopher is a party member.

The leading political figures of Polish sociology have a definite ambition to be the diagnosticians and prognosticians for the top ruling hierarchy. For example, J. J. Wiatr in Polityka (Wiatr 1984, 14) postulates a systematic study of internal socioeconomic trends that may lead to major conflicts. He would like to watch, among others, consumer behavior, social pathology, feeling of deprivation, antagonistic relations between various groups, life opportunities of people at various levels of the social hierarchy, and political behavior. It is necessary to mention that all these topics already have been studied by Polish sociologists. The postulates formulated by Wiatr are evidently addressed to the political authorities to convince them that sociology may be useful to learn that something is going wrong.

Polish sociologists are already very divided and polarization will probably grow in the future. Some sociologists are needed by the ruling circles as convenient and obedient analysts or propagandists. On the other hand, as long as a considerable part of the Polish population is dissatisfied, there are strong disincentives to make one's sociological career through the close cooperation with the rulers. Most sociologists have neither interest nor even necessity to sell themselves to the government and the ruling party. They do research, teach, and publish having in mind their professional image in the society with which they share a difficult daily life, frustrated democratic aspirations, and the hope that sometime in the future there will be a chance to change the whole system to something much more efficient and humanitarian. It is possible that the rulers will exert pressure to make Polish sociology a real party discipline, as has happened in all other Soviet-bloc countries. However, so far this has not been done, and even inside the ruling circles there is a fear of doctrinaire approach. A "truncated" Polish version of state socialism has a strong chance of remaining intact, leaving most sociologists relatively free.

The Polish sociology data offer much more insight into the actual functioning of Soviet state socialism than the sociological sources in all the rest of the Soviet bloc. Since 1981 and the suppression of Solidarity this has not changed much and it is still worth reading the Polish sociological publications; unfortunately because of the language barrier they are not adequately known in the west. Censorship prevents a great deal of critical material from being published, but even after the official clearance enough remains to offer valuable insights. The Polish Sociological Association remains an important member of the international sociological community; it is much more difficult for Polish academic workers to finance their participation at the conferences outside the Soviet bloc, and politically "unreliable" sociologists are not cleared by the authorities to attend conferences outside Poland. Still some sociologists manage to pay visits to the "capitalist" west. The major problem is the shortage of new western books and professional journals; Poland does not have foreign currency to pay for them, and Polish sociologists greatly appreciate books mailed to them privately.

It would be in the interest of western societies to support and reinforce the development of the sociological imagination in Poland as potentially contributing to democratization, critical thinking, and better awareness of various alternatives. So far there is enough proof that Polish sociology has not become a weapon of totalitarianism because of the sense of professional independence, the commitment to the liberal creed of the intelligentsia, and the ambition to gain appropriate recognition inside the country (in comparison with other disciplines) as well as outside. Being an important part of the local intelligentsia, Polish sociologists are very sensitive to their image, and their striving for intellectual independence is constantly reinforced by people with whom they socialize. These informal societal bonds play a major part in the formation of motives and personal aspirations. As long as the rulers are not able or even willing to paralyze the social life of the intelligentsia, there is promise that sociology will remain a vivid discipline.

As long as sociologists were internally divided by the uneven distribution of research grants, travel money, promotions and other rewards, it was relatively easy for the ruling party to penalize its enemies and to support its friends. The same mechanisms of control have remained intact, and the manifestation of loyalty may help the careerists. On the other hand informal public opinion is much stronger than before, reinforced by the close friendship ties, the whole network of people who trust and support each other, and by the widespread underground press, which provides uncensored views and news, warns against potential enemies, reveals the blunders of the authorities, and praises the opposition heroes for their deeds. When the dependence on the official support is a mixed blessing and the authorities have little to offer particularly to young people, the informal connection network becomes particularly important. Sociologists have many good reasons to want to appear as honorable people before their professional colleagues, family members, friends, and relatives. In the current "pecking order" official power counts now much less than before and personal esteem counts more.

In Poland since World War II at least two societies have coexisted more or less antagonistically. One is the society run by the Marxist elite building a socialism of their own style, controlling power and resources, rewarding their obedient friends and penalizing their enemies. The other is the society of people who do not accept the official ideology because they follow their own ideology (Catholicism, secular humanitarianism, practical utilitarianism). These people depend on their own informal networks, remain hostile or at least unconvinced by the official creed, and cooperate with the authorities only as far as it seems to be necessary. Since 1981 the gap between the two different societies has widened not only because of the exceptional power claimed by the militarized regime but also because of the bad economic situation. The economic reform promised by the government is developing slowly and is meeting the resistance of managers not accustomed to the risk and responsibility, higher administration trying at any cost to keep enterprises under some control, workers not paid according to their actual performance, in addition to shortages of almost everything needed for production, including labor.

Sociologists in Poland are relatively free to describe many vital problems and pains of the society: the limited perspectives for the youth to find some place for themselves, the changing leisure patterns and the difficulty to satisfy the growing aspirations under limited circumstances, social inequalities between various categories of the population, family problems and the generation gap, careers, religious practices and their role in various groups, social mobility between various strata, etc. It is not up to the state sponsored Polish sociologists to look for deeper political roots of social problems and blame the whole system, as is widely practiced in the west. However, the opportunity to publish outside Poland or in the underground press, although risk is involved, remains relatively open and several more courageous sociologists have taken advantage of it.

There is a good chance that whoever will be in power in Poland in the future, sociological expertise will grow in importance. A nondoctrinaire approach to several urgent issues is evident already and probably will be reinforced in the future. The critical point is the willingness of decision makers to take advantage of expertise. The tradition of Soviet state socialism is to manipulate intellectuals and not to learn from them how to run the country in a better way. It is necessary to remember that the Polish ruling elite consists mainly of the status seekers who are very sensitive about their limited education (many of them have a technical or political education not supplemented by anything broader), feel threatened by the intellectuals, believe in simple solutions, and are constantly pressured by "experts," every one trying to "sell" his or her own solution.

In this tough competition for the court favors, sociologists are in a poor bargaining situation because their own discipline appears "softer" than other disciplines and this is constantly used against them, particularly by the economists who are eager to incorporate some pseudosociological aspects into their discipline. It is also true that sociologists do not have anything particularly positive to offer.

The conclusion from sociological diagnoses quite often shows that much more resources should be spent to improve considerably the well-being of the population. And who among the rulers is actually eager to spend money on common people?

It will probably become more and more difficult to rule Polish society, and this will force the ruling circles to become more sophisticated in governing the people. At the end of 1984 it became clear that the abuse of power so far widely practiced by the secret police will be curtailed at least to some extent, mainly for a better public relations image inside and outside Poland. In all fields of Polish life, and particularly in business management and public administration, sociological expertise may multiply the alternatives of action. The inhumanity of several state socialist policies arises not so much from the evil spirit of the policy makers and the executors, but from sheer incompetence and narrowmindedness. A great deal may be improved by looking closely at what can be done in a different way. The obviously inefficient running of production and distribution in Poland is deeply rooted in vested interest groups that gain from the preservation of the status quo and are willing to do anything to prevent any change. An indepth sociological diagnosis may be beneficial for the whole country if it is done by genuine professionals who have knowledge and courage, not by political appointees oriented mainly to their own security and easy profits.

The black-and-white approach to the global analysis of society, so characteristic of Marxist sociology in Poland until 1980, seems to be abandoned for good in Poland. Room has been made for several other approaches that would illustrate how much more complicated the whole variety of current Polish problems are. The full understanding of the need to have a genuinely pluralistic sociology seems to be growing in contemporary Poland even when progressing radicalization is seen on both sides (the rulers and the opposition) because of the prolonged crisis of an economic, political, and moral nature. Instabilities in the political scene caused by the shaky relationships between five basic organized powers—the military, PUWP, the bureaucratic elite, Solidarity (underground since the martial law), and the Catholic Church—will probably become a permanent phenomenon in Poland of the 1980s, as long as the USSR does not decide to interfere militarily and to impose its own rule similar to the model imposed on Czechoslovakia in 1968 or the East German model. Since December 1981 the authoritarian approach has gained superiority among the ruling political elite. However, it appears that there are no radical solutions that could promise the end of a permanent Polish crisis. The introduction of martial law was a major blow against any reasonable compromise. It was an end of dreams among sociologists to construct a democratic society based on scientific expertise, pluralistic in its nature and appealing to the good will of all major forces within the society.

However, despite the bleak circumstances, there is hope for sociologists that in the long run they may become useful again. The need for reliable expertise has become one of the priorities in Poland, a clear difference from the situation existing before 1980 when the basic function of the social sciences was to justify the regime because virtually all important planning and policy decisions were the result of power struggles within the ruling party establishment. With the decline of authoritarian appeal in the Polish society, the role of independent experts, sociologists among them, is gaining strength. All major institutions of society have their own sociological experts and follow their suggestions more or less consistently. The proof of it may be found in the content of documents produced by various governmental and nongovernmental agencies before the introduction of martial law and in the daily press in Poland in 1980 and 1981.

THE MAIN TRADITIONS

The traditions of Polish sociology still have validity. The memory of Stanislaw Ossowski and his resistance against any form of intellectual slavery is vivid. In relation to the official Marxist doctrine, Ossowski promoted an open-minded approach at a cost of his elimination from academic teaching during the first half of the 1950s. According to Nowak, Ossowski's thoughts were partly "formed either under the direct influence of Marxism, or by way of continuing the study of problems raised by Marxism" (Nowak 1974, 14), but he definitely had an independent and critical orientation. According to Ossowski, "Methods of planned cooperation in a polycentric society must be worked out and the conflict between effective centralized leadership and the humanist values of polycentrism must be resolved" (Ossowski 1968; 4, 196). For him it was clear that economic security should not be achieved on the expense of freedom, spontaneity, and initiative (Ossowski 1968; 5, 297). As an independent scholar, Ossowski was ready to suffer persecution for the pursuit of a truth very uncomfortable for the ruling Marxist authorities. Several of his theoretical concepts, among others the classification of social orders (Karpinski 1979), were continued and developed by his Polish disciples.

Josef Chalasinski (1904-1979) in his own studies, as well as the studies inspired by him, focused mainly on the impact of social change on social consciousness and the self-image of Polish lower classes, mainly peasants. His most important works deal with the young generation of peasants before World War II (published in 1938) and afterwards (published between 1964 and 1980). Chalasinski's critical analysis of Polish traditional intelligentsia (1946) was written in defense of such values as realism, hard work, and national responsibility.

The same concerns inspired his contributions in the field of sociology of education and culture. He defended Polish sociology against too much dependence on foreign patterns that might threaten the self-identity of this discipline and particularly its roots in history. The integration of the nation based on the contributions of various strata, as well as their full recognition, was one of Chalasinski's main concerns. He followed methodology developed by Florian Znaniecki and applied it widely to the Polish reality (see more on Chalasinski in Kultura i Spoleczenstwo, 1980; XXIV, 1-2).

Adam Podgorecki in his global analysis of Polish society relates "the historically determined informal system of relations between the social structure and social stratification on the one hand and on the other the type of personality which functions within the framework of this structure and stratification" (Podgorecki, 1976, 17). Poland, having been partitioned for a long time (1772-1918), did not have until recently a historical opportunity to experience a homemade industrialization and commercialization. Most of the innovation in this respect was foreign-born (and even the recent socialist industrialization was a Soviet import); therefore, several characteristics of a traditional society coincide in Poland with the modern trends. The formal structure of the Polish socialist society (shaped according to the Soviet model) differs widely from the informal that is the product of a long historical experience. The internal contradictions within the formal system invigorate the informal organization as a correction and also as a supplementary structure needed by people who are unable or unwilling to find full satisfaction within the official framework. The traditional ties are destroyed because of the planned reconstruction of the whole society according to the model imposed by the rulers. However, for members of the society to succeed privately as well as officially, they must depend to a large extent on ties of an informal or semi-informal nature as long as formal channels remain slow, inefficient, effort-consuming, and in general unreliable.

The history of Poland during the last 200 years consists of several completely different set-ups to which Polish people had to adapt in order to survive (Podgorecki 1981, 74-77). The art of survival has become very common among Poles and is based on the close family ties (children as idols that consolidate the primary bond), close friendship that sometimes erodes into a mafialike confraternity (Podgorecki calls it a "community of dirty togetherness") (Podgorecki 1981, 82), and individualism manifesting itself in promoting one's own interest justified by need for security (Podgorecki 1981, 78).

On the other hand the long Catholic tradition and the feeling of patriotism have both contributed to the establishment among Poles of a "spectacular principledness," which manifests itself in the particular commitment to a moral decorum. Poles enjoy gestures that show how moral, dedicated, and patriotic they are. It is not "proper" to do things just for personal gain or any other reasons that may appear to be "pedestrian" and "inferior."

> In the Polish society the value of gesture is more important than the value of reasonable behaviour which is likely to solve the task at hand. To be more specific—in that culture, an attempt to do something which assumes a form of a spectacular gesture and approaches the given problem in an impressive way, is valued higher than a pragmatic, logistic, practical, strictly economic solution. In that culture, the social position of a person is not determined by his real skills, qualifications or abilities, but is established by the way of a social how which the given person delivers when faced with the problem. The symbolic values certainly overpass the real ones. . . . Legends and myths become the most crucial factors (Podgorecki 1981, 91).

There is an aura of rigorousness that goes with spectacular principledness and leads to an eager condemnation of others on the basis of their alleged wrongdoing, disloyalty, etc. In the society traditionally characterized by a deep cleavage between the privileged few and the mass of common people, rigorousness is related to the existence of distances. Those who try to overcome these distances are informally penalized for being "rude," not showing proper manners, etc. On the other hand the status seekers use the cliché of egalitarianism to fulfill their aspirations in the field of consumption. Rather than being really egalitarian, status seekers use the phrase as a suitable weapon to gain more for oneself under the guise of equal opportunities (Dyoniziak 1967; Podgorecki 1976a, 19).

Social mobility on a mass scale, promoted since the late 1940s by the socialist government for political and economic reasons, has allowed in the long run considerable homogeneity of the whole society, evident, among others, in the gradual disappearance of local slangs. But this mobility has its side effects. The newcomers to urban areas have brought with them tradition of parochial concerns and priorities. "Traditional, neighbourly methods of doing business, of services mutually rendered, formed in small peasant communities have been transported live into the heart of a rational, pragmatic, and impersonal state administration" (Podgorecki 1976b, 21).

Within the rigid and depersonalized bureaucracy, the above-mentioned methods directly transferred from a small group situation expose the whole formal structure to corruption, especially when the nihilistic approach to life and low respect for law become common phenomena. In the early 1980s under the impact of economic disaster caused by the unrealistic and wasteful governmental policies, the Polish blue-collar workers revolted. They reacted against the false-hood of Soviet-made "make believe," the exploitation of labor, and the inefficiency of formal structures that were supposed to serve their interests but in reality enslaved them (Podgorecki 1981, 95-96). At the same time the youth staged a mass revolt oriented much more in-strumentally than the older generation's, tired with the traditional cult of gesture and showmanship, wanting to reconcile the principles with the reality of their home country.

The events in Poland that started in the middle of 1980 are the product of a progressing homogeneity of the society documented in, among others, the sociological studies inspired and coordinated by A. Podgorecki (1976a, 1977). The urban culture based on instrumental values has deeply penetrated the countryside. The traditional intelli-gentsia has become widely professionalized. The social advancement of lower classes through education has stimulated new aspirations dif-ficult to fulfill within the existing system. The national consciousness has grown but it could not be satisfied under the conditions of high de-pendence on the USSR. The class distinctions have diminished, but under these new conditions the privileges of the ruling elite have be-come exposed even more clearly. The mass culture has an equalizing effect but at the same time discourages any deeper involvement. For-mal organizations penetrate private life more and more, but they re-main depersonalized, immune to genuine social control, inefficient (red tape), and vulnerable to erosion by internal clique struggles. Many people are employed by government agencies under state social-ism, but there is little satisfaction from working for the government and little opportunity to feel useful.

The whole system is supposed to be highly socialized, but the ossified formal structure prevents any genuine social involvement, local initiative, and personal commitment. The system based on high modernization goods needs pragmatic and efficient people, but the bureaucratic reality gives a premium to passivity, blind obedience, and personal avoidance of any genuine engagement. The ambitious goals are formulated at the top, but the lower ranks of the hierarchy have a vested interest in not attaining those goals. Mass aspirations are constantly pampered, but the system remains unable to satisfy them and manifests its obvious dysfunctions (Podgorecki 1977, 37-41).

Showmanship is inherent in the Soviet style of state socialism and leads to the window dressing effects that are supposed to hide in-ternal contradictions of the system. Unfortunately, showmanship is also a part of the Polish tradition of human relations. In Poland, be-cause of specific historical circumstances, many people like to think of themselves as being highly principled and to give others this im-pression of themselves (Podgorecki and Los 1979, 238-246). Unfortunately, these principles are not always genuine and sometimes they function as a window-dressing to hide quiet pedestrian intentions. The ascribed status related to the gentry tradition, continuity of the family life through several generations, and social distances between various strata and social circles inherited from the past are other Polish social characteristics. "Prestige accorded to various occupations in Poland was, until recently, linked with the social structure formed along traditional principles" (Podgorecki 1976b, 25). Both of the factors mentioned above—holding specified high principles (or at least so pretending) and the pride of having an ascribed status—become to a growing extent contradictory to the utilitarian and instrumental approach to life badly needed by the modernized societies, including Poland (Podgorecki and Los 1979, 236-247).

Some tensions and inconsistencies are almost unavoidable under such circumstances, especially when the formal structure is imposed from outside (the Soviet mode of socialism), market shortages force people to use personal connections to gain what they want, and the daily functioning of state bureaucracy remains highly ineffective. Poles are rigorous but mainly for others and not for themselves. The tendency toward social punitiveness remains strong (Adamski 1981, 107), but many "rigorous" people claim themselves above others and demand special privileges for themselves on the cost of others.

According to Podgorecki, close friendly ties exist in Poland almost exclusively when all members hold the same or at least similar social positions. Individuality is attractive for Poles but is practiced mostly for the external use and remains an imposed phenomenon. Concern for survival is very strong among Poles, but it is not proper to admit it in front of others. The instrumental abilities have considerably developed, especially among the young generation, but the framework of the centrally planned society does not account for them (Podgorecki and Los 1979, 200-204). People enjoy primary groups, but the existing institutional framework neglects completely this common need. There is a long tradition of spontaneity and initiative, but they have been systematically discouraged and even persecuted during the last several decades by the rulers of the country (Podgorecki 1976b).

As long as the institutional basis of the society is full of contradictions and people have great difficulty socializing into the system without denying their ego, Polish society remains in an internal turmoil and there is no hope for recovery. The only reasonable alternative is to reconstruct the institutional basis by allowing for much more spontaneity and initiative, as well as by incorporating several informal elements. As long as these elements do not introduce too much deviation, or even corruption, they should be tolerated to accommodate people who need them (Podgorecki 1976b, 1981).

According to Jan Szczepanski, Polish sociologists have a unique opportunity to study the transformation of a capitalist socioeconomic system into a socialist one (Szczepanski 1970, 5). In contrast to other communist countries, in Poland there is a great deal of statistical and sociological data available for analysis. Of all communist-dominated countries, Poland has shown so far the strongest resistance to the materialistic Marxist ideology, and at the same time has maintained a very large private sector of the economy, mainly in agriculture.

Contradictions are quite common in Poland as admits Szczepanski: The ruling Polish United Workers' Party (PUWP) includes half of the white-collar workers and only forty percent of manual labor, but pretends to be a leader of the entire manual working class. Members of the party are supposed to be Marxists, but many of them, especially among the peasants and manual workers, regularly attend Catholic churches and receive sacraments. The nationalized economy is dominant, but the highest incomes are enjoyed by people from the private sector. The Polish society officially advances toward communism, but the individualistic spirit is not weakening, and it is common for Poles to develop private initiative to satisfy their needs by legal or extralegal pursuits (Szczepanski 1970, 65).

Szczepanski approaches the Polish society "as a tremendous laboratory where the experiment of planned social reconstruction has been undertaken on a macroscale. It is a society in transition" (Szczepanski 1970, 193). "The emerging order is indeed more egalitarian and closer to the ideal Marxian image of classless society" (Szczepanski 1970, 146). In Poland sociologists have "the opportunity to study Marxist ideas in action, to study their role in this transformation [of a capitalist socioeconomic system into a communist one-A.M.], and to observe the results of their application to the solution of social and economic problems" (Szczepanski 1970, 5).

Therefore, most of Szczepanski's interest is devoted to the transformations of Polish society under socialism. He considers political institutions and forces (political parties and groups, government, other politically significant organizations, unorganized political forces), economic institutions (objective of a socialized economy, various sectors of the national economy, organization of economic institutions, development of the labor force), social macrostructure (changes in traditional social classes and their consequences, concept of a classless society and its at least partial fulfillment), culture of the nation (traditional values, education, the representative culture, the folk culture, religion, formation of social personalities, subcultures, conflicts in values), and the microstructure (patterns of interaction, patterns of interpersonal relations).

In all these fields Szczepanski looks for factors of continuity and and change. He enumerates the basic new elements introduced by the socialist order of the Soviet style, and he looks for factors of change

that modify the communist influence, such as modernization of industry, scientific progress, diffusion of western patterns of life, and
mentality of a new generation. "The new generation in Poland, instead
of engaging in ideological discussions are trying to change the principles of socialist order. The organization of its institutions, sees them
in the perspective of the emerging technological civilization of Western
high mass-consumption societies" (Szczepanski 1970, 196). Members
of the new generation "have to adjust themselves to the existing order
so as to get jobs, advancement, positions, and so on" (Szczepanski
1979, 196). The "grapevine" helps people adjust by allowing them to
develop informal substitute institutions to meet needs not fully satisfied within the formal framework.

Until 1980 Szczepanski was very optimistic about Polish society,
and he differed in this respect substantially from the criticism common not only among dissidents and émigré refugees (see the volumes
of Kultura published by Institute Litteraire in Maisons-Lafitte near
Paris), but also among several disillusioned prominent leaders of the
ruling party. An example of the latter is W. Bienkowski (1966, 1970)
who developed a theory of petrification of social orders especially
valid for the highly bureaucratized communist societies.

Communism has been for Szczepanski a great turning point that
has dissolved the two upper classes (the land-owning class and the
bourgeoisie), upgraded the peasantry and the wage earners, achieved
ethnic and political unification, pushed forward industrialization, developed mass education and culture, secured the national boundaries,
and found a stable place for Poland in the Soviet bloc. According to
Szczepanski, "No one in Poland thinks seriously about the possible
change" and "the group in power is firmly established" (Szczepanski
1970, 47, 48) even if there are some disagreements within the political establishment. The basic issues are just how to make the state
administration more effective, educate Poles for citizenship ("It is
important to overcome the traditional Polish individualism and anar-
chical inclinations") (Szczepanski 1970, 50), and improve the ruling
party leadership (more pragmatically oriented people are needed, he
believes). With these actions, Szczepanski believes the problems will
be entirely solved. According to Szczepanski, the government "enjoys
the support of the people on many essential issues," and "feelings of
opposition are softening with time" (Szczepanski 1970, 63). This is
asserted even though Szczepanski acknowledges that conditions for
introducing a constructive citizenship "are extremely difficult for the
present ruling political party, because the Poles are not too willing
to learn the lessons of self-restraint," and because most Poles "almost automatically look for an extralegal solution" to satisfy their
needs (Szczepanski 1970, 64-65).

An opposite view widely held by critics of the present regime,

for example the well-known Polish economist J. Drewnowski (1970),
maintains that the system based on one party rule, a very considerable
limitation of individual and group freedom and the monopolization of
the economic power by the state and the party makes "constructive
citizenship" virtually impossible. People who represent such a viewpoint also would not agree with Szczepanski that "the emerging order
is indeed more egalitarian and closer to the ideal Marxian image of a
classless society" (Szczepanski 1970, 146), and that the multidimensional stratification of the new society makes it "hard to foresee the
formation of a social class based on political authority" (Szczepanski
1970, 142). Szczepanski believes there are several effective safeguards
against formation of a well-established ruling class. In this respect
Szczepanski differs profoundly with Bienkowski (1970), who points out
the lack of such safeguards as the basic weakness of the communist
political system.

The tradition of dialogue and mutual tolerance is deeply ingrained
and remains strong in Poland, although it had not much influenced the
politically oriented Marxist group of sociologists up to the late 1970s.
Polish politics has been traditionally more an abstract ideological and
moral problem than the practical issue of gaining power and afterward
implementing it in the pursuit of specific goals (Krol 1979). Debates
about freedom and democracy are not specific, and the people who
claim to be democrats quite often lack the basic skill and knowledge
of how to run meetings in a democratic way. Parliamentary procedure
and the conduct of meetings (rules of order) in the Anglo-Saxon countries are widely applied in daily business of various institutions, and
they socialize people into the democratic approach to problem solving.
The state building practice has been traditionally handicapped in Poland
by several historical circumstances (partitions, underdevelopment of
the middle class, authoritarian rule during the interwar period, the
Nazi occupation, the communist regime since 1945) and by the ideological and moralistic style of political thought dominant among the Polish
intelligentsia, which aspires to exercise the governance of souls (Gella
1971, Matejko 1974).

The introduction of the communist rule in Poland in 1944 from
the beginning was related to the suppression of free exchange. It was
in the vested interest of the new ruling class to promote its own apologists at the expense of other groups. The concentration of all major
material means in the Marxist state and the establishment of official
censorship served as the basic means of gaining the monopoly of thought.
Debate was allowed only as it served the interests of the ruling elite.
For the sake of make believe some differences of opinions were arranged, but they were immediately eliminated in the case of any insubordination (similar to the policy of 100 flowers promoted by Mao
Tse Tung in the 1950s). From time to time the Marxist intellectuals

involved themselves in the public exchange of views with Catholics, non-Marxists, or atheistic or agnostic scholars, but these exchanges always served certain political purposes and were arbitrarily stopped whenever it suited the rulers.

THE OFFICIAL MARXIST LINE

Polish Marxists' analysis has for years tended to go much beyond the dogmatic interpretation prevailing in Soviet social science. For example, J. Mucha and A. K. Paluch (1980), in addressing the modernization theme in the Marxist theory of social development, propose to supplement it by the theory of social diffusion and the specific theory of modernization. Diffusion and modernization are treated by Mucha and Paluch as disturbances of the regular development predicted by Marxism. According to Mucha and Paluch, the traditional Marxist narrow interpretation of how various socioeconomic formations follow each other has negatively influenced the studies of modernization in Asia and Africa (Mucha and Paluch 1980, 29).

Mucha (1980) postulates a conflictual analytical model of socialist society and shows several negative consequences of the consensual model widely followed by most Marxist sociologists, although several acknowledge the existence of contradictions. Wesolowski mentions the diversity of vested interests involved in the distribution of goods and services between various categories of the population (Wesolowski 1974, 219-25). Wiatr acknowledges the diversity of allocation priorities, differences between the general policy and the vested interests of various groups, and differences in the perceptions of interests among people located at various levels of the hierarchy (Wiatr 1973, 320-21). Widerszpil writes about the disparities between needs and their satisfaction, organization and its material basis, central decisions and local initiatives, etc. (Widerszpil 1977, 30, 33). However, any theoretical generalization of conflictual contradictions under socialism must—according to Mucha—be based on a very clear definition what really is socialism in order to recognize conflicts that are characteristic for its true essence: socialized ownership of production means, reward proportional to work contribution, central planning, and democratic centralism of political power (Mucha 1980, 30).

Mucha seems unaware of the fact that the contradiction between the official model of socialism and its implementation is a primary source of conflict and imbalance of the whole model. Recent developments in Poland have revealed the nature of the basic contradiction searched for by Mucha (Mucha 1980, 34). It seems to be unrealistic to promise plenty, equality, and growth under the conditions of enforced unity and suppression of any manifest contradictions that would be loaded with conflict. The tolerance of open conflicts advocated by Mucha (Mucha 1980, 36) was implemented in Poland during the period of September 1980 to December 1981 but was full of tensions and did not promise any easy equilibrium. Martial law, introduced in December 1981, and the imprisonment of most people who supported the pluralistic model of Polish society were the end of a democratic dream widely shared by Marxist and non-Marxist intellectuals.

According to Kolarska (1980), centralization of decision making in organizations may eliminate certain types of conflicts, but it inspires others. The assertion that certain conflicts do not manifest themselves under the conditions of centralization is of little value because latent conflicts, as a substitute of the manifest ones, may be even more dangerous phenomena (Kolarska 1980, 105). This position was very characteristic for these Polish Marxist sociologists who had a genuine interest in social reality and wanted to study empirically the functioning socialist system. It was important for them to reveal the institutional contradictions appearing under the umbrella of central planning.

Wiatr rejects the understanding that Marxism is a status quo apology but at the same time distances himself from the disillusioned who attack the socialist society of today (Wiatr 1975, 10). From this perspective, the problem remains "how to develop the theory which by virtue of its political orientation has direct practical implications" (Wiatr 1975, 11). As a scientific theory, Marxism is not subject to empirical verification. As a political doctrine, Marxism is supposed to remain flexible in its goal achievement. The task of Marxist social theory in socialist societies is to contribute to the optimalization of the strategic decisions that determine the course of social development, the realistic assessment of the limits within which social processes can be centrally directed, and the role of spontaneity in the transformation of the socialist society (Wiatr 1975, 16). The optimal extent of political intervention in various spheres of life should be ascertained on the basis of a systematic social research (Wiatr 1975, 18).

A collective work on Marxism and the processes of social development, edited by W. Wesolowski (1979) and based on the conference held in 1976, summarizes the perspective promoted by establishment-oriented sociologists. This work starts with the condemnation by F. Wiatr of such "bourgeois" critics of Marxism as Wittfogel, Rostow, and others. J. Topolski discusses critically universalistic explanations offered by Popper, Levi-Strauss, Freud, Toynbee, and Teilhard de Chardin. He claims that the Marxist historiosophy is more original and more optimistic than others. T. M. Jaroszewski praises the humanistic values of the socialist industrial revolution, which according to him offers full opportunities for the growth and well-being of people. S. Widerszpil, inspired by the 1973 paper by J. Szczepanski, presents the basic assumptions for the theory of a developed socialist society: the leading role of the party and the state as representative of the "objective" necessities of social development, the rejection of empirical facts as the only source of truth, the plan established by the ruling party, the use of social research to eliminate existing contradictions, etc. J. Pajestka advocates a global approach to social planning under socialism in Poland, but actually he does not go beyond trivia. J. Szczepanski suggests social planners learn more about the spontaneous processes and life-styles to make more sophisticated the official manipulation. W. Markiewicz looks at the question of political culture as a necessary element of socialism. A. Sufin provides data on general improvement in Poland. D. Polinski considers the Marxist concept of production forces. K. Ostrowski emphasizes the crucial role of the ruling party in shaping the whole society. The remaining authors discuss various aspects of manipulating social life according to the directives established by the ruling establishment.

Party sociologists rarely complain that there is not enough Marxism in various fields. At the conference on sociology of work and organization in the fall of 1979, K. Doktor complained that the contribution of W. I. Lenin, "the greatest organizational designer of state and Party," was not adequately recognized (Borkowski 1980, 330). At the same conference several sociologists emphasized some vulnerable spots: disparity between the rapidly developing economy and the inefficiency of planning and organization, the low educational level of managing personnel, excess of managers and shortage of workers, the lack of citizen participation, the concentration of organizations on their own goals at the expense of social goals, etc.

The synthesis of social structure in Poland of the mid-1970s was promoted by Polish Marxists with the firm assumptions that Polish society had already started to become a developed socialist society (Wesolowski, ed. , 1978, 5; Widerszpil 1977) and that the Marxist perspective should definitely become the dominant, if not the only, one. From this perspective, division of labor is treated as a decisive reflection of social stratification instead of the traditional class differences. It is assumed that the main political forces in Poland agree that the official socialist ideology should prevail under any circumstances. The program of PUWP is understood as a decisive factor shaping the political attitudes of the working class. At the same time it is admitted that as long as goods are scarce, the distribution of them among various groups may lead to conflicts of vested interests. It is up to the political system to achieve a harmony (Wesolowski and Slomczynski 1978, 32-37).

Marxist sociologists recognized the disproportional growth of various parts of the "working class" and the growing difficulty of adequately defining the progressing differentiation of this class (Wajda 1979), but they remained slow in making theoretical conclusions. Wiatr even suggested to look at how this difficulty relates to the gradual development of a new society free from classes (Wiatr 1980, 313), but he missed the obvious fact that Marx imagined that society to be rich.

During the 1970s the official-line representatives strengthened their contacts and cooperation not only with their Soviet-bloc colleagues (Wesolowski and Stelmach 1977; Andorka and Zagorski 1980) but also with the west. Several spent a considerable amount of time on visits to western countries (Wesolowski, Wiatr, Sztompka, Jasinska, Galeski, etc.). Western acceptance of their scientific contribution was a common goal of the Polish establishment-oriented sociologists despite their alleged ideological differences. It was in their interest to claim that Poland under Soviet state socialism did not differ much from the developed nonsocialist countries in civil rights, well-being of the population, and participatory practices. On the contrary, from the humanitarian perspective, state socialist Poland in many respects was supposed to be even better off (see writings of J. Wiatr and W. Wesolowski), and, therefore, the Polish population was allegedly strongly behind the system.

By reading the writings of the officially promoted Polish sociologists of that time, western colleagues were expected to conclude that human needs and aspirations in Poland were satisfactorily recognized, even if qualitatively differently under Soviet state socialism compared to western democracies. The sociology establishment has executed very efficiently its party duty to offer an attractive image for PUWP in the field of international relations.

The western writings of Sztompka (1974, 1979) and particularly his book on the dialectical paradigm in sociology may be a very useful example of this image. He makes a distinction between Karl Marx as a scientific theorist and as a political prophet. He wants to overcome the current crisis of sociology by applying a dialectic paradigm based on the Marxist tradition.

Sztompka tries to abstract basic ontological, epistemological, and methodological assumptions from the existing theories and discuss them critically. He uses his own analytical model as a measuring stick. "One must postulate the assumptions that can possibly, or potentially, be formulated, and then check by means of concrete illustrations whether or to what extent they are approximated by actual theories" (Sztompka 1979, 25). Sztompka's analysis of the theoretical contribution of sociology is within the framework of the theoretical dilemmas of:

science or humanities? science of man or science of society? the
    problem of demarcation between sociology and other disciplines;
    and

knowledge or action? detachment or bias? man as object or man as
subject? society as a whole or society as an aggregate? the
problem of the ultimate goals of theory construction, as well
as the structure of a theory.

This distinction of various master models, or paradigms, of
sociology serves the author as a meta-theoretical construct for the
reappraisal of sociology from a Marxist perspective. He attempts to
trace the dialectical solutions to several theoretical dilemmas of
sociology. He claims the five traditional dilemmas are spurious.
Sztompka's way of showing it is based on the combination of the thesis
embedded in one of the extreme assumptions with the antithesis embedded in the opposite assumption to produce a dialectic synthesis in
the form of a third alternative assumption (Sztompka 1979, 35). He
understands his own role as the continuation of the Marxian tradition
with Marxism treated as the point of the arrival and not the point of
departure (Sztompka 1979, 36). "In the scientific, open, undogmatic
Marxian orientation, the road out of the current theoretical crisis of
sociology is to be discovered. . . . The crisis of sociology is due
precisely to the neglect of this vital theoretical tradition, or to put it
more precisely, to the neglect of the scientific, paradigmatic aspects
of Marxism, as distinguished from its ideological and moral appeal"
(Sztompka 1979, 36).
    Sztompka treats the problem of demarcation of sociology versus
other disciplines as "an unfortunate survival of the sociological tradition which generates spurious and unfounded divisions among sociologists, contributing thereby to the crisis of sociology" (Sztompka 1979,
36). The Marxist integralist position "that the world is material entails
the common patterns of science; that all cognition is rooted in experiences entails the common patterns of empirical science; that matter
is differentially organized entails the specific procedures of science;
and that the experience is substantively varied entails the specific
procedures of empirical science" (Sztompka 1979, 81).
    Concerning the opposition of the reductionistic and antireduction-
istic standpoints, the final answer once again is to be found in Marx,
who "was able to solve the problem of demarcation in an original and
fruitful way" by accepting sociology as a distinct scientific discipline,
remaining in partnership with other disciplines (Sztompka 1979, 128).
    The same line of reasoning is presented by Sztompka in all re-
maining topics. The Marxist doctrine of the union of theory and practice is for him the answer to the dilemma between cognitivism and
activism. "A sociological theory reflects the social world, which is
constantly being constructed and reconstructed by people, and also
participates in the construction of the social world, by providing knowledge of its qualities and regularities together with directives for chang-

ing it" (Sztompka 1979, 173). The dichotomy of facts and values, according to Sztompka, can be easily solved from the standpoint of "commitment." "Sociology should employ valuations as the necessary ingredient of an unbiased method leading to unbiased knowledge of social reality" (Sztompka 1979, 223). "Only within a valuational perspective can a complete and adequate knowledge of society be achieved" (Sztompka 1979, 231). It is up to the sociologist to identify with the value and interest of the working class. The consciousness of this class "does not develop spontaneously, but rather requires the organizational and theoretical efforts of the leaders, who instill and promote the 'correct' historically adequate perception of the class interest among the class members" (Sztompka 1979, 240).

The dilemma of subject to object, of passivity and autonomy according to Sztompka again finds a solution within the Marxist framework. "Man is seen as actually autonomous, but genetically restricted: possessing control over his actions, but only within limits determined by the encountered natural environment, by his biological constitution, by the social structures within which he operates, and by his experiences with respect to all earlier factors. . . . Human nature is both universal and historical" (Sztompka 1979, 275-76). Collectives are explained by Sztompka with the following vague conclusions: "Sociology is certainly about people, but this does not follow that it must be written in terms of people" (Sztompka 1979, 310). "The multilevel, complex model of a social structure typical of the Marxist orientation comes closer to a full understanding and explanation of social reality and its ontological pecularities than any of the alternative, one-sided, and simplistic images of the collectivists and individualists" (Sztompka, 1979, 323).

It is easy to agree with Sztompka that sociology is in fact in a state of crisis with respect to ontology, epistemology, etc., and that the real focus of the crisis is to be discovered at the level of the fundamental assumptions (Sztompka 1979, 327-28). However, he is wrong in claiming that "the essence of the crisis is the statement of those assumptions in dichotomous, mutually contradictory terms, with a tendency to a growing polarization of standpoints" (Sztompka 1979, 328). By taking sides, and even exaggerating their theoretical claims, social scientists gain insights impossible to be achieved in another way. Sztompka does a disservice to Marxism by trying to solve the theoretical dilemmas on the basis of the common sense statements that may be easily accepted but do not provide any suitable ground for the pursuit of a better understanding of phenomena here under consideration.

A new, unified paradigm of sociology offered by Sztompka and identified with Marxism as a logical outcome of its tradition looks like a sterile exercise. His suggestions for the dialectical resolution of sociological dilemmas seem to violate the basic tenents of Marxism itself. For example, the socioeconomic and sociocultural background of various meta-theoretical counter-currents is totally ignored by Sztompka in his analysis. To be consistent in his Marxist approach, Sztompka should go beyond a purely intellectual basis for the solution of the crisis in sociology and pay attention also to the material conditioning: growth of the modern society, articulation of its internal and external contradictions, class relations, etc. (For other weaknesses of the position taken by Sztompka, see Stehr, 1982.) It is even not necessary to be a Marxist to admit that the crisis of modern sociology has socioeconomic background, and to solve this crisis satisfactorily it is necessary to recognize this conditioning. It seems strange that Sztompka, while claiming to be a Marxist, does not pay attention to this important point.

Sztompka dissects analytically the existing formulations of various meta-theoretical positions but always comes to conclusions identical with the official version of Marxism preached in eastern Europe. His aim is to show that the theoretical dilemmas of western sociology are spurious and that the official east European Marxism in its common-sense, simplified version should be universally accepted as the final word of modern sociology. This message represents Sztompka's major contribution to the task implemented already for years by the east European Marxists to make their official doctrine fully acceptable and "respectable" in the west. It is necessary to say that Sztompka has fulfilled this task excellently by showing a considerable knowledge and skill.

Sztompka does not find it very difficult to argue that several theoretical claims of sociologists violate his common-sense, moderate approach that appears so clearly in everything he finally says. The problem is that, in reality, he returns to the point of departure and does not offer anything constructive. It would be a disservice to Marxism to reduce so much of its intellectual capacity, as Sztompka does unwillingly, by giving priority to common sense knowledge and stating triumphantly that this knowledge is in agreement with official Marxism as taught in eastern Europe.

The global analysis of Polish society during the 1970s was very much influenced by the vested interest of those who gained material support and official recognition for their more or less rosy sociological image of the Polish style of socialist modernization. J. Szczepanski, a sociologist who was appointed to the top state positions even without being a PUWP member, claimed that inefficiencies in Poland originated from the anarchistic inclinations inherent in the Polish national character (Szczepanski 1970). Szczepanski presented in his book a descriptive and eclectic approach without any leading theoretical idea. The full acceptance of the state authority has been Szczepanski's basic message. The Marxist sociologists on their own behalf did everything they could to show how open-minded the Polish officials were and how much they devoted themselves to the struggle for social justice all around the world (except the Soviet bloc). The general aim was to make Poland a display window of state socialism with a manifestly happy working class, an enlightened Marxist intellectual elite, and a very progressive government.

An entirely different approach to the global analysis of Polish society was presented by such independent scholars as A. Podgorecki, S. Nowak, and many others. It was the intention of Podgorecki to locate the constitutive features of Polish society and expose the social, psychological, and cultural bases of the collective behavior of Poles (Podgorecki and Los 1979, 236-47).

The vested interest of the establishment led to the subjugation of any critical analysis and to an omnipotent control. An illuminating example in this respect may be found in the Institute of Social Prevention and Resocialization established in 1973 (Podgorecki 1980, 1981a). This institution prepared the first critical analysis for global distribution of social pathology in Poland that showed how serious the situation was even when the processes of industrialization and urbanization did not lead to the increase of delinquency (Mosciskier 1976, 54). Several other insightful sociological studies have been done by the institute: a study of the demand of experts in the governmental agencies and their utilization, several studies of delinquency, etc. The fact that the chief promoters of these studies were non-Marxist scholars, as well as that the studies revealed some obviously weak spots of the state socialist system, had earned the attention of the PUWP organs. The local PUWP unit inside the institute was activated against the independent scientists occupying some leading positions and particularly against A. Podgorecki. Students were instigated against their own teachers but without success. Finally the core staff was dispersed through the forceful transfer of people to other places. The authorities were scared of the revealed facts and decided to change the policy, reallocating the academic personnel and getting rid of the most dedicated among them. The new management abandoned entirely the previous ambitious program, and the political control of research activities was strengthened (Dziedzicki and Borowski 1981). Many more such cases happened in Poland during the 1970s. All of them resulted from the political establishment's process of getting rid of people who did not act as obedient servants of power and their ideas.

THE GROWING SPLIT AMONG POLISH MARXISTS

The development of Marxism in Poland before the World War II was influenced by several factors. First of all, the struggle for independence had a strong social justice undertone, and for many people the national cause harmonized very well with the social cause. After 1918 several of the socialist leaders oriented themselves to the reform socialism or even left socialism entirely (Pilsudski and his close followers). However, the international orientation represented on one side by R. Luxemburg and on the other side by pro-Soviet communists remained intact even when its influence was limited mostly to intellectual circles (some of artists and intellectuals were financially maintained indirectly or directly by the USSR), the young Jewish generation, such minorities as Belorussians and Ukrainians, etc. The issue of social justice remained the major source of appeal and this was evident, among others, in the type of social research promoted by Marxists.

After the World War II Marxism became the official ideology, and this fact has influenced the cadre selection, scope of interests, type of sponsorship, and even the nature of argumentation. The system has needed its "priests," but the final control remained almost entirely beyond the Marxist priesthood. The pragmatic orientation of the ruling status and power seekers upgraded from the social bottom or incorporated from the career-oriented young offspring of the previously privileged social strata has never allowed the ideological concerns to dominate the communist scene in Poland. The ornamental and propagandistic function of Marxism has been well-settled, and the social justice orientation has almost disappeared entirely from the domestic ideological market.

For the status seekers trying to make a career under Soviet state socialism, Marxism has become a language of loyalty and potential rewards, such as promotion, travel abroad, security, research grants, etc. The opportunistically oriented part of the young generation took for granted during the 1960s and the 1970s that they had to pay for jobs and promotions by claiming allegiance to Marxism, especially when trying to enter the field of social sciences. They wanted secure and rewarding positions, and they did not mind having to pay an ideological price for such a position. The myth of welfare state socialism effectively promoted during the 1970s by Gierek and his companions was a suitable platform for the new Marxist intellectual generation. Members of this generation had common interest in the liberation from the old intelligentsia and its remnants in the academic world. Young Marxists gained full support from the ruling establishment in monopolizing all attractive resources, the professional and managerial positions, contacts with the western scientific centers, publication facilities, editorial offices of the leading professional journals, etc. In exchange for their own privileges, the new scholars provided the ruling establishment with a scientific decorum (Karkowski 1985). Their obligation was to document the growing happiness of the working class, the popularity of state socialism among the masses, etc. In the international field of social sciences, these Polish scholars played an important role in making their western colleagues believe that there is nothing morally and socially wrong with state socialism as practiced in Poland.

This apologetic function of Marxism has not worked very well for several reasons. One of them was the parvenu orientation of the ruling elite that prevented it from accepting and absorbing the Marxist "priests" as the corulers of the country. The Marxist leading "theologians" were supposed to stay within the role of the obedient servants of power, remaining in the hands of people who even did not care to learn Marxism themselves. The orientation in Marxism (and even the knowledge of Russian) remained very low among the ruling elite, which was busy organizing coalitions against each other or consuming others' privileges. Even by the 1950s the professional Marxists were growing dissatisfied with their exclusively servile position. Several had the ambition to gain the high status of intelligentsia, and they were more and more encouraged to challenge the parvenu leadership on intellectual grounds. The political rulers did not hesitate to purge Marxist rebels substituting them with the young careerists willing to remain fully obedient for the sake of promotion. (This process was even more evident in Czechoslovakia after 1968.)

Since the second half of the 1950s it has become relatively safe to rebel intellectually and Marxists have enjoyed in this respect an even greater margin of freedom than the rest of the population. In a country dominated by Christian ideology, any Marxist, even a rebel, was an asset for the ruling establishment. Only in the late 1960s did the idea of pushing the "revisionists" out of the country gain ground within the establishment. The rebellious Marxists have become a permanent part of the Polish scene even if, depending on historical circumstances, their programs differed. In the 1950s the Marxist reformists oriented themselves mainly against the dogmatic interpretation of the doctrine held by the highest levels of the party hierarchy. In the 1960s the Marxist scholars were dissatisfied with the unsophisticated policy making under Gomulka, who personally became a synonym of a simple-minded version of Marxism.

Since the late 1960s the official Marxist orientation sponsored by the ruling elite has definitely gained the upper hand in Polish sociology. The fast growth of this discipline during the 1970s opened room for a career to many young people. Most of them did not have any deep commitment to Marxism, although several claimed to be Marxists because it was necessary for their professional and institutional careers.

Polish non-Marxist intellectuals remained under the dictate of their Marxist colleagues, who remained in constant touch with the centers of political power and were much better informed regarding the current and future policies. It was very often in the vested interest of the rulers to mystify reality, and Marxist scholars willingly or unwillingly became the executors of policies oriented toward the subjugation of society.

Polish Marxists have substantially differed in their readiness to be obedient "servants of power," and this has created several problems for the ruling elite. Even in the late 1940s there were several cases of insubordination. In the mid-1950s an intellectual revolt was stimulated in Poland partly by Marxists. After a big strike and riots in 1956 in Poznan, the revisionistic trend became one of the main sources of a major political upheaval. Since that time it became common among the Marxist intellectuals to show more and more insubordination although the rulers often substituted the "unloyal" elements with people totally subservient (at least for a time). During the 1970s the intellectual contact with the west was already well-established, and the Marxist professional "intellectual workers" demanded more and more independence. They gradually gained courage to have their own view on various matters and defend it against the apparatchiks.

However, the main challenge came in the early 1980s from the blue-collar workers' rebellion, which manifested a deep contradiction between the working class and the ruling Marxist establishment. Paradoxically, the dream of Marx, to see the workers massively revolting against the oppressive and exploitive regime, has been fulfilled in Poland against the Marxist establishment on a scale never met before. Marxist intellectuals were forced to make an unequivocal declaration: either on the side of the PUWP as traditional sponsor and benefactor, or on the side of the proletariat. Never before in history has such a situation happened in a full clarity. Marxists were among the intellectuals sent by the military regime to the internment concentration camps. Even before the introduction of martial law in December 1981, many leading Marxists solemnly declared their allegiance to the reform movement and distanced themselves from the authoritarian version of state socialism.

This "rebellion of theologians" within the Marxist "church" is a very significant phenomenon. Many of these people took the Marxist road only to make a secure professional career. Instead of serving the party in a more uncomfortable capacity, they committed themselves to academic functions. The party provided them with everything that was in its limited capacity, and their aspirations outgrew these relatively modest limits. Increased contact with western Marxism using slogans of social justice, as well as with the western liberalism, stimulated in the Polish Marxists some new concerns, very different from the narrow intellectual and moral horizons of the professional Marxists in the Soviet bloc. The growing concern for the individual, the revival of the young Marx and his sensitivity to alienation, the acceptance of empirical social research, the refinement of research methodology, the close cooperation with several "progressive" western scholars, the concern for Gramsci and other open-minded Marxist thinkers almost completely neglected in the USSR, all of these factors have shaped the intellectual profile of Polish Marxists since the 1950s.

The function of an uncritical apologist for the system and the rulers is becoming increasingly unpopular among Polish Marxists simultaneously with their growing professionalization, sophistication, and exposure to a whole variety of intellectual experiences. By the 1950s, with the departure from Stalinism, the regime was gradually losing its control over the Marxist "priests." Within the Marxist intellectual circle it has become more and more attractive to take a new role of the critic of the system. In this respect intellectuals could easily find a common ground with the informal public opinion and even in some cases they became the leaders of opposition, promoters of democratization, advocates of reason and common sense, enemies of dogmatism and parochialism. This new social role became particularly attractive for the Marxists of a new generation that is free from fears characterizing the survivors of Stalinism and at the same time is actively involved in the rivalry with the old generation. The obvious errors in the economy, sciences, and culture committed by the ruling apparatchiks representing the older generations were used as weapons by the young Marxists. They gained considerable mileage from the exposure of wrong-doing and stupidity committed by the establishment people. It was very significant how enthusiastically the young Marxists joined the reform movement in the early 1980s, vigorously blaming the political establishment.

The military establishment in Poland since December 1981 has at its disposal relatively few professional Marxists of any stature. This does not mean that Marxism as an establishment ideology is finished in Poland. It is always possible to rebuild the Marxist facade and to promote new ambitious young people who are eager to play the role of ideological propagandists. The problem remains that the ideological group officially claimed to be the backbone of socialism has in Poland a long tradition of rebellion, undermining the system quite effectively. Where is the guarantee that the young generations of professional Marxists will not become rebellious, taking the inspiration from the revisionistic heirs? Will the rulers not be tempted to abandon entirely such an ideology that suspiciously feeds its followers with the spirit of rebellion against the establishment?

Paradoxically, under the new circumstances Marxism not only becomes obsolete in its explanatory potential, but also it has to be treated with the growing suspicion by the status quo-oriented power elite. The peaceful and forgiving Christian spirit fits much better into the needs of those who are looking for all possible compromises just to rescue their positions. In several cases it has been easier for the powerful to find common ground with the moderate church and union leaders who give priority to peaceful solutions, than with the products of Marxist indoctrination who approach history in the terms of class war.

The intensification of oppression, regardless of how it is ideologically justified, can only lead to more trouble and insecurity in the long run. Marxism does not offer any chance of reconciliation, which is badly needed by Poles. There is little hope for Marxism as an active ideology in Poland when taking into consideration that even the radical elements among the trade union underground are totally disinterested in any version of Marxism.

THE REVISIONIST CRITIQUE

The position taken by the Polish Marxist revisionists purged from Poland by the ruling establishment differs widely from the position presented above. The revisionist position questions the benevolent character of the party and state authority, emphasizes the gap between the vested interests of the working masses and the people in power, and the bureaucratization of the whole Soviet–style state socialism.

The allocation of administrative privileges and subordination of the whole society to the party hierarchy is, according to M. Hirszowicz (1980), the central feature of communist rule in eastern Europe. She does not differ in this basic point from several prominent western critics of Soviet communism: Koestler, Deutscher, and others. From this perspective, the advance of the socialist order has to lead to more enslavement as long as the democratic freedom is denied to society. Sovereign bureaucracy dominant in the Soviet bloc is primarily focused on the maintenance of power at any cost, and the monohierarchical order of the party state remains in constant disagreement with several vital interests of the population that are stifled. "The principle lesson that may be drawn from the history of communism in eastern Europe is that bureaucratic dictatorship tends to reconstruct society along bureaucratic lines, a simple truth that has been widely ignored by the apologists of the communist policies" (Hirszowicz 1980, 36). This is a deceptive dream of the totalitarian order into which societies are forced through omnipotent control, omnipresent supervision, and all-pervasive power. The population is mobilized to fulfill obediently the tasks formulated by the ruling elite.

Is there any opportunity to change this system for the better? Hirszowicz is quite pessimistic in this respect, and the events in Poland since the introduction of the martial law in December 1981 verify this pessimism. The party state may change but without necessarily abandoning the bureaucratic dictatorship. Increased administrative and police oppression are widely used by the authorities to suppress disturbances appearing from time to time within the system. The extension of privileges to ambitious individuals and groups leads to the co-optation of them. Modern technology offers many sophisticated organizational and propagandistic weapons. Stalin erected the foundation of the bureaucratic rule, and even with the progressing diversification of organizational forms within Soviet-bloc countries this tradition has managed to survive.

Kolakowski, in his Main Currents of Marxism (1978) says, among others, that the centralized management of the means of production and the abolition of large private ownership have proved to be devasting. "In the event it turned out that, having nationalized the means of production, it was possible to erect on this foundation a monstrous edifice of lies, exploitation, and oppression. This was not itself a consequence of Marxism; rather, Communism was a bastard version of the socialist ideal" (Kolakowski 1978, 3:526). This criticism of Soviet socialism was widespread in Polish independent intellectual circles much before Kolakowski's break with Marxism, and it probably influenced his own growing ideological disillusionment. However, the main role was played by the confrontation of the doctrine with the reality of its implementation. Kolakowski had enough common sense and feeling of justice to break with doctrine that proved to be unworkable.

The greatest emancipation in history promised by Marx has led to a universal rationing under which the more powerful gain disproportionately more and the less privileged receive disproportionately less. Kolakowski emphasizes that perfect equality cannot survive without perfect despotism. Within the socialist societies there are several obvious inequalities that perpetuate themselves because of the omnipotent bureaucracy. Communist parties are overwhelmingly founded on white-collar worker participation and commitment, but there is a long tradition to upgrade the lower classes and to utilize them for the benefit of the system. According to Hirszowicz,

> Contradictions are built into the system, owing to the way individual and collective incomes are allocated. Every section of the population may thus expect a larger share of the national product at the expense of other sections, administrative privilege being the best example of how the higher strata of the bureaucracy can use the means available to them for their own benefit. . . . Stratification appears as a divisive factor that at the same time operates as an integrative force of sorts by destroying the

links between different occupational sectors and reinforc-
ing their dependence on the power centre" (Hirszowicz
1980, 118, 121).

According to several Polish Marxist revisionists, the view that
Marxism should be institutionalized as an instrument of power and
that its content must be governed by the needs of the struggle for
power comes originally from Lenin, but it found a full implementation
only under Stalin. Kolakowski argues that Stalinism was a true development of Leninism. "Stalin as a despot was much more the party's
creation than its creator; he was the personification of a system which
irresistibly sought to be personified" (Kolakowski 1978, 3:5). As regards Trotsky, he was far from being more democratic than other
Soviet leaders. The doctrine of Trotskyism was artificially fabricated
by Stalin to denounce his main rival.

Stalin "realized Marxism-Leninism is the only possible way by
consolidating his dictatorship over society, destroying all social ties
that were not state-imposed and all classes, including the working
class itself" (Kolakowski 1978, 3:419). Stalin decided not to return
to the New Economic Policy (NEP), which would permit free trade
and this way also would limit the omnipotence of the state.

It is necessary to remember that in the USSR freedom was effectively suppressed in the early 1920s. However, at least Marxism
was not still codified and a considerable latitude remained intact to
interpret Marxist applications in various fields. For example, in
Trotsky's view, "it was wrong to canonize any particular literary
style, or label creative forms as progressive or reactionary regardless of their content" (Kolakowski 1978, 3:52). The development of
totalitarianism was related not only to the nature of Leninism or to
the personal inclinations of Stalin but also to the internal power struggle between various pressure groups. "Writers and others seeking a
monopoly for their views accepted and encouraged the baneful principle
that it was for the party and state authorities to permit or prohibit this
or that form of art. The destruction of Soviet culture was in part the
work of its own representatives" (Kolakowski 1978, 3:52). There was
a strong pressure from all quarters to make attractive positions available for the status seekers and careerists willing to pay any price for
their own upgrading. The socialist system, by supporting the promotion
of lower classes, contributed greatly to the above-mentioned pressure.
Stalin, in his struggle against political rivals, used very skillfully the
mechanism of promotion by condemning millions of people to concentration camps and substituting them with the loyalistic and ambitious
new people upgraded from the bottom. There was no effective resistance against what Stalin did because all independent moral and material
authorities were already destroyed. "There is no evidence that any of

the party leaders at any time protested or attempted to prevent repressions or obviously faked trials, as long as none of the victims was a Bolshevik" (Kolakowski 1978, 3:56).

Marxism already in the late 1920s became a dogma, and even the opposition of the natural scientists to philosophic interference was defeated. "Philosophy's service to the party was to consist purely and simply in glorifying its successive decisions. Philosophy was not an intellectual process but a means of justifying and inculcating the state ideology in whatever form it might assume. . . . The significance of Stalinism for philosophy does not lie in any particular conclusions that were forced upon it, but in the fact that servility became practically its whole raison d'etre" (Kolakowski 1978, 3:76).

Great purges of the late 1930s in the USSR had practically eliminated any political debate even inside the ruling party.

> The object of a totalitarian system is to destroy all forms
> of communal life that are not imposed by the state and
> closely controlled by it, so that individuals are isolated
> from one another and become mere instruments in the
> hands of the state. . . . The purge was designed to de-
> stroy such ideological links as still existed within the
> party, to convince its members that they had no ideology
> or loyalty except to the latest order from the high, and
> to reduce them, like the rest of society, to a powerless,
> disintegrated mass (Kolakowski 1978, 3:86–87).

The Soviet society exposed to a series of purges was unable to develop any resistance. People were morally annihilated, and "the victims of persecutions were reduced to the degrading role of accessories to the crimes committed against themselves, and participants in the universal campaign of falsification" (Kolakowski 1979, 3:87).

The official Soviet statements were greatly successful in diverting the attention and moral sensitivity of western intellectuals from the actual suppression of basic human rights in the USSR. "Ideology and wishful thinking were stronger than the most manifest reality. . . . The system had been brought to an almost ideal state of perfection, in which civil society hardly existed any more and the population seemed to have no other purpose than to obey the behests of the state personified in Stalin" (Kolakowski 1978, 3:89, 91). Outside the USSR many intellectuals identified Soviet communism with Marxism and remained totally blind to the reality of society under Soviet state socialism. "Hypocrisy and self-delusion had become the permanent climate of the intellectual Left" (Kolakowski 1978, 3:116).

This situation continued in the USSR after World War II with the intentions to stop kowtowing to the west and to destroy any intellectual endeavor independent of the state. Even cybernetics was condemned as a pseudoscience because being a discipline of a wide scope it challenged the priority of Marxism-Leninism. The Soviet military circles managed to rehabilitate cybernetics as a discipline of a particular utility for them.

The hate of everything that looked different from the Soviet tradition was seen not only in Stalin and his followers but also in the whole bureaucratic parvenu class dominating over the Soviet society.

> The nation's culture was that of a parvenu—its every feature expressing almost to perfection the mentality, beliefs, and tastes of somebody enjoying power for the first time. . . . The Soviet governing class consisted mainly of individuals of workers' and peasant origin, very poorly educated and with no cultural background, a thirst for privileges and filled with hatred and envy towards genuine "hereditary" intellectuals. The essential trait of the parvenu is his incessant urge to "make a show," and accordingly his culture is one of make-believe and window dressing (Kolakowski 1978, 3:144).

The vulgarized version of Marxism was a very suitable ideology for this class of people. According to Kolakowski, "It would be absurd to say that Marxism was predestined to become the ideology of the self-glorifying Russian bureaucracy. Nevertheless, it contained essential features, as opposed to accidental and secondary ones, that made it adaptable to this purpose" (Kolakowski 1978, 3:161). The political life of Marxism as the ideological weapon of communists is understandable as a manipulatory device in the power game. Marxists have learned how to take advantage of the existing confusion and frustration to channel aggressive feelings using in this respect some fragments taken from Marx. "At present Marxism neither interprets the world nor changes it; it is merely a repertoire of slogans serving to organize various interests, most of them completely remote from those with which Marxism originally identified itself" (Kolakowski 1978, 3:530).

The Polish Marxist revisionists pay particular attention to the contradictions within the socialist society. From their perspectives the bureaucratic party state hampers economic growth even when it is vitally interested in giving full support to this growth. The elimination of a genuine social control makes it easier for the ruling elite to practice policy making, but the whole system becomes even more vulnerable to some serious deviations. The lack of institutional flexibility triggers social conflicts. Overcentralization causes unavoidable delays in decision making. A defensive position of functionaries versus clients, customers, and outsiders influences efficiency negatively.

Organizational inducements are not harmonized with the nature of the tasks to be performed nor with the needs and aspirations of performers. Rules and regulations grow excessively. Party organs are constantly busy interfering with the various organizational units, but this is much more a nuisance than a real help. Bending the rules is a common practice. Informal and formal structures penetrate each other in a negative manner. The quest for spectacular achievements is the source of waste and cheating. Various vested interest groups exercise their pressure on planning; they change priorities and introduce chaos. The social costs of many economic programs are not considered, and this harms the public interest. All these contradictions impose limits on the rationality of a planned society.

The contradiction between the intelligentsia and bureaucracy is also an important factor of imbalance. On one hand, the ruling bureaucrats need experts whose number is constantly growing. On the other hand, the members of the intelligentsia maintain the tradition of social consciousness foreign to bureaucratic communism and potentially dangerous to its rule. For example in Poland, "the educated and articulate carriers of opposition not only regard themselves as the heirs to the old Polish intelligentsia but for some observers they are the intelligentsia in the proper sense of the word. . . . As fighters for the cause and guardians of public interests they are encouraged and supported by members of the public who sympathize with their demands and expect them to be the advocates of social justice" (Hirszowicz 1980, 198).

EXAMPLES OF SOCIOLOGICAL INSIGHTS AND DIAGNOSIS

Until the late 1960s it was possible for several independently minded Polish sociologists to question, at least indirectly, the wisdom of political leadership. With the deaths of Stanislaw Ossowski in the 1960s and Maria Ossowski in 1974, as well as the elimination of several Marxist reformists from the academic life during the late 1960s, not much remained in sociology to maintain its previous high intellectual and moral spirit. Young sociologists who were dissatisfied with the status quo had to find allies outside of the government-controlled discipline. The underground political opposition, since 1976 tolerated by the government at least to some extent, became a basis of global diagnosis of society much different from the more-or-less rosy picture presented by official sociologists (Matejko 1981b).

With the economic situation clearly deteriorating since the mid-1970s, the gap between the official version of Poland's fate and the underground version has widened considerably. According to the loyalistic creed, everything was fine in the Polish society with some transitory difficulties arising from the rapid growth. According to the gloomy diagnosis of the dissidents, Poland was a highly unequal society with very large pockets of poverty; a self-appointed establishment that relies on force and on the party; and a young generation much limited in its chances to succeed in life. It is quite significant that sons and daughters of prominent party elite move to prestigious, more secure, and less demanding positions in the academic world, scientific institutes, cultural facilities, journalism.

Since the second half of the 1970s relations between the ruling establishment and almost the whole nation have rapidly deteriorated in Poland. After the successful strike of shipyard workers in Gdansk, various groups—mainly blue-collar workers, professionals, and postsecondary students—declared their autonomy from the government and party authority. In the fall of 1981 even the police force, before absolutely loyal to the regime, established its own union and declared its allegiance to the democratic principles. According to a survey done at the end of 1980 and based on a national quota sample of about 2,500 people, the agreement made between the government and Solidarity was supported by 92 percent of the adult population and almost 60 percent of the PUWP members (Adamski et al., 1981, 10). The government definitely appeared to be unpopular, especially among blue-collar workers. The full support for new arrangements was shown by 82 percent of blue-collar workers, about 40 percent of farmers and intelligentsia respectively, but only a small percentage of the ruling apparatus (Adamski et al., 1981, 17). Even among the trade union members remaining outside Solidarity, only 10 percent evaluated the new movement negatively. The survey also revealed the farmers' great concern for the delivery of agricultural machines and spare parts, the urban population's concern with housing shortage, bad food supply, and family, as well as the lack of public credibility suffered by the governmental institutions.

Even more interesting are the options taken by respondents for the pluralistic model of society: higher role of nonparty members—92 percent; workers' self-government—86 percent; more control of those in power by the society—92 percent; freedom of information—83 percent; decentralization—80 percent; stronger role of the church in public life—79 percent. Only 11 percent preferred a stronger role for PUWP in the exercise of power (Adamski 1981, 104-105). There was a clear demand for more equality in society, but at the same time there was a demand for more discipline.

Events in Poland until the introduction of martial law in December 1981 reflected a growing mass pressure to liberate the individual and the group initiative, as well as to limit the role of the state. Free trade unions in the urban and rural areas pushed for the limitation of central control for the benefit of local initiatives. Yet, the ruling political elite had a vested interest in maintaining the state control and in promoting the model of a socialist mass society thoroughly penetrated by the ruling party and the governmental bureaucracy. To stay in power, the elite did not hesitate to use the martial law and to imprison thousands of people.

In this confrontation of two opposite models—democratic and totalitarian—the essence of society is at stake. In the first of these two models socialization is treated as a spontaneous process in which individuals choose voluntarily between various personal and social patterns depending on their own preferences. The defense of basic freedoms is much in the tradition of Poles, who during the whole nineteenth century suffered under partitions forced on Poland by neighboring states. Poles had to learn to defend their own national and religious identity against hostile foreign powers. In the totalitarian model socialization is treated as an artificial imposition on immature people such patterns that would be handy to shape the society according to the superior preferences of the rulers, who enjoy a monopoly of final truth and final answers.

The collectivistic elements are still quite strong in the Polish traditional social consciousness, but they are gradually weakening. The tragedy of Polish history has strengthened the inclination of Poles toward individualism (Leslie et al., 1980). The unattractiveness of the state socialist model during the last forty years was so obvious to a large majority of Poles that the public appeal of collectivism was very limited. Now the economic crisis, mass repressions, and the general turmoil in Poland encourage many young Polish people to take any occasion to leave the country for good.

An important side effect of the present day confrontation in Poland is the growing ability to reconcile the public and private interests manifested in Solidarity and other independent bodies. The artificial suppression of private concerns for the benefit of public concerns is much in the tradition of Soviet state socialism and has led in Poland to the opposite effects. People widely concentrate their attentions on their own interests hidden under the clever disguise of the public interest. Some openly reject public for the benefit of their own private ends. The spontaneous development of various autonomous and self-governmental bodies in Poland between September 1980 and December 1981 led to an authentic socialization on a scale so far unknown in the Soviet bloc. People started to trust each other and were ready to join forces to contribute to the common good.

According to the official doctrine, people in Poland were supposed to become much more socially oriented than under conditions of a market economy. Taking into consideration hardships of a rapid industrialization and the heavy burden imposed on society (low wages and very modest housing conditions) it would be reasonable to expect at least some sociomoral advantages. There are several sociological studies that provide an insight into this problem.

Being officially the backbone of socialist society, the blue-collar workers were expected to be particularly supportive of the ruling PUWP. In industry every fourth worker was a PUWP member in the early 1970s (Jarosinska and Kulpinska 1978, 162). However, workers faced the consequences of mismanagement in the nationalized enterprises that are the result either of local failures or of the ineffectiveness on a marco scale. Mismanagement harms workers directly because they do not receive expected bonuses (Waclawek 1974, 141). The 1979 study of about 1,200 male employees in thirteen heavy-industry work places in Upper Silesia (Poplucz 1980) shows a high tendency to move even among the workers with a generally positive work attitude. The relatively high labor turnover is one of the acute problems of the Polish industry.

It was well-documented by 1980 that those institutions assigned to represent the working class were malfunctioning, but that documentation did not go far enough. Several official sociologists functioned as apologists of the existing system. For example, according to K. Ostrowski (1970) the role of trade unions is to articulate the expectations of their members and to mobilize the membership to implement the goals formulated by the political authorities. The fact that there may be a considerable gap between the genuine interests of workers and the official PUWP line was neglected by Ostrowski's analysis.

The study done in the first half of the 1970s on a sample of 2,858 blue-collar workers representing the 163 greatest industrial enterprises in Poland shows a considerable difference between the actual functioning of workers' councils or trade union councils and the desired role of them. In general, respondents wanted local councils to focus more on representing worker's interests and comanagement of enterprises and less on how to mobilize workers to work harder (Hryniewicz 1980, 260). More than half of the workers (but only about 3 percent of the top administration) felt that they did not have enough influence on the councils; 40 percent of them also felt that the workers' councils and the trade unions had too little say in the enterprise (Hryniewicz 1980, 262-63). The same was documented in the previous studies (Owieczko 1970, Gilejko 1970).

In Hryniewicz's study about 20 percent of the workers claimed that the influence of PUWP and the top administration was too high (Hryniewicz 1980, 263). Most of the workers felt that their expectations regarding safety, pay, and participation were not satisfactorily met by the enterprise organs: top administration, supervisors, PUWP committee, trade unions, and workers' councils (Hryniewicz 1980, 266). From 36 percent to 47 percent of workers were aware of conflicts between their group interests and the vested interests of other groups.

This was especially valid for the establishment of work norms and bonuses as well as the allocation of housing space, jobs, and a subsidized stay in the tourist hostels (Hryniewicz 1980, 27). There was also a lack of belief that making requests through the official channels counted much (Hryniewicz 1980, 274).

Contrary to the official PUWP policy to politicize blue-collar workers favorably, the sociological data reveal an evident concern of these workers with issues far from politics and the official ideology. A comparative study done in 1973 on two samples of the industrial labor force—young (2,059 people in the ages of 17-30) and "old" (1,091 people in the ages 45 and over)—shows that in both cases workers give priority to personal happiness in family life and occupation. To be a political activist was the least attractive alternative (Adamski 1980, 147). Family life is given priority more often among more educated workers than less educated workers, and the opposite is true for the occupational expertise. The same is valid for differentiation according to socioeconomic position (Hryniewicz 1980, 153, 155). Young people concern themselves much less on material well-being than the old generation and much more to knowledge (Hryniewicz 1980, 158).

The 1975 study of how people spend their free time and money among the families of urban workers and employees in Upper Silesia shows that 41 percent of free time and 68 percent of cultural expenditures were allocated to family and friendship contacts; only 4 percent and 3 percent respectively were allocated to local cultural institutions. On the other hand, 56 percent of free time was devoted to the external cultural services, mainly TV (Milic-Czerniak 1980, 242).

The impact of the traditional intelligentsia on contemporary intellectuals is quite substantial. Sicinski claims that writers' social composition and problems remained essentially the same as during the interwar period, even with the influx of the people from lower strata (Sicinski 1971, 124). Among the young intelligentsia, dependence on parents is lower now than it used to be. Still, although the young intellectual "considers himself an adult person he relies on his parents' material financial aid. He does not take full responsibility for this life" (Los 1977, 125). The great housing shortage and very low salaries of people beginning their professional careers make material dependence on parents a necessity. Having this support, the young intellectual remains to some extent isolated from reality, and is allowed to indulge in principalism and idealism. "Hypocrisy, routine, ideological opportunism receive his disapproval. . . . He stresses education and development of his own personality and individuality" (Los 1977, 125).

The ethics of contemporary Polish people have been influenced by their growing education, as well as by exposure to mass media and social mobility. In this respect there are some clear differences between the intelligentsia and the rest of the population (Los 1977, 1979).

For the intelligentsia already occupying some important positions there is not much more to look for in terms of social upgrading; among other strata there is great aspiration to improve one's well-being as well as life perspectives.

The study done in 1972 on a random sample of 5 percent of the Polish labor force has shown considerable social mobility (44 percent of respondents were in a different socioeconomic group than their fathers), and this was especially valid for the white-collar workers. The outflow from farming to other occupations is typical not only for Poland but also for other Soviet-bloc countries. For example, in Poland, Czechoslovakia, and Hungary, the outflow from the farmer stratum to the blue-collar stratum is a little over 40 percent, and to the white-collar stratum is about 30 percent. Forty percent of blue-collar workers in Poland and Czechoslovakia are of peasant origin (in Hungary 55 percent). About 20 percent of Polish blue-collar workers move to the white-collar stratum, 25 percent in Hungary, and 35 percent in Czechoslovakia (Zagorski 1976).

By 1960 social mobility started to stabilize due to the declining number of openings in the white-collar ranks. The children of the white-collar stratum more and more were forced to satisfy themselves with blue-collar jobs (Zagorski 1976, 29). In the period 1970-76 the share of young people entering the vocational schools had grown from 31 percent to 54 percent. Among them only 7 percent were from the white-collar families in 1976. Vocational education is the main vehicle of social upgrading among the blue-collar workers and peasants. However, it would not be justified to assume that formal education is the only factor that counts for Poles. In the survey based on a national sample of about 6,000 people between the ages of 15 and 45, it was found that 56 percent of Poles do not treat formal education as the only factor of being sophisticated, and 38 percent of them concentrate on intellect, character, good manners, etc. to describe a well-educated person (Wisniewski 1980, 209).

The review of various surveys dealing with occupational prestige done in between 1958 and 1975 (Pohoski et al., 1976) shows professionals being at the top and followed consecutively by semiprofessionals and technicians, supervisors, skilled manual workers, individual farmers, office workers, service workers, craftspeople, and skilled manual workers. At the top and the bottom of this hierarchy there is a considerable homogeneity. Occupational categories in the middle are heterogeneous and partly overlap with each other. As regards division of labor between sexes, Poles are still quite conservative. The majority of them think that child care and upbringing belong only to women. Shopping and the household duties are mostly done by women (Sokolowska 1976, 42).

Because of the general shortage and the red tape, there are

usually so many difficult situations that friends are constantly needed. "The bureaucratized administrative apparatus especially in the case of state-owned economy becomes so routinized, inelastic, decentralized and powerless that the central organs may know no other way to keep this apparatus functioning than by saturating it with their own ramified 'mafia'" (Podgorecki and Los 1979, 200).

The formal structure becomes a front for the informal network of private mutual interests, commitments, and loyalties (Podgorecki and Los 1979, 202-203). Within the framework of reciprocal arrangements, people make deals of various kinds and use institutions for their own benefit, even if this is contrary to the official purpose and against the public good as understood by the rulers. Conformism within the circle of friends is the cost that people are willing to pay to maintain psychological and material support found in these circles.

For Poles success means locating themselves vocationally in an exclusive position (Narojek 1976, 47) that offers some privileges, secures a good bargaining position, offers personal freedom, and has barriers against competition. Because such positions are rare, there is some sense of deprivation. People strive to achieve high vocational skills, but even with those skills an exclusive position is not necessarily available. For example, many young people become disillusioned with higher education when opportunities so greatly differ from expectations. Yet, channels of social upgrading other than education are limited or unattractive. It is significant that in Poland positions of power (manager, party boss) are not very attractive among the young generation (Narojek 1976, 45).

At the same time under the bureaucratic dominance there is not much opportunity to gain a real satisfaction from work. "Only an insignificant minority expect work to satisfy demands of a different sort—perfection of one's talents, the sense of self-realization or acting for the good of others, in exceptional cases fame and public approval" (Nowak 1980, 7). Dissatisfaction with work is partly related to the fact that in the Polish public opinion economic virtues are not of primary importance, although in the 1975 survey of around 2,500 Poles these virtues were mentioned much more often (43 percent) than military virtues (26 percent). Deviant behavior (alcoholism, bad mutual treatment, stealing, laziness, etc.) dominated among the factors of shame (Makarczyk 1979). In the same survey professional experts, except popular scientists and artists, were rarely mentioned as contributing to the past or present fame of the nation. PUWP was mentioned in this capacity only in 5 percent of cases. On the other hand, 30 percent of choices for the present contributions to fame were given to sports figures.

The main problem seems to be located in the overbureaucratization, which diminishes the motivation of people to be promoted to higher positions (in which there is too much of red tape and boring routine), lowers job satisfaction and creates many tensions (Matejko 1980a). Several big economic projects lack human touch. They were designed and implemented without any real concern for people as producers and consumers. The grandiose projects were promoted at any cost to satisfy the ambitions of influencial people involved in their own struggles for more power and prestige. The study by Sufin (1979) of a new industrial center in Pulawy is very characteristic in this respect. The author shows all the advantages of this ambitious project but does not pay enough attention to the human cost related to the underdevelopment of local services, poor housing, long and cumbersome travel to work and back, etc. (these shortcomings of the study were shown by Jalowiecki 1980). Many investments in various fields of life do not provide adequate results due to bureaucratization. It is evident even in the field of public health.

A comparison of morbidity and health services functioning in Lodz and Liverpool at the end of the 1960s shows morbidity indicators much higher in Lodz (three times higher chronicity with disability, as well as high severity; twice as high anxiety; 30 percent more of sick days), but at the same time a much less efficient delivery of health services. Polish hospitals are overburdened by cases that should be treated outside and much earlier to prevent the further deterioration of the patient's health (Rychard 1979, 94).

Polish sociologists, in order to earn a reputation at home as well as abroad, become involved in the global analysis of all the phenomena mentioned above. A sound scientific background of the social economic policy is now needed more than before. After December 1981 again there is no independent authority in Poland able to question decisions made by the top levels of party and government except the Catholic Church.

The active role of sociologists in Polish society is much more complicated due to the deepening confrontation between the government and the dissident social forces. The apologetic role played by the politically trusted sociologists for PUWP's benefit is totally bankrupt. The information monopoly has been effectively broken in the consciousness of the Polish masses.

To be trusted and considered seriously in society, sociologists have to provide well-documented insight into the social problems of their society, free from any obvious biases in favor of their institutional sponsors. Especially vulnerable in this respect are any studies that used to be politically doctored: the working and living conditions of the working class, economic delinquency and its sources, the dysfunctions of state bureaucracy, the dependence of employees on their bosses, managerial problems, politics. Poland badly needs the honest and reliable sociotechnics that would provide a bridge between research and social practice, social scientists and administrators, thinking and doing (see Podgorecki 1975).

It is difficult to imagine a new beneficial role of sociology in the contemporary Polish society without the recovery of civil rights and the elimination of all free centers of public opinion. The quality of sociological expertise suffered considerably under the regime that existed until September 1980 and the same, unavoidably, has to happen under the rule exercised by the military junta. On the other hand, the democratic spirit is definitely stronger among Polish social scientists than in the rest of the Soviet bloc, and it will be difficult for the state and party authorities to suppress it entirely. The liberal tradition of Polish sociology has a great appeal among the young generation of the intelligentsia, and there is a great promise that the devotion to intellectual freedom will not disappear under any circumstances.

The essential features of contemporary Polish society do not seem to fit to the basic concepts of the Marxist social analysis. This was a limiting factor in sociology, which was so strongly dominated by official Marxists particularly during the 1970s. The doctrine of PUWP has shaped the minds of sociologists occupying the most responsible and influential positions. Neither the transformation of the economic basis due to the socialist industrialization nor the Marxist indoctrination on a large scale nor even the mass promotion of lower class people through the educational and bureaucratic channels has led to a social order that would become established in the actual behavior or consciousness of people.

It is necessary to remember that in Polish society mimicry is a long-practiced way of survival. It was needed in partitioned Poland to protect Polish culture and interest in the Polish nationhood. In that period an author would sometimes write "society" but he had "nation" in mind. In the sociological vocabulary "association" stood for "partitionary powers" and "community" did for "nation" (Kurczewska 1975, 64). The distinction between the nation and the state has traditionally been much better understood by Poles than by members of many other nations. In modern times mimicry also plays a major role. Even under the name of Marxist official studies, several insightful critical approaches have been practiced in Poland. This phenomenon is impossible in the USSR, East Germany, or Czechoslovakia.

NOTES

1. In the period 1975-83 the share of science in the governmental budget has diminished from 2.4 percent to 1.1 percent.
2. A half of them are under 40 years old.
3. Sixty-five percent of young scientists do not have their own apartments.

6 EPILOGUE

Work systems differ considerably in their relative "openness" and "closeness": this distinction has much to do with their adaptability to internal and external change. Many tensions and even most catastrophies in the western industrial relations systems result to a large extent from their openness. New people and new trends become easily absorbed and the system has afterwards many problems of digesting the additions. Adaptation, though, is many times a superficial phenomenon, more a window dressing than a reality, as is true in many places with participatory management, minority rights, junior executive training, etc. On the other hand, the acceptance of the fact that the system is naturally imperfect keeps it potentially innovative.

A much different story is found in the systems that assume some perfection which is the case of Marxism, among others. As long as they are accepted and maintained on the basis how naturally "good" they are supposed to be, any critique and any attempt to modify them encounters a very strong resistance. People in power feel personally endangered. The broader systems of a political nature do not tolerate any deviation of established schemes. Innovators are identified with trouble-makers and are pushed into the margin or neutralized in another way. Even people at the bottom of the hierarchy are suspicious of potential reform because they have a vested interest in hiding and preserving their own informal way of beating the system. In the battle between "innovators" and "mediocrities" within the well-established bureaucracies often the former become the victims of the latter (Matejko 1984, ch. 7; Mohan 1979, ch. 1).

The pursuit of policy contrary to self-interest is seen not only among individuals but also among public bodies, including work systems (Brewer and Leon 1983). According to Tuchman, "Wooden-headedness, the source of self-deception, is a factor that plays a remarkably large role in government. It consists in assessing a situation in terms of preconceived fixed notions while ignoring or rejecting any contrary signs. It is acting according to wish while not allowing oneself to be deflected by the facts. . . . Wooden-headedness is also the refusal to benefit from experience" (Tuchman 1984, 7).

It is not very difficult to demonstrate that the work systems widely practiced in the Soviet bloc under the name of state socialism are demonstrably unworkable or counter-productive from the perspective of a general social welfare. They meet the resistance of the population and result in informal reactions oriented toward the promotion of the private good at the expense of the public good as imagined and represented by the official authorities. In Poland this has become more evident than in other parts of the bloc because of the peculiar characteristics of Polish society presented in this book.

Poles even under the Soviet state socialism have preserved their humanity and spontaneity: The informal organization in Poland has flourished behind the ossified formal facade probably more than in the Soviet Union. The Polish traditional culture and spirituality have been relatively well preserved even under the tough Stalinist period of the early 1950s; strong family bonds are intact despite the long hours of work of all adults and the daily irritations of consumer shortages and a deepening generation gap. The main sociotechnical question is how to incorporate the natural human assets of Poles into the modern complex organizations.

One of the paradoxes of the official Marxist optimistic global analysis of society was the a priori exclusion of any unexpected change. The assumption about the socioeconomic development according to scientific laws from presocialist stages through various levels of socialism up to communism in the far future excluded, in practice, the serious attention paid to any major spontaneous deviations; especially when the path of socialism was well-secured within the Soviet bloc by the power of one-party states. This reliance on laws reveals a conservative inclination of official Marxists who do not have any intellectual tools to meet the unexpected.

By identifying himself with a "permanent" order, the conservative looks for security and self-assurance. According to Kolakowski, the conservative

> loves to boast of his consistency, of the stubborn persistence of his own ideals and kinds of behavior, for he acquires a feeling of identity and authenticity only when he is able to link this with the highest sum of stable qualities. . . . While nihilism represents camouflaged adaptation to any reality and is ready to adapt itself to any change, while

it abandons responsibility by questioning the effectiveness
of every moral enterprise, conservatism gains the same
end by using different means" (Kline 1971, 159-61).

As long as they dealt with the monolithic structure, the Polish
official Marxists enjoyed a free hand in dealing with the analysis of
society. According to Wesolowski, the Polish working class was integrated primarily through party organizations and additionally through
official union organization and official workers' self-government
(Slomczynski and Krauze 1978, 46). Wesolowski treated the leadership of the party and its ideological dominance in the society as the
basic dimensions of the political and doctrinal hegemony of the working class (Slomczynski and Krauze 1978, 47). The present day Polish
working class, which articulates its program and demands outside of
the ruling Marxist party and even against it, represents for official
Marxists a theoretical and practical problem. The legitimacy of official power has been shaken by the phenomenon of Solidarity and this
is a matter of survival for the PUWP.

During 1981 Solidarity was able to increase involvement in
workers' self government and economic reforms only because the
government was so ineffective in these areas. This involvement led
to more and more confrontation with the government and the ruling
PUWP and finally to the imposition of martial law in December 1981.

Sociologists do a very good diagnostic job of trying to establish
institutional conditions under which the socially constructive initiatives
of task-oriented people may be adequately initiated, maintained, and
implemented. The collapse of productivity and institutional control in
most Polish governmental institutions is related to a large extent
exactly to their impersonality and inability to socialize people into
the meaningful work teams representing something more than just
the organizational units.

Changing historical circumstances in Poland have forced the
ruling authorities to switch from time to time to a different policy
model. All these models have had an ultimate goal of strengthening
the allegiance of Poland to the Soviet bloc and to implement a socialist
society based on industrialization, the nationalization of production
means, Marxist ideology, one-party rule, etc. To achieve these goals,
it seemed necessary for the ruling elite to weaken very considerably
the traditional social bonds, religious commitments, even family
bonds.

The tough policy promoted under the assumption that "we know
better what is good for all of us, including you" was fully developed
in Poland already since the first half of the 1950s. Between 1947 and
1975 capital accumulation has grown from 15 percent to 36 percent of
the national income at the expense of consumption; while later, accumu-

tion has declined to 22 percent in 1983 (Maly 1984, XXIX). Industrial growth was fast, but it occurred at the cost of the living standard, enforced mobilization of the labor power, a very serious restriction of civil rights, and the application of coercion in the case of meeting any resistance.

The results were very impressive in heavy industry, but the neglect of agriculture had laid the ground for the future food shortages. Official ideology imposed upon the population led to the lack of mutual trust between the ruling and the ruled. Omnipotent bureaucracy contributed to the ossification and provided ground for the growth of counter-cultures and informal dealings of an illegal or semi-legal character. People withdrew from the public field and concentrated themselves on their private interests, paying lip service to the official order. The ruling party disposed of everything available in the society, but the feedback from the rank and file did not work anymore. People were just too scared to say openly what they thought. The cost of an enforced socialization was substantial in terms of low productivity, disguised privatization, semiaristocratic rule by a self-appointed elite, formal rigidity, communication gaps, and the growing market shortages.

All attempts after 1955 until the 1970s to liberalize the model were not successful, and a more ambitious reform was tried in the early 1970s. The proposal to modernize Poland with generous loans from the west won the leaders' approval. In the 1970s the western money, mostly from western Europe, was used to buy technical equipment and even food. It was an ambitious plan to create in Poland a basis for future handsome profits gained from the foreign trade. The authorities were willing to intensify their contacts with the west and even remain lenient toward the political opposition in order to open room for foreign credits. The population gained much more freedom to go abroad; there was much greater opportunity for consumerism; cultural contacts with the west were tolerated.

The modernization program promoted during the 1970s by Gierek and his collaborators was supposed to make the state even stronger and more dominant, thanks to the extensive application of modern technology, organizational concentration, the much more sophisticated manipulation of citizens and the whole society, the use of methods other than force for policy implementation, a much more penetrating political socialization of the youth (the school reform), the consolidation of the ruling elite, the improvement of the general educational level (emphasis on gaining a diploma), and the strengthening of the security forces (very generously funded). Poland was supposed to become a sophisticated mass society cleverly manipulated by the self-conscious elite accepted in the east as well as in the west, with the investment funds coming from the rich nonsocialist countries and a docile local population working hard for the relatively meager wages to achieve a modest consumer standard of living.

This model failed mainly because of the inability to adequately utilize what was coming from the west. The ossified economy based on the rigid central planning was wasteful and could not digest profitably the sophisticated imports. Under the pressure of growing world oil prices, it became even more difficult than before to position Polish products on the western markets. The necessity to import food became burdensome. It was necessary to raise food prices to lower the state financing of mass consumption, but this appeared to be almost impossible.

In the second half of 1980 and until December 1981, a democratic alternative gained the upper hand in Poland. The basic gain was the recovery of public spirit among the people, who regained courage and ability to run their own affairs. The internal contradictions of the system were at last openly discussed, and there was a genuine search for new solutions. Very soon it became obvious that the situation could not be improved without some major reshuffle: different priorities (agriculture and consumption instead of heavy industry and armament), financial discipline, rule of the market (instead of rigid planning), local initiative (socialized enterprises becoming self-dependent), pluralism (within the limits imposed by the monopoly of the Communist Party), egalitarianism (abolishment of previous group privileges), and even less dependence on the USSR. This alternative was so shocking for the USSR and other Soviet-bloc countries that under the collective pressure exercised by them, the Polish ruling elite decided to apply drastic measures.

The rule existing in Poland since December 1981 is supposed to rescue state socialism of the Soviet style from the growing pressure coming from the spontaneously organized Polish blue-collar workers, the members of the intelligentsia, and private farmers. Relying on secret police, military forces, and the special troops ZOMO, the ruling elite crushed the centers of democratic revival in Poland, arresting the several thousands of activists, including top leaders. The prices of basic goods went up dramatically with the government's decision to cut drastically food subsidies and to make agricultural production more profitable. The mass media had been dramatically curtailed; many people were ordered to sign the loyalty oath; any free associations were abolished. In the outcome of these dramatic events the productivity of the economy had further deteriorated; the underground resistance movement started to develop vigorously; many intellectuals lost their jobs and purpose to act; the deterioration of the ruling party became even more evident.

The promoters of state socialism in Poland originally intended to establish a mass society cleverly manipulated from the top, consisting of individuals unable and unwilling to create any free coalitions among themselves; all institutions of the society remaining under a very strict control from the top; all activities within society being concentrated on the fulfillment of tasks arbitrarily formulated at the top of the official hierarchy; the internal and external order benefitting the Soviet bloc, primarily the USSR. This "ideal" has failed entirely in Poland due to the economic failure, weakness of the myth that communists are omnipotent, local tradition of resistance against any externally steered form of government, low popularity of the USSR, the traditional nationalistic spirit of Poles, the relative autonomy of the Polish culture, vivid contacts with the west, and the corruption of the ruling elite.

Poles have preserved the close primary ties, as well as their religious commitments and affiliations. This factor has helped them successfully resist the external manipulation based on an atheistic program and foreign interests. The public sphere of life has been identified by Poles as something strange and decisively disadvantageous. Secondary ties and formal organizations have been sacrificed for Poles' withdrawal to the private sphere (therefore, socioeconomic institutions function in Poland much worse than in East Germany and Czechoslovakia), but at the same time the withdrawal allowed people to preserve much internal freedom. Under the suitable circumstances in 1980, moral resistance against the corruptive influence of the system grew very fast. The spiritual and social revival on the mass scale became possible in Poland. Very fast and without much hesitancy people from various strata and spheres of life committed themselves to the establishment of a new organizational infrastructure that effectively challenged the existing official structure. Although suppressed since December 1981, this successful mass revival will remain in the tradition of the Polish nation, inspiring future generations.

The future of Poland remains very unclear, but it is obvious that any other manipulatory type of state socialism will meet resistance in the whole country, which may appear in the whole spectrum of forms: from a passive decline to work hard to even guerrilla movement in the urban as well as in the rural areas. The suppression of freedoms has its obvious limits of effectiveness in a society that is at a relatively high level of sophistication.

What will the rulers do to remain in power but at the same time establish some modus vivendi with the nation? It is difficult to say because the main decisions in this respect will be made not in Warsaw but in Moscow. However, the quality of expertise available to the rulers, as well as their willingness to seriously consider it also play some role. In this book we consider, among others, the question of how adequate has the expertise offered by sociologists been in Poland. Of course, there are some obvious difficulties related to the role of experts in serving bureaucrats. However, those roles become even more difficult when the bureaucratic state dominates the whole society as has happened in the Soviet bloc, including Poland.

REFERENCES

Brewer, Garry D. and Peter de Leon. The Foundations of Policy Analysis. Homewood: The Dorsey Press, 1983.

Kline, George L. ed., "A Leszek Kolakowski Reader." Tri Quarterly. 1971.

Matejko, Alexander J. Beyond Bureaucracy? Cologne: Verlag fur Gesellschattsarchitektur. 1984.

Mohan, Raj. P. ed. Management and Complex Organizations in Comparative Perspective. Westport: Greenwood Press. 1979.

Slomczynski, K. and T. Krauze. Class Structure and Social Mobility in Poland. White Plans: M. E. Sharpe. 1978.

Tuchman, Barbara W. The March of Folly. From Troy to Vietnam. New York: Alfred A. Knopf. 1984.

BIBLIOGRAPHY

Adamski, Franciszek. "Model Concepts of Marriage in Poland." The Polish Sociological Bulletin. 1976, 3: 51-60.

Adamski, Wladyslaw W. "Women in Contemporary Poland: Their Social and Occupation Position and Attitudes Towards Work" in Women in Eastern Europe and the Soviet Union, T. Yedlin, ed. New York: Praeger. 1980.

_____. "Typy orrientacji zyciowych mlodego i starszego pokolenia Polakow" (Types of life orientation among the young and the old generation) Studia Socjologiczne. 1980, 1: 147-67.

Adamski, Wladyslaw W., et al. Polacy 80. Wyniki badan ankietowych, Warsaw: Polish Academy of Sciences. Institute of Philosophy and Sociology. 1981.

Allardt, Erik and W. Wesolowski, eds. Social Structure and Change. Finland and Poland. Comparative Perspective. Warsaw: Polish Scientific. 1978.

Anasz, Marian and Wlodzimierz Wesolowski. "Changes in Social Structure of People's Poland," in Transformations of Social Structure in the USSR and Poland, M. N. Rutkevitch et al., ed. Moscow-Warsaw: Publisher. 1974.

Andorka, Rudolf and Krzysztof Zagorski. Socio-Occupational Mobility in Hungary and Poland. Comparative Analysis of Surveys 1972-1973. Budapest-Warsaw: Central Statistical Offices. 1980.

Ascherson, Neal. Polish August. Penguin Books. 1982.

Beskid, L. Zmiany spozycia w Polsce. Warsaw: KIW. 1972.

Bielasiak, Jack, ed. Poland Today. The State of the Republic (compiled by the Experience and the Future discussion group in Warsaw). Armonk: M. E. Sharpe. 1981.

"Bibliography of Selected Sociological Works 1970-1974." The Polish Sociological Bulletin. 1975, 1-2: 87-106.

Bienkowski, Wladyslaw. Problemy teorii rozwoju spolecznego. Warsaw: PWN. 1966.

_____. Motory i hamulce socjalizmu. Paris: Institute Litteraire. 1970.

Bilbo. Jadwigi Staniszkis poszukiwanie sprzecznosci. Warsaw: Krytyka. 1978.

Blazynski, George. Flashpoint Poland. New York: Pergamon Press. 1979.

Bokszanski, Z. et al. Wspolczesna polska klasa robotnicza. Warsaw: KIW. 1975.

Borkowski, Tadeusz. "Konferencja nt. Teoretyczne i metodologiczne problemy socjologji pracy i organizacji" Studia Socjologiczne. 1980, 2:329-34.

Bromke, Adam. Poland. The Last Decade. Oakville: Mosaic Press. 1981.

Bromke, Adam and Teresa Rakowska-Harmstone, eds. The Communist States in Disarray. Minneapolis: University of Minnesota Press. 1972.

Bromke, Adam and Derry Novak. The Communist States in the Era of Detente. Oakville: Mosaic Press. 1981.

Brus, Wlodzimierz. Socialist Ownership and Political Systems. London: Routledge and Kegan Paul. 1975.

Chalasinski, Josef. Przeszlosc i przyszlosc inteligencji polskiej. Warszawa: Ludowa Spoldz. Wydawnicza. 1958.

Davies, Norman. Poland: Past and Present. A Selected Bibliography of Works in English. Newtonville: Oriental Research Partners. 1978.

Dissent in Poland. London: Association of Polish Student and Graduates in Exile. 1977.

Dobrowolska, Danuta, Ireneusz Reszke, and Irena Reszke. "Zawody w strukturze spolecznej" (Occupations in the social structure) in Kszalt struktury spolecznej, W. Wesolowski, ed. Wroclaw: Ossolineum. 1978.

Drewnowski, Jan. Socjalism w Polsce (Socialism in Poland) Kultura (the Polish exile journal). 1970, 9 (276): 25-39.

_____. Wladza i opozycja. London: Veritas. 1979.

_____. Development of Social Structure and the Concept of Interest. The Polish Sociological Bulletin. 1980, 1: 23-38.

Dyoniziak, Edward. "Potrzeby konsumpcyjne a problem 'falszywej swiadomosci'" (Consumer needs and the problem of "false consciousness") Kultura i Spoleczenstwo. 1967, XI, 2.

Dyoniziak, Ryszard, et al. Wspolczesne Spoleczenstwo Polskie. Warsaw: Panstwowe Wydawnictwo Naukowe. 1978.

Dziedzicki A. and C. Borowski. "Na tropach patologii" (On the path of pathology). Kierunki. 1981, 49: 1, 6.

Dziewanowski, K. M. The Communist Party of Poland. Cambridge, Massachusetts: Harvard University Press. 1976.

_____. Poland in the 20th Century. New York: Columbia University Press. 1977.

Felice, Micheline, and G. Mink., eds. "Egalities et inegalites en Europe de l'Est." Problemes politiques et sociaux. Paris: La Documentation Francaise. 1979.

Gella, Alexander. "The Life and Death of the Old Polish Intelligentsia." Slavic Review. 1971, 30: 1-27.

Gella, Alexander, ed. The Intelligentsia. Sage: Beverly Hills. 1976.

Gilejko, L. "Formowanie sie i rola samorzadu" (Development of self-government and its role) in Struktura i dynamika spoleczenstwa polskiego, W. Wesolowski, ed. Warsaw: PWN, 1970.

Hirszowicz, Maria. The Bureaucratic Leviatan. A Study in Sociology of Communism. Oxford: Robertson. 1980.

Hryniewicz, Janusz T. "Dzialalnosc organizacji samorzadowych w przedsiebiorstwie" (The activity of self-governmental bodies in the enterprise) Studia Socjologiczne. 1980, 3: 255-76.

Jalowiecki, Bohdan. "Book Review of S. Sufin, Pulawy." Studia Socjologiczne. 1980, 3: 316-19.

Jarosinska, Maria and Jolanta Kulpinska. "Transformation of the Working Class in People's Poland" in Transformations of Social Structure in the USSR and Poland. M. N. Rutkevitch et al., ed. Moscow-Warsaw: PAN, 1974.

_____. "Czynniki polozenia klasy robotniczej" (Condition of the working class), in Ksztalt struktury spolecznej. W. Wesolowski, ed. Wrocla: Ossolineum. 1978.

Jarosz, Maria. Nierownosc spoeczna. Warsaw: KIW. 1984.

Jasinska-Kania, Aleksandra. "The Study of National Character: Theoretical and Methodological Problems." The Polish Sociological Bulletin. 1980, 1: 5-17.

Jasinski, Jerzy. Przewidywanie przestepczosci jako zjawiska masowego. Warsaw: Wydawnictwo Prawnicze. 1980.

Jedlicki, W. Klub Krzywego Kola. Paris: Institute Litteraire. 1964.

Kaminski, Antoni Z. "General Public Interest in the Non-Dialectic Theory of Planning, and Obstacles to Participation." The Polish Sociological Bulletin. 1979, 4: 5-10.

Karpinski, Jakub. "On Types of Social Order." The Polish Sociological Bulletin. 1979, 1: 33-40.

Kline, George L., ed. "A Leszek Kolakowski Reader." Tri Quarterly. 1971, 22.

Kloskowska, Antonia. Kultura masowa (Mass culture). Warsaw: Panstwowe Wydawnictwo Naukowe. 1980.

Kocik, Lucjan. "Przemiany stosunkow pracy w rodzinie chlopskiej" (Changes of labour relationships in the peasant family) Studia Socjologiczne. 1980, 2: 131-54.

Kolakowski, Leszek. Main Currents of Marxism. The Founders, vol. 1, The Golden Age, vol. 2, The Breakdown, vol. 3. Translated by P. S. Falla. Oxford: Clarendon Press. 1978.

Kolarska, Lena. "Formalization, Standardization and Centralization. A Critical Analysis of Selected Research." The Polish Sociological Bulletin. 1977, 2: 63-74.

_____. "The Functioning of Voice in the Polish Economy." The Polish Sociological Bulletin. 1980, 1: 39-47.

Kolarska, Lena and Andrzej Rychard. "Wplyw organizacji przemyslowych na strukture spoleczenstwa socjalistycznego" (Influence of industrial organizations on the structure of a socialist society) Studia Socjologiczne. 1980, 2: 155-71.

Kolbanowskij, W. W., ed. Socjalnoe razwitije roboczego klassa w socjalisticzeskich stranach, (Social development of the working class in socialist countries). Moscow: The Soviet Academy of Sciences. 1978.

Koralewicz-Zebik, J. "Niektore przemiany systemu wartosci, celow i orientacji zyciowych spoleczenstwa polskiego" (Some transformations of the value systems, goals and life orientation in the Polish society) Studia Socjologiczne. 1979, 4: 175-90.

Krol, Marcin. Style politycznego myslenia. Wokol "Buntu Mlodych" i "Polityki" (Styles of political thinking. Around "Youth Mutiny" and "Politics"). Paris: Libella. 1979.

Kurczewska, Joanna. "Nation in Polish Sociology." The Polish Sociological Bulletin. 1975, 1-2:59-68.

Kurczewski, J. and K. Frieske. "Z zagadnien prawnej regulacji dzialania instytucji gospodarczych" (Problems of legal regulation of economic activities), in Socjotechnika, A. Podgorecki, ed. Warsaw: AIW, 1974.

Lane, David. The End of Inequality? Stratification under State Socialism. Harmondworth: Penguin Books. 1971.

_____. Leninism: A Sociological Interpretation. London: Cambridge University Press, 1981.

Lane, David and G. Kolankiewicz. Social Groups in Polish Society. New York: Columbia University Press. 1973.

Leslie, R. F., J. Ciechanowski, L. A. Pelczynski, and A. Polonsky. The History of Poland Since 1863. Cambridge: Cambridge University Press. 1980.

Lifsches, Andrzej. "Some Problems of Education and Occupational Adaptation of Sociologists in Poland." The Polish Sociological Bulletin. 1979, 4: 81-88.

Los, Maria. "Group Ethoses in the View of Polish Empirical Researchers." The Polish Sociological Bulletin. 1977, 3-4: 113-80.

_____. "Class Ethos" in Adam Podgorecki and M. Los, Multidimensional Sociology. London: Routledge and Kegan Paul. 1979.

Makarczyk, Waclaw. "Z badan nad samowiedza narodowa" (Research on national self-consciousness) Studia Socjologiczne. 1979, 1: 29-49.

Makarczyk, Waclaw and Jan Bluszkowski. "Przemiany warstwy pracownikow umyslowych" (Transformation of the white collar stratum) in Kszalt struktury spolecznej, W. Wesolowski, ed. Wroclaw: Ossolineum. 1978.

Matejko, Alexander J. "Some Sociological Problems of Socialist Factories." Social Research. 1969b, 36, 3.

_____. "The Polish Executive." The Polish Review. 1971, 3.

_____. "Sociologists in Between." Studies in Comparative Communism. 1972a, V, 2-3.

_____. "Why Polish Workers are Restive." East Europe. 1972b, 21, 7-8.

_____. "Institutional Conditions of Scientific Inquiry." Small Group Behaviour. 1973a, 4, 1.

_____. "Poland's New Social Structure." East Europe. 1973c, 22, 102.

_____. Social Change and Stratification in Eastern Europe. New York: Praeger Publishers. 1974.

_____. The Polish Blue Collar Worker. Ann Arbor: The North American Study Center of Polish Affairs. 1977a.

_____. "The Salent Power: Blue Collar Workers in Eastern Europe" in Proceedings of the First Banff Conference on Central and East European Studies 1977, T. M. Priestly, ed. Edmonton: CEESA: 1977b.

_____. "Basis and Superstructure in Poland." Nationalities Papers. 1979a, VI, 1: 79-93.

_____. "The Obsolescence of Bureaucracy." Relations Industrielles. 1980a, 35, 3: 467-92.

_____. "Canada and Poland: Two Countries, Two 'Big Brothers'" The Jerusalem Journal of International Relations. 1980b, 4, 4: 31-55.

_____. "The Structural Roots of Polish Opposition." The Polish Review, 1982, 1-2: 112-140.

_____. The Phenomenon of Solidarity. An Attempt at Assessment. Nationalities Papers, 1983, XI, 1: 7-2.

_____. The Nature of Polish Crisis. Sociologia Internationalis, 1984, 22, 2: 59-110.

Matejko, Alexander J. ed. "Society and Sociology in Poland: Views from Polish Intellectuals Currently Outside Poland." International Journal of Contemporary Sociology. 1973, Special Issue, 10, 1.

Macshane, Denis. Solidarity-Poland's Independent Trade Union. Nottingham: Spokesman. 1981.

Mervyn, Mattews. Privilege in the Soviet Union. A Study of Elite Life-Styles Under Communism. Boston: Allen and Unwin. 1978.

Michnik, Adam. Kosciol, lewica, dialog (Church, leftism and dialogue), Paris: Institut Litteraire. 1978.

Milic-Czerniak, Roza. "Uczestnictwo w kulturze czlonkow gospodarstw domowych w zespole miejskim GOP" (Cultural participation of the household members in the conurbation GOP) Studia Socjologiczne. 1980, 3: 239-53.

Mink, Georges, ed. "L'opposition ouvriere et intellectuelle en
Europe de l'Est." Problemes politiques et sociaux. Paris:
La Documentation Francaise. 1977.

_____. "Structures sociales en Europe de l'Est." Notes et Etudes
Documentaires. 1, Les Paysanneries, Paris: La Documentation
Francaise. 1977.

_____. Structures sociales en Europe de l'Est. Notes et Etudes
Documentaires. 2, Transformation de la classe ouvriere.
Paris: La Documentation Francaise. 1979.

Misztal, B. Zagadnienia spolecznego uczestnictwa i wspoldzialania
(Problems of participation and cooperation). Wroclaw:
Ossolineum. 1977.

Moczulski, Leszek. "Rewolucja bez rewolucji" (Revolution without
revolution), Droga. 1979, 7.

_____. "Demokratyczna Opozycja i Nurty Polityczne" (Democratic
opposition and political trends). Czas, 1979/80, Dec. 29th,
Jan. 5.

Morawski, Witold. "Funkcje samorzadu robotniczego w systemie
zarzadzania przemyslem" (Function of Workers' Self-Management in Managing Industry) in Przemysl i Spoleczenstwo w
Polsce Ludowej, J. Szczepanski, ed. Wroclaw: Ossolineum.
1969.

Moscickier, Andrzej. "Delinquency in Poland and the Processes of
Industrialization and Urbanization." The Polish Sociological
Bulletin. 1976, 1: 53-64.

Mucha, Janusz. "Konflikt spoleczny jako kategoria teoretyczna
spoleczenstwa socjalistycznego" (Social conflict as the theoretical category of socialist society) Studia Socjologiczne. 1980,
1: 23-37.

Mucha, Janusz and Andrzej K. Paluch. "O miejsce problematyki
modernizacji w marksistowskiej teorii rozwoju spolecznego"
(On the place of modernization in Marxist theory of social development) Studia Socjologiczne. 1980, 3: 25-43.

Najduchowska, Halina. "Drogi zawodowe kadry kierowniczej" (Professional careers of executives) Studia Socjologiczne. 1969, 3,
253-69.

_____. "Dyrektorzy przedsiebiorstw przemyslowych" (Industrial executives) in Przemysl i Spoleczenstwo w Polsce Ludowej, J. Szczepanski, ed. Wroclaw: Ossolineum. 1969.

Narojek, Winicjusz, et al. "The Planned Society-Discussion." The Polish Sociological Bulletin. 1974, 2: 39-59.

Narojek, W. "Przeogranzenia spoleczne z perspektywy losu jednostki" (Social transformations from the perspective of individual life) Studia Socjologiczne. 1975, 3.

_____. "The Psycho-Cultural Premises and Effects of Social Mobility in Poland." The Polish Sociological Bulletin. 1975, 2: 43-56.

Nowak, Stefan. "Changes of Social Structure in Social Consciousness." The Polish Sociological Bulletin. 1964, 2: 43-56.

_____. "Stanislaw Ossowski as a Sociologist." The Polish Sociological Bulletin. 1974, 1: 12-26.

_____. "System wartosci spoleczenstwa polskiego" (The value system of Polish Society) Studia Socjologiczne. 1979, 4: 155-74.

_____. "Value Systems of the Polish Society." The Polish Sociological Bulletin. 1980, 2: 5-10.

_____. "Values and Attitudes of the Polish People." Scientific American. 1981, 245, 1: 45-53.

Ossowski, Stanislaw. Dziela (Works). Warsaw: PWN, 1967.

Ostrowski, Krzysztof. Rola zwiazkow zawodowych w polskim systemie Politycznym (Role of trade unions in the Polish political system). Wroclaw: Ossolineum. 1970.

Owieczko, A. "Robotnicy w samorzadzie przedsiebiorstwa przemyslowego" (Blue-collar workers in the self-government of industrial enterprises), in Problemy struktury i aktywnosci spolecznej. Warsaw: KIW, 1970.

Persky, Stan. At the Lenin Shipyard. Vancouver: New Star Books. 1981.

Podgorecki, Adam. Zjawiska prawne w opinii publicznej (Legal phenomena in public opinion). Warsaw: Wydawnictwo Prawnicze. 1969.

Podgorecki, Adam, ed. Socjotechnika. Jak oddzialywac skutecznie (Sociotechnics. How to act successfully). Warsaw: KIW. 1970.

Podgorecki, Adam, et al. Poglady spoleczenstwa polskiego na moralnosc i prawo (Views of the Polish society on morality and law). Warsaw: Wydawnictwo Prawnicze, 1971.

Podgorecki, Adam, ed. Socjotechnika. Style dzialania (Sociotechnics. Styles of action). Warsaw: KIW. 1972.

_____. Socjotechnika. Funkcjonalnosc i dysfunkcjonalnosc instytucji (Sociotechnics. Functionalism and disfunctionalism of institutions). Warsaw: KIW. 1974.

Podgorecki, A. Practical Social Sciences. London: Routledge and Kegan Paul. 1975.

_____. "The Global Crisis of Polish Society." The Polish Sociological Bulletin. 1976a, 4, 17-30.

_____. Zagadnienia patologii spolecznej (Problem of social pathology). Warsaw: PWN. 1975.

_____. "Calosciowa analiza spoleczenstwa polskiego" (The global analysis of Polish society) Oficyna Poetow i Malarzy. London, 1975-77, 43: 17-24; 44: 34-43.

_____. "The Rise, Development and Downfall of the Institute of Social Prevention and Resocialization (IPSR) in Poland 1972-1976" Newsletter of the ISA Research Committee on Sociotechnics. 1980, 5: 40-66.

_____. "Niezwykla historia pewnej reorganizacji" (An unusual story on a reorganization) Kierunki. 1981a, 49: 6.

_____. "The Polish Burial of Marxist Ideology" Newsletter of the ISA Research Committee on Sociotechnics. 1981b, 6: 74-96.

Pohoski, Michal, et al. "Occupational Prestige in Poland 1958-1975" The Polish Sociological Bulletin. 1976, 4: 63-78.

The Polish Sociological Association. "Social Structure." Polish Sociology 1977. Wroclaw: Ossolineum. 1978.

Poplucz, Jan. "Badanie zawodowych postaw pracownikow przemyslu" (Survey of work attitudes of industrial workers) Kultura i Spoleczenstwo. 1980, XXIV, 1-2.

Program of the Independent Self Governing Trade Union Solidarnosc, adapted by the 1st National Congress of Delegations, Gdansk, October 7th, 1981. Toronto: (191 Lippincott Street, Toronto M5S 2P3) Polish Workers Solidarity Committee. 1982.

Przeworski, Adam. "Democratic Socialism in Poland?" Studies in Political Economy. A Socialist Review. 1981, 5: 29-52.

Raina, Peter. Independent Social Movements in Poland. London: The London School of Economics and Political Science. 1981.

Rodziewicz, Ewa. "Start do zycia mlodziezy w perspektywie edukacji permanetnej" (Starting to live among the youth and the educational perspective) Kultura i Spleczenstwo. 1980, XXIV, 1-2.

Rutkevich, M. N., ed. Transformations of Social Structure in the USSR and Poland. Moscow-Warsaw: PAN. 1974.

Rychard, Andrzej. "Organizational Stereotypes of Economic Reform." The Polish Sociological Bulletin. 1977, 2: 75-84.

_____. "The Use of the Health Care Services: Comparison Between Liverpool and Lodz." The Polish Sociological Bulletin. 1979, 4: 89-96.

_____. "Interakcje polityki i gospodarki" (Interactions of politics and economy) Studia Socjologiczne. 1980, 1: 301-318.

Schaff, Adam. Die Kommunistische Rewegung an scheideweg, Vienne, 1982.

Schopflin, G. "Poland: A Society in Crisis." Conflict Studies. 1979, no. 112.

Sicinski, Andrzej. Literaci polscy (Polish writers). Wroclaw: Ossolineum. 1971.

Sicinski, Andrzej, ed. Styl zycia. Przemiany i propozycje (Style of life. Transformations and prospects), Warsaw: PWN. 1976.

Singer D. "The Road to Gdansk." Poland and the USSR, New York: Monthly Review Press. 1981.

Simon, M. D. and R. E. Kanet. Background to Crisis: Policy and Politics in Gierek's Poland. Colorado: Westview Press, 1981.

Slomczynski, K. and T. Krause, eds. Class Structure and Social Mobility in Poland. White Plains: M. E. Sharpe. 1978.

Smola, Maria. "The Ethos of Young Poles." The Polish Sociological Bulletin. 1977, 3-4: 131-144.

Sokolowska, Magdalena. "The Woman Image in the Awareness of Contemporary Polish Society." The Polish Sociological Bulletin. 1976, 3: 41-50.

Stehr, Nico. "Zwischen Hoffnung und Resignation: Zur Entwicklung & soziologischen Wissens." Philosophische Rundschau. 1982, 29: 178-87.

Szczepanski, Jan. "The Polish Intelligentsia, Past and Present." World Politics. 1962, 14 (April).

_____. "Some Characteristics of Contemporary Polish Society." The Polish Sociological Bulletin. 1964, 2.

Szczepanski, Jan, ed. Empirical Sociology in Poland. Warsaw: PWN. 1966.

_____. Polish Society. New York: Random House. 1970.

Sztompka, Piotr. System and Function. Toward a Theory of Society. New York: Academic Press. 1974.

_____. Sociological Dilemmas. Toward a Dialectic Paradigm. New York: Academic Press. 1979.

Sufin, Zbigniew. Pulawy. Planowe kierowanie procesem uprzemyslowienia (Pulawy. A planned steering of the industrialization process). Warsaw: KIW. 1979.

_____. "Zmiana warunkow zycia i sposobu zycia jako cel rozwoju spolecznego" (Change of living conditions and the way of life as the aim of social development) in Marksizm i procesy rozwoju spolecznego, W. Wesolowski, ed. Warsaw: KIW. 1979.

Szacka, Barbara. "Historical Consciousness." The Polish Sociological Bulletin. 1976, 3: 19-30.

Tellenback, S. The Social Structure of Socialist Society. The Polish Interpretation. Lund: Student Litteratur. 1975.

_____. "Patterns of Stratification in Socialist Poland." Acta Sociologica. 1976, 17, 1: 25-47.

Thomas, W. I. and F. Znaniecki. The Polish Peasant in Europe and America. Boston: R. C. Badger. 1958.

Tokes, Rudolf L. Opposition in Eastern Europe. New York: Macmillan. 1979.

Turowski, Jan. Rural Social Change in Poland. Warsaw: Polish Academy of Science. 1976.

Turski, R., K. Lapinska-Tyszka and W. Nowak. "Przemiany klasy chlopskiej" (Changes of the peasant class) in Ksztalt struktury spolecznej, W. Wesolowski, ed. Wroclaw: Ossolineum. 1978.

Waclawek, J. "Z problematyki grup spolecznych w zakladzie przemyslowym" (Problems of social groups in a factory) Narodziny socjalistycznej klasy robotniczej. Warsaw: CRZZ. 1974.

Wajda, Augustyn, ed. Klasa robotnicza w spoleczenstwie socjalistycznym, (The working class in socialist society). Warsaw: KIW. 1979.

Wesolowski, Wlodzimierz. "Robotnicy o swojej pracy i zakladach" (Workers about their jobs and workplaces) Studia Socjologiczno-Polityczne. 1962, 12.

_____. "Social Stratification in Socialist Society." The Polish Sociological Bulletin. 1967, 1.

_____. Classes, Strata and Power. London: Routledge and Kegan Paul. 1970.

_____. Klasy, warstwy i wladza (Classes, Strata and Power). Warsaw: PWN. 1974.

Wesolowski, Wlodzimierz, ed. Ksztalt struktury spolecznej (The shape of social structure). Wroclaw: Ossolineum. 1978.

Wesolowski, Wlodzimierz, et al. Social Mobility in Comparative Perspective. Wroclaw: Ossolineum. 1978.

Wesolowski, W., ed. Marksizm i procesy rozwoju spolecznego (Marxism and the processes of social development). Warsaw: KIW. 1979.

Wesolowski, Wlodzimierz and Waldemar Stelmach. Klasy i warstwy w spoleczenstwie radzieckim. Studia teoretyczne i badania empiryczne. (Classes and strata in the Soviet society. Theoretical studies and empirical research). Warsaw: KIW. 1977.

Wesolowski, W. and K. M. Slomczynski. "Teoretyczne ujecia struk klasowej i warstwowej w Polsce w latach 1945-1975" (Theoretical approaches to the class structure and stratification in Poland during the period 1945-1975) in Ksztalt Struktury Spolecznej, W. Wesolowski, ed. Wroclaw: Ossolineum. 1978.

Wiatr, Jerzy J. "Stratification and Egalitarianism." Polish Perspective. 1962, 12.

_____. Marksistowska teoria rozwoju spolecznego (Marxist of theory of social development). Warsaw: KIW. 1973.

_____. "The Marxist Social Theory and the Challenges of Our Time." The Polish Sociological Bulletin. 1975, 1-2: 5-18.

_____. "Book Review of A. Wajda, ed., Klasa robotnicza w spoleczenstwie socjalistycznym" Studia Socjologiczne. 1980, 3: 311-14.

_____. Scjsmografy Kagandry, Polityka, 1984, XXIII, 42.

Widerszpil, Stanislaw. Problemy teorii rozwinietego spoleczenstwa socjalistycznego (Theoretical problems of a developed socialist society). Krakow (5th Polish Sociological Congress), Warsaw: KIW. 1977.

Wielowiejski, A. "Christians and Socialism in Poland." Catholic Mind. 1979, LXXVII, 1334: 38-48.

Wisniewski, Wieslaw. "Wzor czlowieka wyksztalconego w swiadomosci spolecznej" (The pattern of a well-educated man in the social consciousness), Studia Socjologiczne. 1980, 3: 205-19.

Wnuk-Lipinski, Edmund. Wir pamieci (The torment of memory). Warsaw: Czytelnik. 1979.

Yedlin, Tova, ed. Women in Eastern Europe and the Soviet Union. New York: Praeger Publishers. 1980.

Zagorski, Krzysztof. "Changes of Social Structure and Social Mobility in Poland" in Transformations of Social Structure in the USSR and Poland, M. N. Rutkevitch et al., ed. Moscow-Warsaw: PNN. 1974.

Zagorski, Waclaw. "Changes of Socio-Occupational Mobility in Poland." The Polish Sociological Bulletin. 1976, 2: 17-30.

_____. Zmiany struktury i ruchliwosc spolecznozawodowa w Polsce (Changes of structure and the sociooccupational mobility in Poland). Warsaw: GUS. 1976.

INDEX

231

ABOUT THE AUTHOR

ALEXANDER J. MATEJKO is professor of sociology at the University of Alberta in Canada. Until 1968 he was a professor at the University of Warsaw and afterwards he was a visiting professor at the University of Zambia for two academic years before finally settling in Edmonton. In the academic year 1957-58, Matejko was a fellow of the Population Council at the University of Michigan. He has been a visiting professor at the University of Moscow, University of Leningrad, Centre National de Recherche Scientifique in Paris, St. Anthony's College at Oxford, University of Rome, University of North Carolina, Carleton University in Ottawa, and other places.

Professor Matejko has written extensively on east European societies, and particularly on Polish society. However, his main field is sociology of work and organization. He has published not only in English but also in Polish, German, French, Czech, Russian, and Serbo-Croatian. His publications in English include Social Change and Stratification in Eastern Europe: An Interpretive Analysis of Poland and Her Neighbours (1974), Social Dimensions of Industrialism (1974), The Social Technology of Applied Research (1975), Overcoming Alienation in Work (1976), The Upgrading of Zambians (1976), Marx and Marxism (together with A. Jain) (1984), and Beyond Bureaucracy? (1984). His new book edited together with A. Jain will be a Critique of Marxist and Non-Marxist Thought (Praeger, 1985). Professor Matejko has published many articles and book reviews in the professional journals in Canada, Czechoslovakia, France, Germany, India, Israel, Italy, Kenya, Poland, the U.K., the U.S., the USSR, and Yugoslavia.

The author received his Ph.D. in sociology from the University of Warsaw on the basis of his thesis on sociology of work and organization in the U.S. He is the vice-president of the Research Committee 26 on Sociotechnics at the International Sociological Association. He is also a member of the Research Council of the same association. Professor Matejko has presented several papers from a sociotechnical perspective on social organization at work.